Magic: The Yoga of the West

Although they differ in methods, magic and yoga share a common goal—to transform the individual's consciousness and life through an inner union with Divine forces. Donald Tyson, a practicing magician as well as a prolific writer, designed this magical curriculum based on the premise that we learn best by doing rather than simply by reading and theorizing. The impetus for engaging in magic is the desire for results—and this book gives the aspiring magician a clear path to that end.

The Magician's Workbook presents a progressive, integrated series of practical exercises in the Western tradition, designed to create proficiency in the essentials of ritual magic quickly and effectively. These are exercises that do not merely teach—they transform. When regularly practiced, they will result in changes to the body and mind that provide the inner foundation for all magical success

You will find much that is unique in this approach, including:

- A complete and integrated system, combined with a forty-week schedule of daily study

- A primary focus on the training and conditioning of the mind and the will, which is far more important than physical actions or material instruments for successful ritual work

- Complete details of each exercise, encompassing internal as well as external activity

About the Author

Donald Tyson (Nova Scotia, Canada) was drawn to science early in life by an intense fascination with astronomy. He began university seeking a science degree, but became disillusioned with the aridity and futility of a mechanistic view of the universe, and shifted his major to English. After graduating with honors he has pursued a writing career. Now he devotes his life to the attainment of a complete gnosis of the art of magic in theory and practice. His purpose is to formulate an accessible system of personal training composed of East and West, past and present, that will help others discover the reason for their existence and the way to fulfill it.

To Write to the Author

If you wish to contact the author or would like more information about this book, please write to the author in care of Llewellyn Worldwide and we will forward your request. Both the author and publisher appreciate hearing from you and learning of your enjoyment of this book and how it has helped you. Llewellyn Worldwide cannot guarantee that every letter written to the author can be answered, but all will be forwarded. Please write to:

Donald Tyson
℅ Llewellyn Worldwide
P.O. Box 64383, Dept. 0-7387-0000-2
St. Paul, MN 55164-0383, U.S.A.
Please enclose a self-addressed stamped envelope for reply,
or $1.00 to cover costs. If outside U.S.A., enclose
international postal reply coupon.

Many of Llewellyn's authors have websites with additional information and resources. For more information, please visit our website at:

http://www.llewellyn.com

THE MAGICIAN'S WORKBOOK

*Practicing the Rituals
of the Western Tradition*

DONALD TYSON

2001
Llewellyn Publications
St. Paul, Minnesota 55164-0383, U.S.A.

First Edition
First Printing, 2001

Cover design by Gavin Dayton Duffy
Illustration on page 115 by Mary Ann Zapalac

Library of Congress Cataloging-in-Publication Data

Tyson, Donald, 1954 –
[ISBN: 0-7387-0000-2 Pending]

Llewellyn Worldwide does not participate in, endorse, or have any authority or responsibility concerning private business transactions between our authors and the public.

All mail addressed to the author is forwarded but the publisher cannot, unless specifically instructed by the author, give out an address or phone number.

Any Internet references contained in this work are current at publication time, but the publisher cannot guarantee that a specific location will continue to be maintained. Please refer to the publisher's website for links to authors' websites and other sources.

Llewellyn Publications
A Division of Llewellyn Worldwide, Ltd.
P.O. Box 64383, Dept. 0-7387-0000-2
St. Paul, MN 55164-0383, U.S.A.
www.llewellyn.com

♻ Printed in the United States of America on recycled paper

Other Books by Donald Tyson

Enochian Magic for Beginners

The Messenger (fiction)

New Millennium Magic

Ritual Magic

Rune Dice Kit

Rune Magic

Scrying for Beginners

Sexual Alchemy

Tetragrammaton

The Truth About Ritual Magic

The Truth About Runes

Three Books of Occult Philosophy

The Tortuous Serpent (fiction)

For Llewellyn's free full-color catalog, write to:

New Worlds
c/o Llewellyn Worldwide
P.O. Box 64383, Dept. 0-7387-0000-2
St. Paul, MN 55164-0383, U.S.A.

or call **1-800-THE MOON**

Contents

 ## LIFE EXERCISES

 ## RECLINING EXERCISES

✳ SITTING EXERCISES ✳

✡ STANDING EXERCISES ✡

✴ MOVING EXERCISES ✴

PRACTICE SCHEDULE

Introduction

Benefits of the Exercises Automatic

The forty exercises in this book are designed to develop the practical skills necessary to work ritual magic in the Western tradition. Their value lies in the doing. They are not meant to be studied or analyzed, but repeatedly performed on a regular basis. When integrated into a daily routine of practice and done consistently over a period of months, the benefits they confer are automatic and universal. They strengthen the will, focus concentration, enhance creative visualization, and awaken the perception of esoteric forces and spiritual creatures.

Anyone who follows the routine of practice set forth in the appendix will experience profound changes of mind and body. The degree of benefit will vary depending on the latent gifts within each individual, but just as no one can lift weights for months without enlarging their biceps, it is impossible to work these exercises of practical magic without expanding and strengthening the occult faculties.

You will become more aware of the processes of your own mind, and increasingly conscious of your dreams. You will sense subtle currents of force moving within your body and through the world around you, and learn to control them. Your intuition will grow keener and more reliable. You will perceive the presence of spiritual intelligences and interact with them. You will be able to project the power of your will as a tangible force to influence spirits and human beings. You will cleanse buildings and places of destructive atmospheres, charge objects with subtle energies, open gateways to higher spiritual realms, awaken the energy centers of your body, and call forth angels and elementals to serve your needs.

All exercises are completely practical. A brief commentary has been added to each, but these commentaries contain no theories or moral cautions or history lessons, only instructions essential to avoid confusion and insure accurate performance. Countless books explain, justify, and analyze various aspects and systems of magic, past and present, in exhaustive detail. These works have their place, but they often suffer from a deficiency of simple directions on how to actually do the magic they describe. Readers are forced to distill procedures from hundreds of pages of general discussion, or must translate abstract references into practical steps.

Exercises Progressive and Modular

This crystallization of the practical from the abstract can prove difficult even for those with prior experience in ritual magic. Beginners find it impossible. They do not know where to start, and are bewildered by the sheer mass of information that confronts them. They are told to draw a pentagram, or project a circle, or raise a cone of power, or ground and center themselves, or charge an object, or open their chakras, or invoke the Light, but are seldom instructed in simple steps how to do these things. The practical directions found in most texts on magic, even in the very best, are woefully inadequate. Rituals are set forth in the form of skeletal outlines. While these outlines may serve as useful reminders to those who already know the rituals, they are insufficient for the larger percentage of readers who come upon the rituals for the first time, never having worked a ritual before.

Even when a ritual is described in detail, it is not enough for the practitioner to know all of the required physical actions and gestures. Much more important are the inner actions—visualization of astral forms, manipulation of energy centers and esoteric currents, vibration of words of power, transformation of the aura and the astral body. In those extremely rare instances where both the outer and inner actions of a ritual are described in precise and exhaustive detail, it is still not enough. The ritual will prove ineffective unless the practitioner has trained and strengthened his or her occult faculties.

You can study the theory of how to ride a bicycle for months, and receive advice from hundreds of expert cyclists, but unless you actually practice on a bike to improve your balance, when you try to ride you are certain to fail. It is the same with ritual magic. You must know in complete detail the physical actions needed for a ritual. You must also know how to visualize subtle forces involved in the ritual, and how to manipulate them both within your body and in the greater world. Even this is not enough, however, unless you also have trained in ritual techniques and conditioned your mind and body through repeated practice in the skills that ritual magic requires.

Each exercise in this book is written out in exhaustive detail. Both the external physical actions and the internal mental actions that are required are completely explained. There is no presumption that the reader already knows any of the steps. This degree of detail may seem excessive to those already skilled in ritual magic, but beginners will find it not only helpful but essential, if they are to perform the exercises accurately. Even those who have worked magic for years may discover in this book aspects of practice that they had not previously considered.

A deficiency of most practical texts on magic is the tendency to present rituals toward the end of the book in a kind of shorthand outline, under the assumption that everything written previously is fresh in the memory. This is fine if the reader has read the book from front to back just prior to attempting the rituals, but not if the reader takes up the book six months after reading it with the intention of working one of its procedures. Once the initial explanatory material has left the memory, these shorthand rituals become incomprehensible, and the reader must reread the entire book before they can be enacted. To avoid this difficulty, all the exercises in the present work are written so that they can be understood without the need to refer back to previous instructions.

The exercises are progressive and modular. The early exercises are simpler than those that come later. The complex rituals toward the end of the book are built up of components previously practiced and perfected, so that the reader is not overwhelmed by them, as happens too often in ritual texts, but recognizes in them known procedures. Because these exercises are intended to develop skills and teach techniques rather than achieve results, they are general rather than specific, and may be adapted to a wide variety of purposes.

Essential Role of the Golden Dawn

Some are training exercises and ritual methods developed independently in my own practice. Others are standard techniques and rituals of Western occultism that were first used by the original Hermetic Order of the Golden Dawn, a secret lodge of English magicians that flourished at the end of the nineteenth century. Still others are original rituals, but based on Golden Dawn components. The single thread connecting the exercises is their utility. I have used them all at various times and have found them effective in advancing my skills and awakening sleeping perceptions and abilities. They work, or I would not have included them.

Readers of my other works will know that I do not agree with every aspect of Golden Dawn symbolism. These disagreements are described and justified at length in my book *New Millennium Magic,* where my personal system of magic is presented. To avoid confusing beginners, all of the exercises in the present work adhere to the Golden Dawn system of occult correspondences. Golden Dawn associations are used by the majority of ritual magicians and pagans practicing magic today, even though many of them have no idea where these symbolic relationships originated. The most important of these correspondences is the assignment of the four philosophical elements, spirits, angels and names of power to the four points of the compass. Also important is the relationship between the twenty-two Tarot trumps and the twelve zodiac signs, seven astrological planets, and three simple elements.

It is essential that beginners learn both the occult correspondences and the basic ritual techniques taught by the original Golden Dawn, even if they have no special interest in the Order and no intention of studying its complex ceremonies and system of magic as a whole. The Golden Dawn correspondences are the nearest thing to a standard that exists in modern Western magic. As for the basic rituals of the Order, no techniques are more effective in awakening latent magical ability. They form the backbone of modern magic, and must be thoroughly understood in a practical way by every serious magician.

The Golden Dawn material in the present work includes the invocation and banishing of elemental forces by pentagram, the technique of centering by the Kabbalistic Cross, the technique for vibrating words of power, the way of charging objects with elemental force, both the Lesser Ritual and the Greater Ritual of the Pentagram, the Middle Pillar Exercise, the Rose Cross Ritual, the invocation of the guardians of the quarters, the use of the tattwas in scrying, and other essential techniques. In presenting the Golden Dawn rituals, I have kept closely to the original structures, but have expanded their descriptions, rendering the rituals much more accessible and effective for the average user. Even those who have been doing magic for years and know the Golden Dawn system may find this presentation of the essential Golden Dawn rituals illuminating.

Arrangement of the Exercises

The exercises fall into five groups. The first group involves mental exercises done during the course of the day while engaged in ordinary activities. The second consists of visualization exercises performed in a reclining posture. The third group is done while sitting in a chair, and combines visualization with physical actions or objects for the purpose of developing increased concentration, strengthening the will, astral projection, and other basic skills. The fourth group of exercises is done standing in place, with at least one foot stationary, and introduces ritual techniques. The fifth group involves more complex ritual techniques, and is done while moving or walking around the practice area.

The earliest exercises have no formal structure or associated body posture. They are practiced entirely in the mind. The final exercises are complex rituals that involve many physical movements and gestures. The rest are roughly graded between these extremes. Those in the first half of the work are predominately mental in their focus, those in the second half physical (though always with a vital mental component). The early exercises tend to be directed inward, while the later exercises tend to be directed outward. There is no rigid adherence to these general rules, but they reveal a gradation to the exercises in which skills gained inwardly are used in outer ritual forms.

I have as much as possible avoided the use of tools and materials. Beginners often have difficulty making or procuring instruments. When employed in rituals, instruments distract beginners from the real work of creative visualization and inner concentration. The tools I have described are simple and inexpensive, and will be available to everyone. They consist of a knife, the tattwa symbols cut from cardboard, various receptacles to hold common substances such as water and salt, candles, regular coins, a deck of Tarot cards, incense sticks and cones, a dowsing pendulum that can be made from a piece of thread and a ring, and simple objects such as a watch and a kettle. No ritual clothing is needed, nor is it necessary to create magic talismans, pentacles, or sigils.

Exercises Complete and Practical

This book was written in direct response to numerous letters received over the years, in which readers have asked for a manual of simple instructions that would allow them to actually begin to practice magic rather than merely reading about it. The exercises will be of greatest help to anyone seriously interested in learning magic, but bewildered by the abundance of texts either too complex and abstract to apply to their own situation, or too simplistic to be of any practical value.

Complexity is inevitable in some areas of magic. It is impossible to write a simple book on Enochian magic without leaving out 95 percent of the subject. Similarly, there is no way to explain the Kabbalah in a handful of paragraphs. These subjects are complex and require complex treatments. Israel Regardie's great work *The Golden Dawn* is over 800 pages of fine print, and needs every page to cover the full system of magic used by the Golden Dawn. However, once the beginner has acquired practical knowledge of the basic techniques of ritual magic, these challenging texts become much easier to understand.

At the other extreme of the scale, there is a distressing abundance of books on magical topics that simplify their subject to such a degree, nothing of practical value remains. These works advocate a sort of "shake-and-bake" instant magic. It is assumed by their authors that no preparation and no inner development is required, merely the mechanical execution of a few physical actions, the utterance of a dozen words memorized by rote, and usually, the lighting of a candle. Add water and stir—miracle follows after fifteen minutes. It is quite obvious that those who write such books have no knowledge of magic. The tragedy is that their books mislead many serious beginners into believing that magic requires no effort—or worse, that magic is an obvious fraud and a waste of time.

It is hoped that the present work finds a middle ground between overwhelming the beginner with detail, and simplifying the subject to such a degree that nothing of practical worth remains. Contained in these forty exercises is all that is needed to acquire the basic skills and techniques of ritual magic. A suggested schedule of study is set forth in the appendix to progressively introduce the material over a forty week period. However, the practice of these exercises does not cease after forty weeks, but continues for a lifetime. Also included in the appendix is a four-week maintenance cycle designed to sustain the level of skill achieved during the forty weeks.

Considerations When Doing the Exercises

All of the exercises should be done when the body is in good health, and the mind tranquil. More than one exercise may be done in a day, but they should be spaced apart from each other. It is best to do the three exercises suggested for each day of the practice schedule separately in the morning, early afternoon, and evening, when this is possible. The exceptions to this rule are the life exercises at the beginning of the book, which are completely internal and extend over the full term of the day. These may be done in conjunction with the daily three external exercises.

Never do two exercises back to back. Also, avoid performing two or more similar exercises in the same day, even when they are divided by several hours. For example, you should not to do two major rituals, such as "Cleansing a Space" (exercise 38) and "Evoking Into the Triangle" (exercise 40), in the same day because the first will deplete a portion of the energy required to successfully perform the second. It is safe to do exercises from different categories in the same twenty-four-hour period—a reclining exercise may be combined with a sitting exercise, a standing exercise and a moving exercise.

Always wear loose, comfortable clothing during practice, and be sure to remove anything that irritates your skin or restricts your circulation, such as jewelry, a watch, shoes, a tight belt, or a hat. This is particularly important for those articles of clothing that distract your attention. Someone who has worn a wedding band for years will not need to remove it because the ring has become a part of the perceived self, an extension of the personal identity. Whenever possible, bathe before practice. It is enough to only wash your hands and face for the simpler exercises, but before major rituals it is better to shower or take a bath. Physical cleansing of the body symbolically washes away the clutter of daily concerns and purifies the purpose.

Nothing in this book should be considered unalterable. This applies not only to the suggested schedule of practice, but to the rituals themselves, even those created by the Golden Dawn. When magic ceases to change and grow, it petrifies. Magic only lives within the mind and heart of the human being who works it. I have done my best to distill the essence of my daily practice of ritual magic over many years. These are the techniques that have proved most fruitful. They suit me, and it is my belief that they will be useful to many others. But if there are exercises in this book that you find unhelpful, by all means change them to meet your needs. There is no such thing as teaching, there is only learning. I can describe the basics of practical magic, but only you have the power to make magic a reality in your own life.

Preface

Yoga of the West

In the first chapter of her book *The Mystical Qabalah,* Dion Fortune referred to the European esoteric tradition as the "yoga of the West." She had in mind specifically the magical Kabbalah, as taught by the original Hermetic Order of the Golden Dawn and its offshoot members and occult lodges, but also intended this description to embrace the discipline of ceremonial magic as a whole.

In order to understand her intention, it is necessary to know that yoga is far more than merely a form of physical exercise. There are numerous types of yoga, some predominantly physical and others mainly mental in their approach. For example, Hatha yoga employs physical postures of the body. Bakti yoga involves the exercise of love and devotion. Mantra yoga relies on chanting. Laya yoga focuses on activating the chakras and the sexual power of kundalini in the body.

All types of yoga have as their common goal the attainment of mastery over both the mind and body, for the purpose of transforming consciousness and achieving personal power. The control the yogi seeks is not power over other human beings, but power over the self, because the yogi recognizes that command of the self results in control over the environment in which the self functions. A human being who has mastered the self cannot be dominated by any other person; to the contrary, there is a strong tendency for others to seek to emulate and follow such a master, because they intuitively recognize the value of self-control.

Western ritual magic at its higher level involves an intense mental and physical discipline that is every bit as rigorous as that imposed by Eastern yoga. The yogi tends to work inwardly, focusing on the body, whereas the magus directs the will outwardly upon the objects of the greater world. This apparent distinction is misleading, since inner world and outer world have no dividing boundary, but are an indivisible universe perceived by a single human mind. The ultimate goal is similar in both practices—to master the personal universe and yoke it to the higher aspirations. Power over the environment is a byproduct of skilled magic, but even more significant is the command of the self attained by the magus.

On the physical level, magic relies on tools such as the wand, the chalice, and the altar to divide space and energize objects. On the sensory level, it uses scents, colors, textures, and sounds to focus and direct the attention. On the emotional level, feelings such as enthusiasm, joy, devotion, love, and desire are employed as engines of the ritual purpose. On the mental level, creative visualization shapes and manipulates the substance of the imagination so that they appear to be materially present before the sight. On the spiritual level words and symbols of power constrain spiritual intelligences to fulfill the will of the magus as faithful servants.

None of these aspects is less important than any other. They all work together to accomplish the higher purpose of self-mastery. The magus not only makes his body and mind his ritual tools, he makes the entire universe his instrument of transformation. The serious student of Western magic soon finds that life itself is a ritual working that must be completed—it is merely of question of doing it well or doing it poorly.

No one would expect to build up their body without daily exercise, or to get through university without regular study, but those who approach magic for the first time often have the childish notion that magic will work independently, without any effort required on their part. This naive expectation stems from the mistaken belief that magic is something external and separate from the self, that its incantations, sigils, and pentacles function by themselves, in much the same way that a car engine runs by itself with a turn of the key. This is false. There is no such thing as a word or a symbol that has power inherent in itself. These things are tools, nothing more, and must be skillful manipulated. Learning how to use them properly takes practice, determination, and most of all, plain old hard work.

The tools of magic must be employed on all levels simultaneously. It is not enough to wave a wand about in the air, it must be actualized and visualized on the astral level. During use, the magus remains keenly aware of its responsiveness and tactile feel. Energy is projected along its length with the force of the will. The words of power that are written on its sides are sustained in the depths of the mind, where they act most effectively. Emotional energy is heightened at the moment of projection, then allowed to fall completely quiescent to prevent a backlash. The magic is not in the wand, it is in the magician. The ritual is not worked in the external environment with physical objects, it is worked in the unity of the personal universe that embraces both inside and outside without division.

Most basic texts of Western ritual magic focus on externals. They describe which physical tools should be used, how to dress, what to say, how to move, which symbols and sigils must be employed, the best color for a given purpose, the most appropriate incense, which zodiac sign or planet to invoke, and so on. There is nothing wrong with this approach, as far as it goes. This information is necessary for the practice of magic. However, it is not enough by itself. Without the ability to focus and sustain the will, to channel the energy of the emotions, to visualize in a concrete way astral forms, to vibrate both inwardly and outwardly words of power, the ritual will fail.

Magic, like yoga, is a total mind-body experience that embraces both the self and the world. In yoga, it is difficult to forget the importance of the self because yoga is directed inwardly at controlling the thoughts and disciplining the flesh. In magic, which appears on superficial inspection to involve only external objects and symbols, it is much easier to fall into the error of supposing that mental discipline and focus are unimportant, or at least are less important than external movements, gestures, and symbols.

This workbook redresses the imbalance so common to basic ritual texts, by emphasizing equally both the external aspects of ritual and the internal aspects that must accompany them. Each exercise describes in detail what to do with your body and hands, but also what you must do with your emotions, will, and imagination. These inner requirements of ritual, so well-known to every skilled Western practitioner, are hidden from those seeking to learn magic, simply because internal requirements of ritual magic are not examined in most instructions books. The way the fundamental rituals of Western magic are described in this workbook is the way they are actually performed by knowledgeable practitioners.

Even a detailed description of the actual manner in which rituals are done is not enough to do successful ritual magic. The mind must be conditioned and trained before the inner aspects of ritual can be successfully worked. It is not enough to know how to do magic, you must build up your skills until you attain a level of competence that allows you to actually work rituals effectively. A thin and unconditioned man may know, in very precise detail, how to lift a bar with three hundred pounds of weight attached to it, but unless he has trained his body he will never be able to actually raise the weight. Similarly, even with the detailed description set forth in this book of what must be willed and projected and visualized during ritual, the beginner will not be able to do magic successfully until he or she has strengthened the will, gained control over thoughts and emotions, and attained proficiency in visualization of astral forms.

Many of the exercises in the workbook are designed to build up the mental and physical abilities essential for ritual magic. Among them are exercises for sustaining concentration on a single point for prolonged periods, for projecting the will at a distance, and for visualizing complex astral forms both inside and outside the body. Controlled breathing exercises are prominent since mastery of the breath is essential for controlling the subtle forces of the mind and body, particularly the fiery energy of kundalini. Also vital to success is the skilled vibration of words of power, both inwardly and outwardly, a technique that is often mentioned but seldom taught in detail.

Ceremonial magic truly is the yoga of the West. It has not been accorded the importance it deserves because its virtue as a serious discipline of self-transformation has remained overshadowed by the flash and glamour of its outward show, and by the false expectations and erroneous beliefs of cynics who reject it without even trying to understand it. It is only a matter of time before it is recognized as a precious legacy of our European heritage, able to liberate and transform human consciousness to an unparalleled degree and give complete mastery over both the self and the world. As an instrument of personal empowerment, Western magic has no equal.

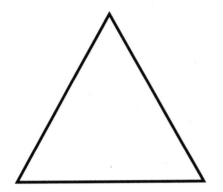

LIFE
EXERCISES

EXERCISE I

Self-Awareness I:
Ego Denial

THIS LIFE EXERCISE is performed over the full span of the day for seven consecutive days. It begins the moment you get out of bed in the morning, and ends when you get into bed at night. Practice is suspended while you are lying awake in bed prior to getting up in the morning, and before falling asleep at night, since at these times your thoughts are unfocused and erratic.

Each day for a full week, refrain from using the words "I," "my," "me," "myself," and "mine" in your conversation. Structure your words so that you do not need to say "I" or these other words regardless of what subject you talk about.

Avoid referring to yourself in the third person by saying such things as "Anne needs a drink" when you mean "I need a drink." Avoid referring to yourself by some cute expression such as "this humble person" or "this entity" or "the practitioner." The benefit of the exercise is lost through this form of cheating.

Cut your ego out of your conversation entirely. For example, if your boss asks whether you completed the report you were

3

working on, instead of saying "I finished the report," or "The report was finished by me," say "The report is finished." If you cannot think of a way to respond without referring directly to yourself, remain silent.

Carry paper and a pen with you throughout the period of the exercise. Each time that you forget your resolve and employ the words "I," "my," "me," "myself," or "mine," make a small stroke on the paper. If at any point during the day you suddenly realize that you neglected to mark down a stroke immediately upon uttering one of the forbidden words—for example, if you were distracted and forgot—put down five strokes as a penalty. At the end of each day, add the strokes and record their number alongside the date.

When you have done this exercise with diligent attention for seven consecutive days, perform the same exercise cycle for another week, but this time refrain from using the words "I," "my," "me," "myself," or "mine" both outwardly while speaking to others, and also in your own thoughts or when talking to yourself under your breath. Strive to eliminate references to yourself in your internal monologue. Each time you refer to yourself in your own thoughts with one of the prohibited words, mark down a stroke on paper, and at the end of the day, add up the strokes. If you suddenly realize at any point during the day that you forgot to mark a stroke, put down five strokes as a penalty.

The seven-day exercise cycle can be repeated on consecutive weeks, or done on individual weeks that are separated by periods of rest. Greatest benefit is derived during the first week, before habit patterns develop that allow the exercise to be completed more easily. In the suggested schedule at the end of the book, the second week of practice is separated from the first week by two weeks.

Commentary

This is a modified form of the exercise taught by Aleister Crowley to his students. In Crowley's version, when the student made the error of using the word "I" he was advised by Crowley to slash himself on the forearm with a straight razor. Crowley believed that pain acted as a useful tool for concentrating the awareness more keenly. Israel Regardie advocated Crowley's exercise, but taught his own students to wear a rubber band on their wrist and snap hard it against their skin each time they used the word "I." Contrary to these examples, neither self-mutilation nor self-inflicted pain is necessary during training, only continuing attention.

The goal of the exercise is vigilance and a sustained clarity of the mind on a particular subject. It is designed to combat mental laziness. Sometimes it is claimed that this exercise reduces egoism. This is false. By the constant effort to keep from using the word "I" or similar words that refer to the self, the mind of the student is repeatedly directed to the ego during the period of practice, and the awareness of self is heightened. However, a strong ego is not a hindrance in the working of practical magic.

The exercise illustrates how consistently human beings tend to view the world from the narrow perspective of their personal needs and desires verses the rest of the universe. By avoiding words generally used to refer to the self, a broader view of the integrated wholeness of creation will be intuited.

Self-Awareness II: Criticism of Others

THIS LIFE EXERCISE is performed over the cycle of a week. Each day, for seven days, from the moment you get out of bed in the morning to the moment you get into bed at night, avoid saying anything critical about any other person. It makes no difference whether the person is known to you or is a public figure, or whether the person is living or dead. Equally irrelevant is whether or not the person deserves criticism. If you find yourself engaged in conversation, and someone invites you to criticize someone in any way whatsoever, remain silent. Do not indicate agreement with words, facial expressions, or body gestures.

Carry a pen and paper during the seven days of your practice, and each time you find yourself outwardly expressing criticism of another person, or of what another person has done or said, whether by words, sounds, body posture, gestures, or expressions, mark down a stroke on the paper. If you neglect to mark down a stroke immediately, and later realize your omission, mark down five strokes as a penalty. At the end of each day, add up the strokes and record the sum beside the date.

After you have performed this exercise for a week with diligent attention, you should at a later date do the same exercise for another week, but this time in addition to not criticizing others outwardly by words, expressions, or gestures, avoid mentally criticizing any other person in your own thoughts, even if you believe they merit censure, or have done or said something to injure you. Each time you catch yourself speaking ill or having a harsh thought about someone, set down a stroke upon the piece of paper you keep with you for this purpose. If you neglect to mark down a stroke and later realize your omission, set down five strokes as a penalty for your lapse of attention. At the end of every day, add up the strokes and record the sum beside the date.

This exercise in inner attention can be done on two consecutive weeks, or on separate weeks interspaced by a period of rest. In the suggested practice schedule at the end of this book, the weeks are separated.

Commentary

Rare individuals not in the habit of thinking or speaking critically about others will find this exercise easy, but the majority will discover that much of their waking energy is devoted to denigrating others in an effort to feel better about themselves. The goal of the exercise is to become aware of this automatic tendency in your own nature.

In the first hour or two of practice you may find that you have made no marks at all, but as the exercise progresses through the week, ingrained habits of thought assert themselves, and you will discover that you criticize others so automatically that you have difficulty being aware of it. This is the real challenge of the exercise— to actively monitor your mental processes so that you can consciously notice critical thoughts or words when these arise.

It is best to begin weekly practice for all three of the daily life exercises on the same day of the week. Monday is the normally accepted beginning of the week, and a good day to start the seven-day exercise cycle.

EXERCISE 3

Self-Awareness III: Criticism of Self

As with all life exercises, this focus of awareness on self-criticism is performed from morning to evening daily over the span of a week. It begins when you get out of bed and ends when you get back into bed. During the course of the day, strive to avoid saying or doing anything critical of yourself or your actions. Whenever you disparage or denigrate your own behavior, intelligence, appearance, personality, or worth as a human being in front of others by word, sound, posture, gesture, or facial expression, mark down a single pen stroke on a piece of paper carried with you for this purpose.

You must record these strokes even for very minor acts of self-criticism, such as a shrug of the shoulders that expresses to others something such as "Oh, there I go again, being clumsy," or habitual expressions such as "Silly me" or "My mistake." Even if you sigh in exasperation at yourself when others can hear, put down a stroke. If for any reason you forget to make the mark at once, record five marks as a penalty for your inattention. At the end of each day of practice, add up the strokes and record the sum beside the date.

When you complete a week-long cycle of daily practice, perform the same exercise for another week, but this time mark down a pen stroke not only when you express self-criticism before others, but also each time you criticize yourself in your own mind. When you become aware that you have cursed yourself—for example, when you drop something and swear—or have mentally said to yourself "I'm stupid," or have remembered some error made in the past with feelings of anger or embarrassment, mark down a stroke. Whenever you belittle yourself or are harsh with yourself in your thoughts, mark down a stroke.

If you realize later during the day that you have been critical about something you did, or some remembered event, but neglected to put down a stroke, record five strokes as a penalty. As before, add up the strokes each day and record the sum beside the date.

The two seven-day cycles of practice for this exercise can be done back to back, or separated by a rest period. In the schedule at the end of the book they are divided by two weeks of other work in order to insure complete attention during the second cycle.

Commentary

Some individuals are habitually more self-critical than others. They apologize for their actions, and attacks upon their own behavior, a part of their social identity. This type of self-abuse is not useful. Before it can be amended, it must be recognized.

Perform the exercise with a detached awareness, as though observing the behavior of somebody else rather than yourself. Avoid the tendency to gloat over few pen strokes or chastise yourself over many. There is no right or wrong number. The goal of the exercise is the process.

It is best when engaged in these life exercises of self-awareness not to tell others what you are doing, and if possible, not even to give them a clue that you are doing anything out of the ordinary. This insures that others continue to act naturally toward you. One trick to use, if you find that it draws attention to yourself when you mark down pens strokes on paper, is to carry coins in your left pocket, and each time you need to mark a stroke, instead transfer a coin to your right pocket. At the end of the day, count the number of coins in your right pocket and record the sum beside the date.

RECLINING EXERCISES

Inward Perception I: Stepped Relaxation

L IE ON YOUR back on the floor in what will hereafter be referred to as the reclining posture, with your feet about six inches apart, arms at your sides, and your thumbs turned slightly outward. If you find the bare floor uncomfortable, lie on a mat or rug, and put a folded towel or other clean cloth under your head. Close your eyes. Breathe slowly and deeply with a regular rhythm.

Focus all your attention on your left leg. Lightly tense the muscles in your leg and raise it an inch or so off the floor. Curl your toes. Be aware of all the muscles, nerves, and bones from the sole of your foot up to your hip. Feel the muscles gripping the bones, the blood flowing through your veins and arteries, the tightness of your skin. Hold this awareness for ten seconds.

Let your left leg fall gently back to the floor, and at the same time, completely withdraw your awareness from your left leg. Without thinking about it, maintain the quiet certainty in the back of your mind that your left leg has ceased to be a part of you. It is no more connected to you than the clouds in the sky.

Turn your attention to your right leg. Tense its muscles and raise it slightly off the floor. Curl your toes. Feel the solidity and weight of the leg's muscles from your hip down to your foot. Be aware of the bones in the leg beneath the muscles, then turn your attention to the skin that contains it all. Hold all these parts of your right leg in your mind for around ten seconds, then let it fall back to the floor, and immediately withdraw your attention from it as though the leg were no longer a part of you.

Tense your left arm and lift it an inch from the floor with your fingers stiff and straight. Be aware of its sensations, its bones and joints, its muscles straining against each other, its nerves, its enclosing skin. Hold your left arm in its entirety in your awareness for ten seconds, then allow it to fall nervelessly to the floor and regard it as separate from your body. Turn your attention to your right arm.

Tense your right arm and raise it an inch with your fingers stiffened straight. Be aware of all of its sensations, its weight and warmth, the blood flowing through it, the bones beneath its muscles. Maintain this awareness for ten seconds, then allow your arm to fall back to the floor and completely remove your attention from it, as though it were no longer a part of you.

Turn your awareness to your buttocks. Lightly tighten the muscles in your buttocks and squeeze your bottom cheeks together. Tighten your anus. Be sure to keep the rest of your body completely relaxed and detached from this activity. Hold this tightness for ten seconds while focusing all your awareness on the sensations it causes. Relax your buttocks and anus.

Focus attention on your lower belly. Tighten the muscles on the front of your belly below the level of your navel and between your hips. Be aware of your lower belly and the upper surface of your pelvis, including your genitals. Let your mind contain every sensation of this area of your body for about ten seconds. Then relax and move your awareness upward to the level of your abdomen just under your rib cage.

Tighten the muscles of your abdomen and lower back, and feel with total awareness the entire mass of your lower torso, with all its organs and fluids. Hold this awareness as you maintain the tension. Relax and let your awareness leave the lower torso as the tension leaves it. Know without actually having to consider it that your lower torso has ceased to be connected to you.

Your awareness shifts naturally upward to your chest. Tense the muscles on the front, sides, and back of your rib cage, and as you maintain this light tension direct your mind to the stiffness of your ribs and spine, the weight of your lungs, the beating of your heart. Hold the tension of your chest for ten seconds, then shift your awareness upward to your shoulders.

Tense the muscles across the top of your shoulders and be conscious of their stiffness and heaviness. Feel where they join onto the sides of your neck. Hold this tension for ten seconds with full conscious awareness of all aspects of this area, then allow your shoulders to relax and separate yourself from them. They are no longer a part of you. Nothing exists below the level of your neck.

Focus on your neck and tense its muscles lightly. Feel the tension in the cords on either side of your throat and the muscles at the sides of your neck. Tighten lightly the inside of your throat. Be fully aware of your neck for ten seconds. As you let your neck relax completely, shift your attention upward to your jaw.

Clench your jaw lightly, just enough to feel the tension in your jaw muscles and the pressure against your teeth. Press your tongue against the roof of your mouth and press your lips together. Hold this tension for ten seconds or so, then relax your jaw, tongue, and lips. Shift your awareness upward to your closed eyes.

Squeeze your eyelids together and knit your brow. Feel the tension in your skin on your forehead and at the corners of your eyes, feel the hardness of your skull beneath the skin and the weight of your brain. Be aware of the pressure of the floor or the towel against the back of your head. Feel the softness of your hair. Hold this awareness of your skull, scalp, and upper face for ten seconds or so, then relax completely and let all perception of your head slip from your consciousness.

Continue to breathe with a slow and regular rhythm. Be aware of your existence as consciousness separate from your physical form. Imagine that you lie in a comfortable posture in the bottom of a boat that floats upon the gentle stream of a river. Feel the fresh air and gentle sunlight upon your skin. Allow yourself to be borne along by the flowing water. Continue in this relaxed state for five or ten minutes.

Raise your hands and apply them gently to your face so that the heels of your palms press into the hollows of your closed eyes. Draw your hands downward as though slipping off a skin-tight mask. Slowly open your physical eyes, yawn to stretch your jaw, and gently move and stretch your arms and legs. If you feel slightly dizzy, remain lying on the floor for several minutes and it will pass away. When you are ready, arise from the floor and continue with your day.

Commentary

This type of stepped-relaxation exercise has become common in hatha yoga and other forms of Eastern physical culture that emphasize the unity of mind and body, such as martial arts training. It also happens to be an excellent general method for inducing a hypnotic state when done as a guided relaxation during which an instructor continues to speak and tells students what to visualize throughout the exercise. Usually the direction is given that the student will feel relaxed and wonderful, and if a light hypnotic state has been achieved, this suggestion can have a potent and healthful effect.

Refrain from performing this exercise immediately after eating—wait at least an hour after a meal. Do not do it in bed or you may fall asleep. Do not do it when you are extremely tired, or sleepy, or sick. It is essential that you focus your awareness keenly throughout the exercise for it to produce useful results. It is also essential that the exercise establish its own time frame. Never set an alarm, or do the exercise when you have only a limited amount of time, or when you are likely to be interrupted by a visitor or a phone call. When performed properly, it usually takes around ten minutes.

Pressing the palms against the face and sliding them down is a way of symbolizing with a physical gesture the end of the exercise. It helps separate your altered state of consciousness, achieved during the exercise, from your usual everyday consciousness.

If you wish, you may extend the exercise by progressively tensing and relaxing smaller parts of your body. Instead of beginning with your left leg, start with your left foot, then move to your right foot, before returning to tense and relax your left calf, then your right calf, and so on. The procedure outlined in the exercise results in the minimum acceptable duration of practice, and should not be shortened, but it may be lengthened with beneficial results.

This reclining posture is known in hatha yoga as the Death Pose (*shavasana*). It should not be confused with the Death Posture of Austin Osman Spare, which was employed by Spare to energize sigils and has no similarity to shavasana apart from its name.

EXERCISE 5

Inward Perception II: Elemental Orientation

LIE UPON YOUR back on the floor, your feet six inches apart and your arms spread wide with palms turned upward, so that your body forms a cross. If you are uncomfortable on the bare floor, lie on a mat and place a folded towel under your head. Take care to orient yourself so that your head points to the north, your left arm to the east, your feet to the south, and your right arm to the west.

Perform the stepped relaxation routine described in the previous exercise. Progressively tense and relax your left leg, right leg, left arm, right arm, pelvic region, lower torso, rib cage, shoulders, neck, jaw, and head. As you relax each part of your body, remove your attention from it. Lie quietly for several minutes. Take regular, slow breaths.

Be aware of the immense mass of the Earth beneath you. Extend your perception downward and expand it on all sides until you can sense the roundness of the planet. Feel its gentle curve. Be conscious of the spine of the world, its axis running from the North

Pole to the South Pole, aligned with your own spine. Expand your awareness outward and become conscious of the planets of the solar system and the more distant stars, like glowing jewels set in the turning dome of a great natural cathedral as they rise in the east and descend in the west. Mentally speed up time so that you can watch the stars arc across the dark sky, and can feel the turning of the Earth.

Shift your awareness into your left hand, and open your mind to catch a gentle spring breeze blowing from the east that stirs the fine hairs on the back of your hand and tickles the palm. The breeze is temperate and pleasant. Your left arm becomes light and almost seems hollow, as though filled with warm, dry air. Your left hand wants to move in the breeze like a feather, or rise up like a balloon. Fill your imagination with a bright yellow color similar to morning sunlight, along with the fragrance of flowers and the rustle of leaves. For several minutes hold this combined awareness of the lightness of your left hand, the bright yellow color, the rustling breeze, and the flower scent.

Withdraw awareness from your left hand and move it into your right hand. Feel dampness surround your fingers and palm like a soft glove, just as though your right hand lay enveloped in a cool mist. The mist moves up your arm. After a time your hand and forearm feel distinctly moist. Imagine that your hand floats upon the surface of clear water over which hangs a white mist. Feel droplets of water condense on your palm and trickle across your wrist. Fill your imagination with a deep blue color, and at the same time smell the salty dampness of the sea and hear the distant, rhythmic sigh of waves on a sandy beach. Maintain for several minutes this combined impression of wetness on your right hand and forearm, the deep color blue, the damp scent of the sea, and the sound of waves.

Withdraw awareness from your right hand and shift it into your feet. Feel warmth radiate against your toes, the balls and arches of your feet, and your heels, just as though the soles of your feet were a comfortable distance away from the dancing flames and glowing embers in a fireplace. The feeling of heat is distinct but pleasant. Notice the difference in temperature between your soles and the cooler sides and tops of your feet where the radiance from the fire does not reach directly. Your feet grow dry and hot. Be aware of their dryness and the tingling sensation of warmth. Fill your imagination with bright red color, and at the same time smell the scent of wood smoke and hear the soft flutter of flames. Maintain this combined awareness of warmth, redness, smoky scent, and the sound of flame for several minutes.

Withdraw awareness from the soles of your feet and transfer it to the top of your head. Imagine that the top of your skull presses gently against the side of a large rounded stone. Feel the chilliness and hardness of the boulder against your scalp. Feel its weight pressing upon your head. It is cool but dry as dust. It soothes your scalp as it presses upon it. Fill your imagination with a uniform blackness, and at the same time smell the dusty scent of dry earth and hear a deep but distant rumble that vibrates through the top of your head down to your teeth. For several minutes, maintain this combined awareness of blackness, the smell of dust, and the sound of rumbling earth while continuing to feel the cool weight of the boulder press against the top of your skull.

Split your awareness so that you simultaneously feel a fresh breeze around your left hand, wet mist envelop your right hand, the warmth of fire-glow against the soles of your feet, and the hardness of smooth stone pressing on the top of your head. Hold this fourfold awareness for a minute.

Lay the palms of your hands against your face so that the heels of your palms press lightly on your closed eyes, then draw your hands down over your face as though sliding off a skin-tight mask. Take a deep breath, open your eyes, move your jaw to relax it, and stretch your body. When you feel ready, get up and go about your day.

Commentary

The assignment of the four philosophical elements to the four directions of space is fundamental in magic. In order to ritually manipulate the forces of the elements, their essential natures must be understood, and they must be clearly associated with the four directions. In this exercise, the Golden Dawn arrangement of the elements upon the points of the compass is used because it is the generally accepted arrangement in modern Western magic: Air—East, Fire—South, Water—West, Earth—North. This arrangement is neither correct nor incorrect—it is merely the most common.

It is important to intuitively feel the qualities of each element dynamically flow forth from the four directions of space, not merely to visualize them in a mechanical way. For example, rather than telling yourself that you will now imagine the sensation of warmth, you must accept that the sensation of warmth is already present by becoming conscious of it. You do not pretend to feel warmth begin on the soles of your feet—you become aware that your feet are already warm and accept this reality without question, below the level of critical judgment. This trick of the mind is essential in magic.

EXERCISE 6

Inward Perception III: Astral Projection

FOR THIS EXERCISE you need a new penny. It should be as bright and clean as possible. Before using it, wash it thoroughly with soap and water and dry it.

Lie upon your back on the floor in the reclining posture with eyes closed, a folded towel under your head, your arms at your sides, and your feet around six inches apart. Using your right hand, place the penny upon your forehead between your eyebrows in such a way that it is stable, and not in danger of sliding off your head.

Perform the stepped relaxation technique. Tense and relax your left leg, your right leg, your left arm, your right arm, and work your way up your body until you reach your eyes and forehead. Be aware of the separation between your consciousness and your body, and for several minutes imagine yourself floating gently in a boat on a gliding river.

Focus your attention inwardly upon an imaginary red dot on the inside of your forehead just between your eyebrows, where you can feel the weight of the penny. Do not try to focus your eyes on this place, merely shift your attention and concentrate on a large red dot between your eyebrows as though seeing it float in space against a soft, dark background, like the great disk of the setting sun. As you mentally look at this dot, imagine it slowly expand to take up more and more of your field of view.

Feel yourself as a point of consciousness in the void, without a body. Feel yourself rise up like a soap bubble lifted on a light breeze, and float toward the red dot, which has grown enormous in your inner field of view. The red dot becomes so large, it completely fills your astral vision. You drift forward and pass gently through its center as through an open doorway. You are surrounded by warm, glowing redness, the color that sunlight makes shining against your closed eyelids.

Float within this nurturing red world for a minute or so. Your mind is completely detached, sufficient unto itself. Savor the pleasure of drifting weightless without sensation and without physical limits. Hold the awareness of yourself as a separate, bodiless consciousness. Gradually become aware that you possess a subtle body, and that the red glow is caused by light shining against the closed eyelids of this imagined astral form. It is like lying on a sunny beach with your eyes closed.

Open your astral eyes inwardly, without opening your physical eyelids. Regard the clear, cloudless blue sky that seems to surround you on all sides. If you see a vision of something else, mentally observe all the details of the scene. But if you see nothing but soothing blue all around you, do not be disappointed. The success of this exercise lies in its process, not in any specific result.

Close your inner eyelids once again and be aware of the cheerful red glow all around you. Allow your point of consciousness to sink gently backward until the red light around you has become a large red disk in front of your mental sight. Watch as this circle gradually grows smaller and more distant, until it is only a red dot against a dark background. Regard this dot for a minute or so without haste, and once again become aware of the pressure of the penny against the skin of your forehead.

Remove the penny with your left hand and set it on the floor beside you. Press your palms against your face so that the heels of your palms fit into the hollows of your closed eyes. Slid your hands downward, then open your eyes, stretch gently, and rise to go about your normal day.

Commentary

This simple exercise can be used to initiate astral visions and astral journeys. The red dot acts as a doorway through the Third Eye, or *ajna* chakra, between the eyebrows. The ajna chakra is the psychic center of the body that controls astral sight. Regular use of this exercise will awaken and heighten your natural scrying ability, and enable you to visualize more realistically astral objects and landscapes. This ability is essential in ritual magic.

The penny acts as a physical focus. Pennies are composed of bronze, a mixture of copper, the metal of Venus, and tin, the metal of Jupiter. Venus and Jupiter are both positive, helpful deities. In traditional astrology, Jupiter is known as the Greater Fortune and Venus as the Lesser Fortune. Red is the color associated with the ajna chakra. Azure blue is the color of Jupiter, the sky god. Think of the penny as payment for your astral passage through the heavenly gateway of your ajna chakra.

The contact of the penny will stimulate your ajna chakra and help to activate it. This center is more active in some individuals than in others. To gauge its level of sensitivity, perform this test. Get a sharp pencil and hold it in both hands about four inches away from your forehead with the point aimed directly at the place where your nose connects between your eyebrows. Close your eyes. Slowly move the pencil toward your head. Be aware of any sensations between your eyebrows and in the upper bridge of your nose. If your ajna chakra is active, you will feel a tightness and pressure between your brows before the tip of the pencil touches your skin. The closer the pencil comes, the stronger the sensation. When you notice this pressure, open your eyes and observe how far away the pencil point is from your skin. Release one hand without moving the pencil and estimate the distance by touch. Ideally, the point of the pencil should be more than an inch away from your forehead.

Do not be disheartened if you fail to experience spontaneous astral visions after passing through the circular red doorway and opening your inner eyelids. Specific visions are not the object of the exercise. It is designed to enable you to separate your consciousness from your body, and to become better aware of your astral form. On the other hand, do not be surprised if you find that after practicing the exercise regularly for several weeks, images spontaneously appear against the imagined blue background when you open your inner eyelids. If you begin to see astral images, record them following the exercise sessions either by writing them down in words, or by drawing them as pictures.

EXERCISE 7

Inward Perception IV: Tattwa Awareness

GET A PIECE of heavy cardboard, of the kind you would find making up a shoe box or as backing for a writing pad, that is white on both sides. Draw and cut out the five tattwa symbols, each about two inches on its longest dimension: a circle, a triangle, a crescent, a square, and an egg. With colored pencils, markers, or paints, color on both sides the crescent mist-gray or silver, the triangle red, the egg black, the circle blue, and the square yellow. Make the colors as even and as opaque as possible (see Figure 7-1 on following page).

It is best to perform this exercise in a cycle of five consecutive weekdays, one day for each symbol, in the following order: Monday—crescent, Tuesday—triangle, Wednesday—egg, Thursday—circle, Friday—square.

Lie on your back in the reclining posture and with your right hand place upon your forehead the symbolic shape that corresponds with the day of the week on which you are doing the exercise. On Monday, use the crescent, on Friday use the square, and so on. The tattwa symbols are aligned as in the accompanying illustration—the horns of the crescent should be even and point toward the top of your forehead, as should the large part of the egg.

Perform the stepped relaxation technique, successively tensing and relaxing your left leg, right leg, left arm, right arm, pelvic region, lower torso, rib cage, shoulders, neck, jaw, and head. For several minutes allow yourself to drift free of your body, as though lying in the bottom of a boat upon a flowing river.

Become aware of the pressure of the cardboard symbol upon your forehead. Visualize its shape and color floating above you against the darkness of space, and allow your point of awareness to rise up toward it like a gently rising soap bubble. Approach nearer and nearer, until the symbol fills your sight and surrounds you completely. As it surrounds you, pass through its center and open your astral eyes, while keeping your physical eyelids gently shut.

When you open your astral eyes after passing through the gateway of the silver crescent, visualize all around you beautiful blue; after passing through the red triangle, bright scarlet; after passing through the black egg, pearl white; after passing through the blue circle, rich yellow; after passing through the yellow square, deep black.

Hold these colors around your point of awareness for half a minute or so before allowing them to fade. You may at this point spontaneously see an astral landscape or image that expresses the element connected with the symbolic shape on your forehead. The silver crescent will produce watery visions; the red triangle fiery visions; the black egg ethereal or spiritual visions; the blue circle airy visions; the yellow square earthy visions.

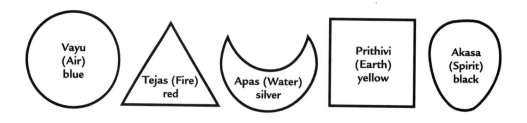

Figure 7-1. Five tattwa symbols of the elements

A vision can sometimes be encouraged by imagining the element that corresponds with the symbol. Even if no vision results, you should spend several minutes filling your imagination with the element associated with the symbol in order to link the two firmly in your subconscious.

On Monday after passing through the gateway of the silver crescent and opening your astral eyes to a beautiful blue that surrounds you on every side, focus your imagination on water. Visualize it flowing and running in streams, fountaining upward, falling as rain, rolling as waves of the sea.

On Tuesday, after passing through the red triangle and opening your astral eyes to a scarlet radiance on all sides, imagine fire blazing, running along sticks of wood, glowing in the form of embers, showering bright clouds of sparks heavenward, and burning with a silent constant flame.

On Wednesday, after passing through the gateway of the black egg and opening your astral eyes to a featureless pearl-white radiance, visualize the shimmering bands of a rainbow all around you, each colored band dancing with tiny sparks of brilliant white light. The seven bands are red, orange, yellow, green, blue, indigo, and violet.

On Thursday, after passing through the gateway of the blue circle and opening your astral eyes to bright yellow on all sides, visualize beams of sunlight shining down from a blue sky upon swirling white clouds to gild them with golden light, and observe the invisible wind make the clouds tumble and move like living creatures.

On Friday, after passing through the gateway of the yellow square and opening your astral eyes upon a featureless blackness, see mountains and rolling hills gradually appear in the distance, and become aware all around you of the ripe fruits and vegetables of a garden growing from dark, rich soil.

When you have visualized the elemental quality of the symbol, close your astral eyes and allow yourself to sink back down through the gateway, so that the tattwa symbol diminishes in size, and once again you can distinguish its outline and color against a dark background. Become aware of the light pressure of the cardboard shape on your forehead. Remove the tattwa symbol from your forehead with your left hand and set it on the floor, then press the heels of your palms gently into the hollows of your closed eyes and draw your hands down your face as though sliding off a skin-tight mask. Open your eyes, stretch gently, and when you feel ready, rise and go about your day.

Commentary

The five Eastern tattwa symbols were used in the Hermetic Order of the Golden Dawn to graphically represent the five elements: Fire, Water, Air, Earth, and the quintessence or fifth element, known in the Golden Dawn system variously as Akasa (Akasha), Aether (Ether), Spirit, or Light. The elemental colors of the tattwa symbols do not agree with the common Golden Dawn colors for the elements. No attempt was made to reconcile this conflict, and it often causes confusion in the minds of students.

Elements	Tattwas	Tattwa forms	Tattwa colors	Element colors
Fire	Tejas	triangle	red	red
Water	Apas	crescent	silver	blue
Air	Vayu	circle	blue	yellow
Earth	Prithivi	square	yellow	black
Spirit	Akasa	egg	black	white

The tattwa symbols were used mainly as astral gateways during scrying in order to access the elemental planes of the astral realm, or as representatives of the elements during meditations upon the natures of the elements. They were also sometimes employed to graphically embody the forces of the elements on talismans, amulets, and sigils. They are encountered in modern systems of magic that have descended from the original Golden Dawn teachings, so it is necessary to be familiar with their meanings and functions.

The correspondence that I have set forth between the five workdays of the week and the five tattwa forms is not exact, but is close enough to be serviceable. Monday, the day of the Moon, is watery in nature; Tuesday, the day of Mars, is fiery; Wednesday, the day of Mercury, partakes of the quality of mind and in this sense is linked with the fifth element of Spirit; Thursday, the day of Jupiter, is airy because Jupiter is a sky god; Friday, the day of Venus, is earthy. This correspondence is not found in the Golden Dawn system, so far as I am aware, but it makes good symbolic sense.

Most persons have some notion concerning the qualities of the four lower elements, but no understanding of the fifth element, Spirit or Aether, that underlies and pervades the lower four. It is the essence of universal mind, and may be conceived as a subtle fire borne upon the breath and stored up in the blood of living things. It is the *pneuma* of the Greeks, the *spiritus* of the Romans, and the *chi* of the Chinese. It is the ether that was supposed by primitive science to pervade all of space between the stars and act as a conducting medium for light. Due to its universal nature, it was assigned both white (all colors) and black (no colors). The rainbow, which also embodies all colors, is appropriate to represent it.

When imagining the black egg against the black background of space, visualize an aura of silvery light around its edge. This radiant aura will distinguish the shape of the egg from the darkness behind it.

The founder of the Golden Dawn, S. L. MacGregor Mathers, specifically instructed against placing the tattwa symbols on the forehead, on the grounds that it would cause headaches. I have not found this to be the case. On the contrary, placing the tattwa symbols on the forehead seems to facilitate their activation. If you find that you get headaches while performing this exercise, try doing it without using the physical tattwa cutouts.

Inward Concentration I: Mantra

THE PURPOSE OF this exercise is to still the chaos of your thoughts by replacing them with a single repeated word known as a mantra. Any mantra may be used, but one that works well is the word "Omega," the name of the last letter in the Greek alphabet. It represents both totality and fulfillment.

Assume the reclining posture upon the floor with a folded towel under your head, and perform the technique of stepped relaxation by first tensing, then relaxing successively your left leg, right leg, left arm, right arm, pelvic region, lower torso, rib cage, shoulders, neck, jaw region, and head. Allow yourself to float gently apart from your physical body for several minutes, as though drifting along in a boat on a river.

Draw a deep, regular breath. As you exhale, mentally sound the word "Omega" in your mind, just as though you were vibrating it upon your voice. Actually hear the word in your mind. Pronounce it inwardly in three extended syllables that flow together without pause:

Ooooooooom-maaaaaaaaa-gaaaaaaaah.

Repeat in your mind this silent mantra when you inhale. Keep your breaths even. Resist the temptation to form the mantra in your throat—keep your throat relaxed. Each time you exhale, mentally sound the mantra once, and each time you inhale, mentally sound it once.

Focus almost all of your attention on the mantra. Leave only a little awareness apart to monitor your breathing and posture. When you find yourself breathing irregularly or holding your breath, relax and smooth out your breaths. When you discover yourself unconsciously tightening various muscles in your body, such as the muscles in your throat or abdomen, deliberate relax these muscles.

Continue to sound the mantra silently within your thoughts for five minutes or so. Resist the urge to form an image in your mind. Do not allow your mind to wander, and if it does, bring it gently but firmly back to the sound of the mantra. The mantra should be mentally sounded around a dozen times a minute, so that each expression occupies five seconds. This results in six cycles of breath each minute, with two mantra soundings on each cycle.

Allow the imagined sound of the mantra to vibrate resonantly within your head as though your skull were hollow. The initial syllable "Om" is particularly important, since it establishes the tone and intensity of the mantra.

After sounding the mantra inwardly for five minutes, take a deeper than normal breath, press the heels of your palms gently into the hollows of your closed eyes, and draw your hands down your face as though sliding off a mask. Open your eyes, stretch your body, and when you feel ready, rise and go about your day.

Commentary

The primary function of any mantra is to prevent the mind from thinking by occupying its attention on a single thing. It was believed in the East that merely by stilling the mind, even for a short time, great spiritual benefits would result. Since it is impossible for the student to empty the mind completely, he or she is provided with something that fills the vacuum created by the temporary cessation of thoughts.

The belief exists that some sounds have special or unique occult virtues. The general mantra "Om" is one such sound. It is also believed that mantras transmitted in secret to the student directly from a teacher possess magical properties when used by that student, but only by that student, and only if these mantras are never revealed to anyone else.

The first syllable of the word "Omega" is the greatest of all mantras, "Om" or "Aum," which may account for the efficacy of the Omega mantra. It has proved to be of great utility in my own practice. "Om" is the first part of the longer mantra Om-mane-padme-hum, which has been translated "Hail the Jewel in the Lotus," but "Om" is often used as a separate mantra.

To still the thoughts is one of the most difficult tasks in Western occult training. You will discover that your mind struggles to free itself from the burden of listening with attention to the sound of your mantra, and will play any trick to cause a lapse of concentration. Your heart will pound and the blood will sing in your ears, your body will itch and ache, your muscles will tense, your breathing will become uneven, your stomach and intestines will churn and gurgle, you will pass gas from both ends, noises in your outer environment will seem enormously magnified, external interruptions to your practice will become more frequent, and your thoughts will wander across every trivial incident in your memory.

Be persistent. Continue the mantra. Focus your mind on the imagined sound, and only on the sound, and when your thoughts wander, as they assuredly will, guide them gently back to the mantra. This course of action will yield results over time.

EXERCISE 9

Inward Concentration II: Thought Stream

L IE DOWN ON the floor, or on a mat upon the floor, in the reclining posture. You may be more comfortable if you fold a towel and place it beneath your head. Perform the stepped relaxation technique by successively tensing and relaxing your left leg, right leg, left arm, right arm, pelvic region, abdomen and lower back, rib cage, shoulders, neck, jaw region, and head. Take several minutes to drift in a bodiless state, as though lying in a boat that floats gently down a river.

Turn your attention to your own thoughts. Do not interact with your mental process in any way, merely observe it as though you were suddenly able to see and hear into the mind of another person. Continue to notice your thoughts with awareness for about fifteen minutes.

At first you will discover that your focused attention immediately stills your mind. You will be able to think nothing other than "What am I thinking?" or "What am I supposed to be thinking now?" However, it is not in the nature of the mind to remain quiet. If you are patient for several minutes, it will slip into its old habit of reviewing memories and concerns of the day. You will begin to daydream, or think about some worry or problem that is vexing you.

Each time you fall into reverie, gently become aware of your thoughts as though watching them and listening to them from outside your own head. This return to attention will halt your thought process for a short time, but soon you will begin to ruminate once again, as you mind resumes its long-established habits.

There is no success or failure in this exercise. It is the process itself that has value in making you aware of your own habitual thought patterns, and in separating for a brief time your conscious point of view from those thoughts. It is better not to set a time limit. Start the exercise with the intention of doing about fifteen minutes work, and end it when you feel you have fulfilled this goal.

To conclude the exercise, press the heels of your palms into the hollows of your closed eyes and slide your hands down and off your face. Take a deeper than normal breath, open your eyes, stretch gently, and get up to continue your normal day without brooding over the exercise or its results.

Commentary

It is important in this exercise not to try to direct your thoughts to any particular subject. The purpose of the exercise is to sustain an awareness of your own thought process. Think of your observing awareness as a part of your higher self, and your automatic thought stream as a function of your lower self. Ordinarily your awareness inhabits your lower self—or more accurately, it seems to inhabit your lower self—but with a small amount of mental effort it is possible to shift its point of view to your higher self. Whenever we step back from something, we are then able to see it in its entirety as separate from self.

The thought process of the average person is mechanical and repetitive. We tend to mull over the same issues and concerns endlessly but are seldom aware of this obsessive and cyclical working of the mind. We also tend to reinforce prejudices and fears by constant mental repetition. If we did not automatically reinforce these things, they would melt away of their own accord since they seldom have any basis in reality. For example, those with low self-esteem regularly tell themselves that they are stupid, worthless, clumsy, ugly, fat, unlovable, and so on, and this reinforcement of destructive thoughts prevents feelings of freedom and happiness.

Simply by becoming aware of this mechanical action of the mind, even for fifteen minutes, we gain some measure of control over it. In order to clearly see what the mind is doing, it is necessary to watch its stream of thoughts without interfering in any way. Once we learn the tricks of the mind, we can begin to train it to avoid repetitive thoughts of self-hatred, fear, and prejudice against others that have no justifiable basis.

Inward Concentration III: Daily Recall

THIS EXERCISE IS best done during evening hours while lying on the floor in the reclining posture. However, it can also be done in bed at night, just before going to sleep.

Adopt the reclining pose, and perform the technique of stepped relaxation, which by this stage in your practice should be second nature. Tense and relax your left leg, right leg, left arm, right arm, pelvic region, lower torso, upper torso, shoulders, neck, jaw, and head. Allow your mind to drift free of your physical form for several minutes.

Direct your thoughts to the early morning of that day and begin to review your actions. Try to remember the events of the day in as great a degree of detail as possible by tracing them in a continuous sequence from when you awoke until the time you began the exercise. As clearly as possible, visualize the events of the day in your imagination. You will find that gaps exist in your recollection. Do not brood over these lapses but pass on to the next event that you remember.

When you have completely reviewed the day, ask yourself what you should have done that was not done. Avoid thoughts of self-recrimination; simply consider useful actions omitted from the day for whatever reason. Perhaps you intended to mow the lawn, or replace a burned-out light bulb, or read a book. Mentally note these lapses, large or small.

Turn your mind to the things done during the day that were worth doing. Enumerate every useful action that you are glad to have accomplished during the day. Most of these actions will be of a minor nature. You may have done your laundry, or smiled and waved hello to your neighbor, or mailed off a bill payment. Avoid an attitude of self-congratulation while making this mental inventory, merely consider the useful actions of your day.

Take a deeper breath, press the heels of your palms over your closed eyes, and draw your hands down and off your face as though sliding off a skin-tight mask. Open your eyes and stretch your limbs. If you do this exercise in the reclining posture on the floor, rise and continue with your evening. If you do it while in bed, roll over and go to sleep.

Commentary

The advantage of performing this exercise in bed at night is its placement at the very end of the day. This allows the recollection of the events of the entire day from morning to night. The disadvantage is that you will find yourself drifting off to sleep before the exercise has been concluded. This is a very bad habit to get into. The reason for performing the reclining exercises on the hard floor is to combat the natural tendency to fall asleep while doing them. They require mental effort, and the mind attempts to shirk this effort by escaping into sleep.

Try the exercise a few times in bed. If you lapse into sleep before finishing it, do it while lying on the floor shortly before you go to bed for the night. Do not persist in attempting it while in bed if you find yourself falling asleep in the middle, since this will establish a very poor habit and will make it difficult for you to perform the exercise properly under any conditions.

Its purpose is the enhancement of your self-awareness, and also the establishment of a balanced attitude toward your daily life. We tend to focus either upon the praiseworthy things we do from day to day, or upon our lapses and omissions. Every life consists both of daily successes and failures. By examining them together, we can achieve a fairer and more accurate impression of the wholeness of our lives.

SITTING
EXERCISES

Breathing I:
Color Breathing

P LACE AN ORDINARY kitchen chair so that it faces a blank wall, a plain curtain, or some other featureless surface that will not distract your attention. Sit in the chair with your back straight, both your feet flat on the floor and about six inches apart, and your hands on the tops of your knees. You should lean slightly forward, with the lower part of your back arched so that it has a hollow—do not allow your lower back to curve outward. Keep your shoulders relaxed and avoid the tendency to hunch them. Imagine that a string attached to the top of your skull is pulling gently upward. This will help you to maintain this position, which will hereafter be referred to as the sitting posture.

It is best to remove any constricting article of jewelry or clothing before you begin exercises that involve the sitting posture. If you are comfortable in your shoes, you may retain them for this exercise, but if you feel more at ease without them, take them off.

Decide beforehand how many repetitions of the exercise you will do. Keep track of the repetitions by means of a rosary, a string of regular beads, a short length of chain, or a length of cord with knots tied close together along its length, that is held in your left hand. In my own practice, I use a length of brass chain. Before beginning, count out the number of repetitions you intent to perform on the beads, knots, or chain links. Each time you complete a breath, pass one of the beads, knots, or links between the thumb and index finger of your left hand until there are none left. This allows you to concentrate on the exercise, not on the count.

Gaze directly in front into the infinite distance, as though you are able to look through the wall at the far-off horizon of the Earth itself. With your eyes open, imagine that the air all around you is a vibrant violet color, almost like a transparent violet haze or mist.

Exhale lightly, then begin the first breath. Slowly draw the violet-colored air into your lungs, concentrating only on the region of your belly. Be aware of the violet air swirling into your nose and down your throat. As you inhale, allow your belly to expand outward without strain or effort. Visualize your entire torso hollow on the inside, and watch with your inner awareness as the region of your belly fills with bright violet mist.

While your belly is expanding, mentally count out three regular beats. The duration of each beat should be around a second. You may wish to mentally voice the words "one-thousand one, one-thousand two, one-thousand three" in order to maintain this duration. Any other word or phrase can be used to set the duration and rhythm of each beat. It is best to choose a word or phrase that has meaning for you, so that it can act as a mantra. The word "Omega" can be used for this purpose.

When your lower torso has expanded as far as it wants without pushing or discomfort, raise your awareness to the middle of your chest, just behind the point of your sternum where your solar plexus is located. Continue to inhale smoothly for three more beats and allow the bottom of your rib cage to expand with violet-colored air. Watch with your inner vision as the level of violet air inside your hollow torso rises to fill the middle portion of your chest.

When your middle chest has expanded to a comfortable size, shift your awareness upward to the zone of your chest between your nipples and your shoulders. Allow your upper chest to expand and your shoulders to rise very slightly without strain or discomfort. Watch inwardly for three regular beats as the violet mist swirling into your nose fills up the top part of your hollow torso.

Hold your breath lightly for a moment or two with your throat relaxed and open, while watching with your inner vision as the swirling violet mist inside your torso becomes quiet.

Begin to exhale by allowing the violet mist in the upper part of your chest to escape through your nose in an even, controlled fashion for three regular beats. Watch inwardly as it swirls out of the top of your hollow torso and mentally see it issuing in a plume from your nose. Allow your shoulders to fall slightly and contract your upper rib cage gently without strain.

Shift your awareness to the middle part of your torso at the base of your rib cage. Continue to exhale for three regular beats and observe the violet mist as it leaves the center of your chest and escapes through your nose. As you do so, contract your upper abdomen slightly.

Direct your mental vision to the lower part of your hollow torso and watch the mist escape upward from your belly as you breath out for three regular beats, at the same time contracting your lower abdomen with light effort. At the end of the third beat, your entire torso is empty of the violet mist.

Hold your lungs empty for a moment or two with your throat open and relaxed. As you keep the air outside from entering your body, visualize the violet mist all around you, a beautiful vibrant coolness against your skin.

This completes one cycle of breath. Allow a single bead, or knot of your cord, or link of your chain, to pass between the thumb and index finger of your left hand. Repeat the cycle of breath, slowly and evenly drawing the violet mist in through your nose to expand your lower abdomen while you visualize it entering your nostrils and swirling down into the bottom of your hollow torso. Continue as already described until all of the beads have been counted.

Draw a natural breath and begin to breathe with your usual rhythm. Set down your rosary, close your eyes, and press your palms over your face with the heels of your palms located in the hollows of your eye sockets. Slide your hands down and off your face. Open your eyes, stand up, and go on with your day.

Commentary

This is an exercise that combines controlled breathing with visualization. It is effective in stirring to life kundalini, the occult power that usually remains coiled and asleep at the base of the spine in most individuals. It also helps to develop astral sight.

By visualizing different colors, different energies can be absorbed into the body. Violet, associated with the quintessence of Akasa or Light, awakens spiritual perceptions. Red, linked with elemental Fire, is energizing and invigorating. Blue, associated with elemental Water, is soothing and loving. Yellow, linked to elemental Air, enhances clarity of thought and improves memory. Green, one of the colors of elemental Earth, heals and strengthens the body. The more common Earth color, black, should not be used in this breathing exercise, since it tends to have a depressing effect.

The visualization of the torso as hollow and the division of the in-breath into three stages are a useful tricks that help to expand all regions of the lungs. While you visualize the violet-colored air entering your body, your physical eyes should look directly in front at the unseen distant horizon. Remember to blink so that your physical eyes do not become dry and red.

In the beginning, you will probably find beats of one second too long to sustain for more than half a dozen breath cycles. If so, shorten the beats to half a second by mentally sounding the mantra more quickly. It does not matter how long each interval is, only that all intervals are regular. The inhalation should occupy the same length as the exhalation.

I must emphasize strongly that you gain nothing by trying to exceed the natural limits of your body. If you attempt to take too much air into your lungs during this exercise, or if you try to empty them too completely, you will hurt yourself. You should avoid the urge to close the back of your throat during the brief retentions of breath. The usual sign that you are doing breathing exercises incorrectly is a tendency to cough after the exercise is concluded. By the time this persistent cough appears, you have already strained your lungs, and it may take weeks, or even months, for them to regain their perfect health. An occasional impulse to cough during the exercise is normal and should not be viewed with alarm.

Always work within the natural limits of your body. When you have done this breathing exercise for a week or two, you will have a clear understanding of where that limit lies. The capacity of your lungs will extend themselves without being pushed, and you will find that you can lengthen the duration between each beat effortlessly.

When you first start to do this exercise, count out only around ten or twelve beads on your rosary. If you discover that even this number of repetitions causes you physical discomfort, reduce the number to six or eight. After a week or so, you can safely begin to increase the number of breaths in each practice, a few beads at a time, to an eventual maximum of around thirty.

It is best to always breath through your nose, but for those with sinus problems, this may prove impossible. When the nose is blocked, either chronically due to a sinus condition or temporarily due to allergies or a cold, open your mouth slightly and breath in and out through your mouth, visualizing the colored mist flowing in between and out through your parted lips. From time to time, moisten your lips with your tongue to avoid drying them out. When you briefly retain your breath, close your mouth.

Breathing II: Pore Breathing

SIT IN A plain kitchen chair facing a wall or other surface that will not distract your attention. Hold a rosary or other counting instrument in your left hand, having predetermined the number of repetitions you intend to perform. Adopt the standard sitting posture, with your feet flat on the floor six inches apart, your hands on the tops of your knees, and your lower back concave as you lean slightly forward. Imagine a string attached to the top of your skull that pulls your head and spine gently upward, and remember to keep your shoulders relaxed.

Direct your gaze forward with your eyes focused on the unseen distant horizon on the other side of the wall. Visualize the tiny molecules in the air around you dancing and vibrating with golden energy. With your mental vision, see them as small flecks of light that vibrate and mingle so rapidly, they merge into a kind of energized golden mist. Be aware that this mist is really composed of ultrafine particles. Exhale completely, but without strain.

Inhale evenly through your nose for four rhythmic beats without overfilling your lungs. Use a silent mantra such as "Omega" to time these beats—repeat the mantra four times in your mind. As you do this, mentally see the golden dancing mist enter your body through the pores in your skin. Visualize it entering uniformly through every part of your body. Have the impression that the air is not entering your body in the usual way at all, but is only entering through your skin.

During the four beats of inhalation, watch with your astral vision as the golden mist fills up not just your lungs but your entire body—your chest, your pelvis, your legs and arms, fingers and toes, head and neck. Watch and feel it permeate every muscle, every nerve, every organ including your brain. Watch and feel the golden mist settle into your bones right down to the marrow.

At the end of the count of four, your entire form is filled with golden energy that you can feel swirling and coursing throughout your blood vessels and along your nerves. Hold it inside for four more regular beats while silently repeating the mantra, and observe it dancing within you. Keep your throat relaxed and open during this retention.

Exhale evenly for four beats while voicing the mantra in your mind. As you do so, watch and feel the molecules of radiant air issue uniformly out through every pore in your skin like golden steam escaping through ten thousand tiny holes. As you breathe out through your nose, maintain the conviction that the air is not leaving your body through your nose, but only through your pores.

Hold the golden mist outside your body for four regular beats as you repeat the mantra you have selected, while you visualize the mist dancing and swirling all around you. Keep your throat relaxed and open during this period. Extend your astral awareness inwardly to see your body empty and dark inside. At the end of this interval, allow a bead of your rosary or link of your chain to pass between the thumb and index finger of your left hand. This marks one complete breath.

Continue in this way until you have completed all the breath cycles of your exercise. Set down your rosary, close your eyes, and press your hands to your face so that the heels of your palms cover the hollows of your eye sockets. Slide your hands down your face as though sliding off a skin-tight mask. Open your eyes, rise from your chair, and go on with your day.

Commentary

It is important to understand that during this exercise, although you breathe in and out through your nose in the usual fashion, you visualize yourself breathing in and out only through the pores of your skin. Although you fill your lungs with air, you turn your awareness away from your lungs and visualize the golden mist filling the entire volume of your body.

Your body and face will become covered with a fine sheen of perspiration if you are doing this exercise properly. This is normal. If you attempt to set too long an interval between the beats, you will find that your body begins to tremble and yearn for oxygen during the retention phases of each cycle. This is a sign that you must shorten the duration of each stage in the breath cycle by quickening the repetition of the mantra. All four stages of the breath cycle must be kept the same length, and all must be equally shortened until you can hold your lungs empty for four regular beats without great discomfort.

Note this distinction between pore breathing and color breathing. In color breathing, the air is visualized as brightly colored mist that resembles a rarified liquid. In pore breathing, the air is visualized as dancing bright particles similar to a fine golden dust that floats in sunlight. You should see with your astral sight the individual energized particles vibrating upon the air.

After you have practiced this exercise for several weeks, you may discover that you no longer need to imagine the air around you filled with dancing golden particles. It is common during this type of controlled breathing for the air to actually take on this appearance to the physical sight. However, you do need to continue to visualize it entering through the pores of your skin as you inhale, and exiting through your pores as you exhale.

This exercise charges your entire body with vitality. It is excellent in the early morning, shortly after waking, because it stimulates the body for the rest of the day. Ten or twelve breath cycles are enough at the beginning of practice. If you find this number of breaths too taxing, reduce it to six or eight.

Breathing III: The Nine–Seven Breath

BEFORE BEGINNING THIS exercise, determine how many repetitions you will do, then count out the same number of beads, links, or knots on your counting device. Hold it in your left hand during practice.

Sit on a plain wooden chair facing a blank wall or other featureless surface. Adopt the standard sitting posture, your feet flat on the floor six inches apart and your hands on your knees, your torso inclined slightly forward with a concavity in your lower back, the top of your head extended upward, and your shoulders relaxed.

Gaze through the wall at the unseen distant horizon as though the wall were transparent. Deepen your breaths slightly, and for a minute or two continue to breathe slowly and deeply with your awareness focused on the rhythm of your breath. Remember to blink so that your eyes do not become dry and irritated.

Exhale completely before beginning the first controlled breath cycle. It is best to use a mantra to regulate the durations of the stages. Any mantra may be employed. The mantra "Omega" works well when silently voiced in the mind. Imagine that your torso is hollow. For three slow repetitions of the mantra, inhale to fill your lungs. On the first mental voicing of the mantra, visualize air flowing into your lower abdomen; on the second, visualize it filling your middle torso in the region of your solar plexus; on the third, visualize air filling your upper torso from your nipples to your shoulders. Raise your shoulders slightly during this third phase of inhalation, but take care not to hunch them.

Lock your throat shut by tightening the muscles inside the base of your throat and pressing the back portion of your tongue upward and backward, while at the same time inclining your head forward and tucking in your chin. This creates a tightness at the pit of your throat. Take care not to strain the muscles in your throat. Continue to gaze at the unseen horizon beyond the wall in front of you. Retain the air in your lungs for nine repetitions of the mental mantra.

Unlock your throat by lifting your head and relaxing the muscles inside the base of your throat and at the back of your tongue. Exhale in a slow, controlled manner for three repetitions of the mantra. On the first, roll your shoulders down and empty the top of your torso; on the second, exhale from the middle part of your torso; on the third, empty the air from your lower abdomen completely with gentle force, taking care not to strain yourself.

Lock your throat by tightening the muscles inside the base of your throat and at the back of your tongue, and tucking in your chin. Hold your lungs completely empty for seven repetitions of the silent mantra.

This completes one full cycle of what I refer to as the Nine–Seven Breath. Allow a bead of your rosary, or a link of your counting chain, to pass through the thumb and index finger of your left hand. Begin the next cycle by unlocking your throat and inhaling for three repetitions of the mantra, and continue until you complete the number of cycles determined prior to beginning your exercise.

Successful practice will be indicated by a profuse cooling perspiration that covers the entire body after the fifth or sixth cycle of breath. You may also become aware of a vibration in your body that is almost like a high-pitched humming in your muscles.

When you have completed the set number of breath cycles, put down the rosary and close your eyes. Press your hands over your face with the heels of your palms covering the hollows of your eyes and slide them down and off as though drawing off a skin-tight mask. Open your eyes and sit for a minute or two, breathing normally, until your heart returns to its usual rhythm. Stand and go about your usual day.

Commentary

The Nine–Seven Breath is extremely effective for awakening esoteric perceptions and abilities. It can be done in concert with color breathing and pore breathing, but in the beginning it is best to perform it without these added visualizations until you become familiar with its asymmetric rhythms.

Its structure is predicated on the physiological reality that it is easier to stop the breath with the lungs full than with the lungs empty. In order to more evenly distribute the effort of the exercise, the retention with lungs empty has been made briefer than the retention with lungs full. The rapid threefold inhalation and exhalation have the beneficial effect of charging the lungs with etheric energy, while the unequal periods of inhalation and exhalation necessitate a high degree of concentration that keeps the mind focused.

The most difficult part of this exercise is holding the breath expelled for seven repetitions of the mantra. If you have set too long an interval, you will struggle to keep the air out and find yourself rushing to inhale. This indicates that you must shorten the durations of each of the four parts of the cycle by an equal degree. Accomplish this either by changing the mantra to one that is shorter, or by mentally sounding the mantra more quickly. The regulating factor is how long you can comfortably keep your lungs emptied. This will establish the interval for the other three parts of the breath cycle.

You must find a balance between moderate effort and excessive strain. If the exercise it too easy, you will not derive benefit from it; if it is too difficult, you may injure your lungs by over- or underinflating them. When stopping the breath, be aware of the urge to gasp for more air, but do not allow this yearning to become physically painful. If you grow dizzy, or see blackness or sparkling lights in your field of vision, you are exerting too much effort and should shorten the phases of each breath cycle either by choosing a briefer mantra, or mentally voicing the mantra more quickly. Other signs that you are attempting too much are an inability to control your exhalations, a wildly pounding heart, or a pronounced trembling in the muscles of the legs and arms.

The Nine–Seven Breath is an advanced exercise with a higher degree of difficulty than those previously described. Anyone with medical problems such as hypertension or heart disease should not attempt it, and should only practice breathing exercises that do not involve rigorous retentions of the breath.

Outward Concentration I: Time Watching

POSITION A PLAIN kitchen chair in front of a table in such a way that when you sit in the chair, you face a blank wall or other nondistracting surface across the surface of the table. On the bare table in front of you put a watch or small clock. You must be able to see the dial and the hands of the timepiece clearly. Adopt the standard sitting posture in the chair with your feet flat on the floor six inches apart and your hands resting lightly on your knees. Breath deeply with a regular rhythm that is somewhat slower than your normal rate of breathing.

Look at the dial of the watch or clock. Note where the minute hand is located. Concentrate your gaze and your attention on the tip of the minute hand and do not allow either to wander for five full minutes. Keep your eyes and your mind relaxed, but never allow their focus to stray from the end of the minute hand. Be aware of its almost imperceptible movement.

Empty your mind of thoughts. Do not mentally tell yourself to concentrate on the tip of the minute hand—simply do it.

Remain motionless during the exercise apart from minor movements such as the need to blink, swallow, and breathe.

When your attention slips, and you find yourself thinking of other matters or daydreaming, gently but firmly guide your awareness back to the minute hand. If your eyes become fatigued, blink several times and deliberately relax the muscles around your eyes without letting your focus on the minute hand waver. If you become conscious that your breathing is uneven, or that you have held your breath, re-establish your regular breath rhythm and immediately return your concentration to the timepiece. Do not fidget in your chair.

At the end of five minutes, close your eyes for several seconds to rest them. Gently press the palms of your two hands over your face, and slide them downward as though slipping off a skin-tight mask. Open your mouth and work your jaw from side to side to relax it. Stretch your arms and back, taking care not to strain your muscles. Rise from your seat and go about your day.

Commentary

Those with poor eyesight will find it easier to see the dial of a small table clock, such as an alarm clock, than the dial of a wristwatch. If possible, use a watch or clock without a second hand—but if a second hand is present, ignore it during the exercise.

A five-minute duration is more than long enough in the beginning. It's very likely you will find it impossible to concentrate on the end of the minute hand for a full five minutes without thinking of something else, such as your breathing, an itch that you wish to scratch, the need to swallow, the rumbling of your stomach, noises outside the room, and countless other minor distractions. A small portion of your attention must remain split off to monitor your body and prevent it from tensing its muscles, holding its breath, and so on, but the greater part of awareness should remain focused on the minute hand.

When your mind or gaze wander (your mind will always stray first), bring them back to the task you have set for them gently but firmly. Do not be angry with yourself for your weakness. Observe the lapse in attention without emotion, correct it, and continue with the exercise. It is inevitable that you will sometimes daydream or think of other matters. What is important is that you remain alert to catch these distractions of the attention quickly. The distance covered by the minute hand on the watch face will show you how long you have been woolgathering.

Do not perform this exercise more than once in a day. After you have done it half a dozen times for five minutes, extend the duration of the exercise to ten minutes.

Ritual magic requires the ability to direct the attention intensely on symbols and objects, and to hold it focused for extended spans of time. The ability to concentrate is essential for success. All exercises to develop concentration tend to be tedious, simply because the human mind hates to focus on something in which it has no active interest. Disciplining the mind to overcome this tedium is the aim of the exercise.

EXERCISE 15

Outward Concentration II: Candle Burning

INSERT THE TIP of a stick pin or other small pin with a weighted head into the side of a white candle about half an inch below the level of the wick, so that the pin projects horizontally when the candle is placed in a candle holder. The tip of the pin should penetrate the candle to a depth between one-eighth and one-quarter of an inch.

Arrange a kitchen chair before a small table as described in the previous exercise, so that when you sit in the chair you will face a blank wall or other undistracting surface. Set the candle in its candle holder on the table and light it. Sit in the chair in the standard sitting posture with hands resting lightly on knees and feet flat on the floor six inches apart. Establish a regular rhythm of slow, deep breaths.

Gaze at the flame of the candle and focus your awareness solely on the flame, to the exclusion of every other thought. Note its shape, its color, and its motion in the same way that a camera records a scene. Do not think about the flame, merely observe it with unwavering attention. Let the flame fill your mind.

When you realize that your attention has strayed to daydreams, memories, or mental reflections, gently but firmly guide it back to the flame of the candle. Each time your mind wanders, bring it back to the flame. Allow yourself to become the flame, alive and aware but without thoughts. Concentrate on the flame keenly and remain fully aware of all its aspects throughout the exercise.

If your eyes water, allow them to close for several seconds and deliberately relax the muscles around your eyelids. Even when your eyes are shut, your awareness should remain on the flame of the candle.

When the heat from the flame causes the metal pin to become warm and drop out of the side of the candle, the exercise is finished. Close your eyes for a few moments. Gently press the palms of your two hands over your face and slide them downward as though slipping off a skin-tight mask. As you do this, allow the tension in the muscles of your face to slip away. Blow out the candle. Stretch and rise from the chair to go about your usual day.

Commentary

Candles burn more slowly than is generally realized. When you do this exercise, you will become acutely aware of this fact. It is best to insert the stick pin into the side of the candle no more than half an inch below the wick in the beginning of practice to prevent an intolerably long exercise. A duration of from five to ten minutes is appropriate. When you become better able to sustain your concentration, you may insert the pin further away from the wick.

A pin with a head is best because the weight of the head insures that the pin will fall cleanly from the candle when heated. Alternatively, a very small nail called a brad can be used. Avoid using pushpins with plastic heads that may melt in the heat from the candle flame, or light pins without weighted heads that may droop down and become embedded in the side of the candle. The pin or nail should drop out cleanly.

This exercise is best done is a dim room so that the attention naturally gravitates toward the brightest object, the flame. However, if the room is completely dark, the glare from the flame may strain the eyes and cause them to water. A level of ambient light in the room equivalent to early twilight works best.

Outward Concentration III: Water Boiling

POSITION A PLAIN chair without arms from four to six feet away from your kitchen stove. Put a small amount of water into a whistling kettle and set it on a burner of the stove to boil. Sit in the posture described in previous exercises, with your feet flat on the floor six inches apart and your hands cupping your knees, your spine straight and your torso leaning slightly forward to create a hollow in the small of your back.

Direct your gaze and your attention at the spout of the kettle and keep it there throughout the exercise. As the water begins to heat, concentrate part of your awareness on the sounds made by the kettle.

First you will hear small creaks and pops as the heated bottom of the kettle expands on the metal burner of the stove. A seething will begin, and grow progressively louder. There are pings and other noises as the body of the kettle warms. The seething turns into a boiling, and small puffs of steam escape from the whistle hole in the spout. These thicken and turn into a constant blast of steam, and the whistle of the kettle begins and steadily rises in volume and pitch.

When the kettle is boiling furiously, relax and close your eyes, then press your hands over your face with the heels of your palms resting upon your eye sockets. Slide your hands downward to cleanse the fatigue from the muscles of your face. Open your eyes and stretch gently. Rise from the chair and take the kettle off the burner, then make a cup of tea and enjoy it.

Commentary

Contrary to popular folk wisdom, a watched pot does eventually boil. Concentrating awareness on the process merely makes it subjectively seem to take much longer.

The special value in this exercise is the need to focus the sense of hearing, as opposed to the sense of sight. Two senses, sight and hearing, are employed, but the attention is primarily devoted to the sounds involved. The gaze is fixed on the spout of the kettle to prevent it from wandering, then the attention of the mind is turned to the sounds of the heating water.

Concentration of awareness through the sense of hearing is useful when using audible (as opposed to mental) mantras, and when vibrating names of power aloud on the breath. It also has a function when music is employed during rituals. It is possible to use the energy in music to project the will more powerfully, but this technique requires the ability to sustain an intense focus of awareness on sound for extended periods of time.

If you do not own a whistling kettle, use a regular cooking pot, and continue the exercise until the water is boiling furiously and the pot emits large amounts of steam. A glass pot works best because you can watch the boiling process as it progresses.

Visualization I:
Geometric Shapes

TAKE UP THE sitting posture in a kitchen chair facing a blank wall or curtain. Gaze directly ahead and focus your eyes on the distant horizon of the world that lies on the other side of the wall in front of you. Look through the wall without straining your eyes, as though the wall and the obstructions beyond it were transparent.

Turn your awareness inward and with your inner sight look upon a colorless void that stretches infinitely away in all directions. Reach out with your mind in several directions to verify that it has no limits. No matter how far you stretch the invisible hand of your awareness, the void continues to extend forever in the same direction. It is neither dark nor light, but a leaden, transparent gray, like an overcast sky at twilight. Contemplate the void for ten seconds or so.

Visualize an infinitely tiny black speck in the void. It is so small, it is almost invisible to your sight. By extending your mind you can feel its position and shape against the gray background.

Project your awareness closer and closer to this point. You discover that no matter how closely you approach it, the point always remains a speck of black without shape or dimension. Just as the void is limitlessly large, so the point is limitlessly small. Contemplate the point.

Create a second black point some distance away from the first. Both are featureless and dimensionless, mere locations in space. Contemplate the two points.

Draw a perfectly straight black line through both points that extends endlessly in opposite directions. Because the points are not thicker than this infinitely thin line, it is impossible to distinguish them from the line itself. Only the line exists. Reach out with your awareness along the line, as though you had two invisible arms that could stretch forever. Feel the infinite length of the line. No matter how far you extend your awareness in both directions, the line continues endlessly onward. Contemplate the straightness, thinness, and endlessness of the line.

Create another point some distance away from this line. Contemplate the relationship between the point and the line.

Extend the line sideways to meet and pass through the point, and at the same time extend the line sideways away from the point. The result is an infinitely thin plane that has no edge but continues forever through the void. Visualize this as a flat sheet of tinted glass that is so thin, it has no measurable thickness. It is like the flat place where two soap bubbles press together, transparent and colorless, but slightly darker than the void. Since the point was no thicker than the plane, it has become lost in the plane. Only the plane exists, dividing the void into upper and lower zones. Contemplate the plane.

Create a point some distance above the plane. Contemplate the relationship between the point and the plane. Let your awareness drift downward through the plane, and mentally look upward through the plane at the point on the other side, as though looking through a windowpane. Drift back up until your awareness is on the same side as the point.

Extend a second plane perpendicularly up from the first to pass through the point, and at the same time extend it downward on the far side of the first plane. The extended plane absorbs the point into itself, so that the point is no longer visible. Like the first, this second plane continues away infinitely on all sides. These identical planes intersect each other at right angles, dividing the void into four equal zones. Allow your awareness to drift from one zone to another as you contemplate the relationship between the planes.

Note that where the planes pass through each other, you can perceive a thin bright line glowing against the grayness. This line is so thin that it is almost invisible. It extends like a laser beam forever in both directions. Reach out with your invisible mental hands and feel the infinite length of this glowing line. Contemplate the relationship between the glowing line and the perpendicular planes.

Create a black point in one of the four zones of the void. Contemplate the relationship between the point and the planes by moving your awareness through the planes from zone to zone as you consider the point. Return your awareness to the zone occupied by the point.

Extend a third plane perpendicularly out from the first two so that it passes through the point and merges the point into itself. At the same time this third plane extends in the opposite direction on the far sides of the first two planes. All three planes intersect at right angles, and divide the void into eight equal zones. Let your awareness drift from zone to zone, passing through the planes, as you contemplate the relationship between the planes.

Note that where the three planes intersect each other, you are able to perceive three glowing lines. Like the planes, these three lines intersect at right angles. Extend your awareness along them to verify that they are infinitely long, without ends.

As you contemplate the lines defined by the intersections of the planes, notice that where the lines themselves intersect there is a brightly glowing point. This point glows twice as brightly as the lines. Consider, for a time, the relationship of this central point to the three lines that cross through it.

Allow the three planes to fade from your awareness like transparent sheets of black smoke, so that only the three glowing lines and their central point of intersection are visible in the void. Contemplate the lines.

Allow the three dimly glowing lines to fade from your awareness until only the brightly glowing point that was their center remains. Contemplate the point.

Allow the bright point to fade away from your inner sight so that there is nothing but the transparent gray void. Contemplate the emptiness of the void.

Relax your body. Close your eyes for a few seconds to rest them. Press the heels of your palms over your closed eyelids and slide your hands down your face as though pulling off a skin-tight mask. Open your eyes, stretch your arms and back gently, then rise from the chair and go about your day.

Commentary

Although I have described the void as transparent gray, the tiny points as specks of black, and the planes as panes of tinted glass, it is best to remove all qualities from these visualized forms other than those necessary to define them. The point has no size or shape, only location. The line has no breadth or width, only length. The plane has no width, only length and breadth. All are colorless.

Rather than trying to see the void as a picture in your mind, it is better to try to feel the existence of the points, lines, and planes. This is a difficult trick to explain. It does not involve pretending to reach out in your mind with an invisible hand (although this is the simplest way to describe it), but rather, a kind of inward projection of awareness that allows you to feel the created forms as parts of yourself.

When you test the infinite length of the line by reaching out in both directions along it, you are actually extending awareness in both directions along the line like electricity running along a wire.

During this visualization, keep your physical gaze directed forward and your eyes focused on infinity. If you notice your eyes wandering, or focusing on some crack or mark on the wall, let your gaze extend through the wall once more. Remember to blink from time to time, or your eyes will dry out and become red and irritated.

You can, if you wish, do this exercise with eyes shut in the beginning. However, it is best to get used to visualizing with eyes open from the start of practice, since this is necessary in subsequent ritual work. If your find your eyes straining to see what is only in your mind, deliberately relax them.

This exercise has proven extremely useful to me over the years. I do it more often than any other visualization. It is especially valuable as a conditioning exercise when preparing to draw sigils and other symbols on the astral level.

Visualization II:
Leaving the Body

S IT IN A plain wooden chair without arms facing a blank wall or curtain in the sitting posture already described, with both feet flat on the floor and your hands cupping the tops of your knees. Look straight ahead and focus your gaze on infinity, as though you are able to look through the wall. Take several deep, regular breaths.

Visualize yourself standing up from your chair and walking behind it on its right side to the center of the room in which you are practicing the exercise. Stop with your back to the chair. Examine the scene in front of you and be aware of all the furniture in the room, the woodwork, the floor, the ceiling, pictures on the wall, and the window or door if they are in your field of view. Notice the colors and textures of the walls and furniture. See the room in as much detail as possible.

Slowly turn around to face the wall so that your projected astral form gazes at the back of your physical body seated in the chair. Observe the color of your clothing, the appearance of your hair, your collar, the shape of the chair, your posture. Examine the room on either side of your seated body with your astral vision. Pay attention to details.

After spending several minutes examining the room, approach the chair on the left side (the opposite side from which you left your body) and sit back down in it. Allow your awareness to re-enter your body. Close your eyes for a few seconds to rest them and take a deep breath.

Open your eyes and leave the chair physically on the right side, walk around to the center of the room and stand with your back to the chair, exactly as you did earlier in your visualization. Look closely at the scene in front of you and compare its details with the memory of your visualized scene. Notice the discrepancies between the image you visualized and that actual image before you.

Turn around and look at the back of the empty chair. Pay attention to its shape and color, and compare it with your visualization of it. Study the details of this side of the room, just as you did earlier in your imagination. Be aware of all the things you missed during the visualization.

Walk around the left side of the chair and sit down. Adopt the sitting posture, feet flat on the floor about six inches apart and hands on knees. Let your gaze focus through the wall in front of you at the unseen distant horizon. Spend a minute or two being aware of your body. Close your eyes and take a deep breath. Press your hands to your face and draw them downward. Open your eyes, stretch gently, and rise to go about your day.

Commentary

This exercise strengthens the ability to perceive the astral forms that overlie the physical forms of objects and places. For effective rituals, it is necessary to be able to see the astral world that is usually overwhelmed with the sheer brightness and solidity of the material world.

Notice that by leaving your chair on the right side and resuming your seat on the left side, you describe a circle around the chair clockwise. It is also best when you turn to face the chair during the exercise, both in your astral and physical forms, that you rotate your body clockwise. Clockwise motion imitates the course of the sun across the heavens and is used in constructive, healthful works of magic, whereas counterclockwise motion is contrary to the sun and is used in works of destruction and malice (there are exceptions to this rule, as later exercises will show). The habit of moving and turning clockwise when performing ritual magic should be established early in your training.

During the course of your astral examination of the room, your physical gaze may have a tendency to wander as you turn your astral awareness from place to place. When this happens, gently but firmly look forward and refocus your physical eyes on infinity. It requires practice before you can completely detach your conscious attention from your physical sight, because we are accustomed to focus our attention on what lies in front of our eyes. This is a survival mechanism, and we tend to revert to it automatically.

You will also find that from time to time your awareness snaps back into your physical body during this exercise. One instant you will be standing in your astral form regarding the room, and the next instant sitting in the chair looking at the wall. Simply project your attention back to the same point of view it occupied just before this recoil occurred. Keep doing this whenever you experience recoils of awareness. After several weeks of practice they will cease.

The exercise should be conducted in many different surroundings to prevent boredom. It is essential, when you visualize your astral form leaving your seated body to study the room, that you have new details around you to maintain your interest. It should not be performed in exactly the same setting more than three or four times. If you do it more than once in the same room, turn your chair to a different wall, or rearrange the furniture. Try the exercise in various rooms in your house or apartment, and also experiment with public places where you can sit undisturbed and face an undistracting wall surface, such as the library, a doctor's office, houses of friends, and so on. It can also be done outdoors.

EXERCISE 19

Visualization III: Astral Temple

ADOPT THE STANDARD sitting posture in a plain wooden chair that faces an eastern wall, with your feet flat on the floor separated by six inches and hands on knees. Look directly forward and focus your gaze on the distant horizon beyond the wall and other intervening structures.

Visualize in your mind a white paneled door on the wall in front of your chair, while continuing to gaze forward into infinity. In your imagination, rise from the chair and step forward to approach the door. Put your right hand on its ornate brass knob. Feel the cool smoothness of the brass as you turn and open it. The door swings on its hinges away from you to the left. Walk through the doorway into a room with an oak floor and pale-gray walls that are almost white. The ceiling is painted the same pallid gray. Close the door behind you without turning to look through its opening.

You stand in the northwest corner of a large square chamber. There is no window in the room, but ample light streams in from above through a circular dome made up of many small triangular panes of clear glass crystal. Blue sky can be seen through the dome. In the middle of the floor rests a black marble altar in the shape of a double cube. The altar is two feet square and four feet high. Its sides are featureless. On the center of the bare altar top a white candle burns in a short brass candlestick.

Around the altar a white circle nine feet in diameter has been painted on the dark floorboards. The band of the circle is three inches wide. There is space to walk around the outside of this circle, since the room is exactly sixteen feet across. Between the sides of the altar and the ring of the circle is a gap of almost three and one-half feet; between the ring of the circle and the outer walls is a gap of three and one-half feet.

As you slowly walk around the outside of the circle in a clockwise direction, you pass on your left an inverted green triangle painted in the center of the north wall at the level of your heart. It is quite large, about three feet across on each side, and completely filled with solid evergreen color. The east wall in front of you bears an upright triangle filled with yellow that is of similar dimensions. The south wall on the right bears a similar upright triangle in red. As you walk around the white circle, you see that the door through which you entered is set in the west wall near its right-hand corner, and that the wall bears an inverted blue triangle in its center. All four triangles are the same elevation above the floor, their centers at the level of your heart.

When you have completed your circuit of the room and once more face east with your back to the closed panel door, step across the white circle and approach the altar. Stand on its western side facing east, and place your hands flat upon its polished surface to feel the chill of the black stone. Hold them there for a minute or so while gazing at the candle flame. Remove your hands and pass them one after the other slowly over the candle near enough to feel the heat from its flame against your palms, but not so close that you burn yourself. The candle flame flutters slightly.

Study the room for a minute or so to impress its dimensions and features in your memory. Notice that the crystal dome in the ceiling is six feet across, two-thirds the size of the painted circle, and centered exactly above the altar. Walk slowly once around the altar clockwise as you examine the room, keeping the fingers of your right hand in contact with the chill stone of the altar. Feel the sharpness of its edges and corners.

When you have observed every detail, release the altar, turn to the west, and step over the white circle on the floor to approach the paneled door. Place your left hand on its ornate brass knob, and as you start to open the door, turn to face the room once again, so that you do not see anything that lies on the other side of the door. Step backward out of the room and pull the door shut while still facing into the room. Step backward again without turning and sit in the chair occupied by your physical body.

Close your physical eyes for several seconds to rest them. Place your palms on your face on either side of your nose, with the heels in the hollows of your eye sockets, and draw them downward as though sliding a skin-tight mask off your features. Take several deep breaths, open your eyes, stretch your body, and rise from the chair to continue with your day.

Commentary

This is one of the most important preliminary exercises. The room visualized is an astral temple. Magic is always worked on the astral level—the physical gestures and movements of ritual are mere foundations for this astral work, which requires advanced visualization skills. Eventually you will design your own astral temple, and it will become your habitual place of working. In the beginning, the appearance of the astral temple is not so important as your ability to clearly experience it with your inner senses.

The four triangles of the elements have been colored and placed according to the Golden Dawn system of correspondences: Air, yellow, east; Fire, red, south; Water, blue, west; Earth, green, north. This is not the only possible assignment of the elements to the directions, but it is the most common assignment, and must be known by every serious practitioner of Western magic.

In my own work I have adopted a different assignment, for reasons too complex to enter into—Earth, green, east; Fire, red, south; Water, blue, west; Air, yellow, north. However, before you abandon the Golden Dawn associations of the elements to the quarters, you should understand them both on an intellectual and an intuitive level, and this understanding can only be gained by using them during rituals over a period of months.

The usual Golden Dawn color for elemental Earth and the north is black. However, olive green, russet brown, and citrine yellow are also used to represent Earth in the Golden Dawn system. Green is a more vital and productive color than black, symbolizing as it does the green plants that grow from the soil. In my opinion, green more equally balances the colors of the other elements individually, whereas black balances all three active elements together. When the four elements are given equal importance, as they are in this exercise, green is a better choice for the north than black.

It is best to begin the visualization of the astral temple by opening the door, and end it by backing out of the temple and closing the door without turning around. In this way, all of your attention is concentrated on the temple itself, without being distracted by externals. The temple occupies a plane of reality separate from the physical plane, and by passing through the doorway you pass from one dimension to another.

For best results this exercise should be repeated regularly. As you gain a sense of how you would like your own astral temple to look, you can visualize the features of your own temple replacing those described in the exercise. Over time you will want to add ritual furniture and instruments to your visualizations, but in this pre-liminary exercise I have made the temple quite plain.

Projection of the Will I: Affecting an Object

S IT IN A plain wooden chair before a table, with a blank wall or other featureless surface in front of you. The front edge of the table should be close enough to touch your abdomen. Place your right hand on your right knee. Keep your spine straight with a slight concavity in your lower back, and your feet flat on the floor about six inches apart. Do not hunch your shoulders.

Between the thumb and forefinger of your left hand hold the thread of a small pendulum so that its bob hangs freely an inch or so above the surface of the table. Rest your left elbow on the surface of the table with your left forearm vertical and your left wrist bent. The bend in your wrist insures that the pendulum is far enough away from your forearm to swing unhindered. It is easier to support the pendulum if you wrap its thread around your left index finger several turns. Any bob may be used for the pendulum, such as a ring or pebble, provided that it is small and light. Its support should be fine thread or a very fine chain.

Direct your gaze at the bob. With the power of your mind, will the pendulum to move. Keep your mind detached from your left arm, as though the arm belonged to somebody else. Do not deliberately move your left arm. Focus all your attention on the pendulum.

After a minute or two, it will begin to move in small circles. Will these circles to become larger and more regular. When the pendulum is swinging in large circles in one direction, will it to swing in an arc toward you and away from you. When you are able to achieve this change of motion, will the pendulum to begin swinging in an arc from side to side. Continue to concentrate your attention upon it until its motion changes. Finally, will the pendulum to swing in circles in the opposite direction.

After ten or fifteen minutes, regardless of your degree of success, set the pendulum down on the table. Relax your left arm, close your eyes and take several deep breaths. Press both hands over your face and draw them downward. Open your eyes and go about your normal day.

Commentary

Not everyone can achieve such exact control over the movements of a pendulum, but almost everyone can cause some movement. The more you practice this exercise, the more precise your control over the pendulum will become.

The pendulum is not set swinging by telekinesis but by the unconscious movements in your left hand. These muscular impulses are so small, they are impossible to detect by the unaided senses. The purpose of this exercise is the use of the will to affect the subconscious mind, and cause it, or its independent intelligent agents, to move a physical object. Regular practice opens a channel between your subconscious and conscious, and enables your subconscious to affect your body subliminally.

The pendulum is an excellent instrument for interacting with spirits, especially for the solitary practitioner. These bodiless beings communicate with human awareness through the subconscious mind. Before spirits can employ the pendulum to answer questions you put to them, they must be able to set the pendulum into motion by affecting your muscles below the level of your deliberate control. Then they respond yes or no to questions by making the pendulum swing back and forth or side to side; or by making it revolve in circles either clockwise or counterclockwise.

When communicating with spirits through the pendulum, it is only necessary to establish in the beginning which motion will signify yes and which will signify no in response to your questions. Simply project the thought at the bob of the pendulum that back and forth will mean yes and side to side no, or clockwise will mean yes and counterclockwise no. This establishes the convention the spirits will use for their communications.

The deliberate effort by the practitioner to control the motions of the pendulum by willpower facilitates the ability of spirits to control the pendulum. It primes the pump, so to speak, and allows a flow of communication upward from the deep mind to the conscious mind. In my view, when you move the pendulum by willing it, the pendulum is actually moved by spirits acting in obedience to your intention, who control the muscles of your arm and hand on the subconscious level. It is a small step from moving the pendulum in compliance with your will, to moving the pendulum in answer to your questions.

The limitation of the pendulum for spirit communication is that all questions must have yes or no answers. It is possible to use a modified form of pendulum for more complex responses, in which the motions of the bob point out letters inscribed on the rim of a bowl to spell words, but this ancient and difficult instrument is rarely employed in modern magic. Even the great magician S. L. MacGregor Mathers and his mediumistic wife, Moïna, employed the common pendulum described here to receive from a hierarchy of spirits known as the Secret Chiefs a portion of the teachings that compose the Golden Dawn system of magic, so widely used today.

Use of the pendulum is a form of dowsing, and modern dowsers sometimes employ a pendulum in preference to a forked stick or bent metal rod when searching for water or other things hidden in the ground. It is not the general opinion of dowsers that their wands or pendulums are moved by spirit agency, but this seems probable to me.

Silver and rock crystal are good materials for pendulums, because both are lunar materials—the moon is the gateway between the conscious and unconscious mind. The best thread is silk, the best chain silver. If the bob of the pendulum is about the size and weight of a cube of sugar, it will work well. Large, heavy pendulums are unresponsive and tiring on the arm when supported for more than a few minutes. A popular and effective form of pendulum is an ordinary ring suspended on a length of thread—a plain silver band is best, but a gold band or ring set with a stone will also work.

Projection of the Will II: Affecting an Element

THIS EXERCISE IS best done at night when the air inside the practice room is still. Position a plain wooden chair about four feet away from a small table, so that when seated in the chair in front of the table, you face a blank wall or featureless curtain or panel. The practice room should be dimly lit from behind you but not completely dark. Remove any object that might distract your attention from your field of view.

Place a candle in a holder on the table, light it, and sit in the wooden chair in the sitting posture, with feet flat on the floor about six inches apart and hands on your knees, leaning slightly forward with a concavity in the small of your back and your head extended upward along an imaginary vertical line that passes through the top of your skull.

Breathe regularly and deeply. Still your thoughts. Focus your attention solely on the flame of the candle, which must be placed far enough away from your face that the gentle exhalations from your nostrils do not cause even the least flutter—it is for this reason that the chair is four feet from the edge of the table. For several minutes regard the flame passively, until you become completely aware of it.

Using the projected power of your will, make the flame stable and straight. Draw it upward with your mind, lengthening it bit by bit as though pulling on a twist of soft, stretchy, golden toffee. For about five minutes, continue to shape the flame with your mind.

Avoid frowning or straining the muscles around your eyes. It does not aid the projection of the will to squint, but will only make your face twitch as the muscles around your eyes and in your brow became fatigued. Also, keep your jaw relaxed, and when you feel your abdomen or legs tighten, consciously relax them and return your attention at once to the candle flame.

Banish everything from your mind but the flame. Imagine that it grows larger until it is six feet tall and broader than your own body. In your astral form, rise from your chair and step forward into the flame so that it bathes your body and surrounds you with its soft golden fire. The flame feels cool and pleasant on your skin.

Allow the flame to penetrate and flow upward through the interior of your body from the soles of your feet to the crown of your head. From within the flame, continue to will it to lengthen itself straight into the heavens, like a great burning pillar. Extend your awareness on all sides as you stand inside the flame to feel the flowing fire around you, and direct it ever higher as you will your astral body to grow taller and taller. Carry the flame up with you.

While you sustain your astral body inside the flame, continue to look fixedly at the burning candle with your physical eyes. Breathe slowly and deeply with a regular rhythm, and be sure to keep your muscles relaxed. Blink from time to time to prevent your eyes from drying and becoming red.

It is necessary to divide your awareness, so that most of it is present in your astral projection within the enlarged flame of the candle, yet a small amount remains in your physical body to regulate your breathing and keep your muscles from tensing.

After five minutes or so, deliberately separate your astral body from the flame. Allow your astral form to reduce to normal height and mentally step backward to resume your seated posture inside your physical body. Continuing to gaze at the candle flame. Take note of how elongated the actual flame of the candle has become. Hold your awareness on the flame for several minutes.

Draw a deeper breath, close your eyes, and place the palms of your hands over your face, then slide your hands downward as though pulling off a mask. Open your eyes. Shift from your posture to stretch your neck, work your jaw back and forth, and stretch your arms. Sit breathing normally for a minute or so, then rise and go on with your normal routine.

Commentary

If the air is still during the exercise to prevent guttering and fluttering, and you have projected yourself into the flame and made it a part of the fire of your own will, the upward extension will be considerable—two or three times higher then you might think a normal candle flame could reach. I have extended ordinary candle flames as much as seven or eight inches.

When projecting the will, it is necessary to get over the false notion that it requires physical effort. Tightening your muscles and clenching your jaw will hinder your practice, not aid it. What is required is sustained concentration and a projection of the point of self to the thing you wish to affect, so that it becomes an extension of your own mind. Once you make something a part of your self-awareness, you can change it with your will just as you change your thoughts. First let the flame interpenetrate your projected astral body, then lengthen your astral body upward and carry the flame with it.

To avoid eyestrain, do this exercise in low light rather than darkness. The flame of a candle is not bright enough to injure your eyesight, but many persons find it difficult to look directly at a flame for more than a few moments in complete darkness. The exercise requires that you continue to fix your gaze on the flame for at least ten to fifteen minutes.

Projection of the Will III: Affecting a Living Being

PLACE A PLAIN wooden chair six or eight feet away from a large television and tune the television to a live news broadcast. Assume the sitting posture in the chair and focus your attention on the anchorperson.

A news program that shows the face of the news anchor for extended periods is best. It is essential that the anchor look directly at the camera while reading the news so that you can establish eye contact with the anchor. For this reason, live interview shows are not suitable.

Fix your gaze upon the left eye of the anchor—the eye that is on your right-hand side as you look at the television screen. To better focus your attention, mentally extend an invisible ray vertically down through the left pupil of the anchor, and then mentally extend a horizontal ray across from your left to right through the pupil, so that these imaginary rays cross exactly on the left eye of the news anchor.

Imagine that the left eye of the anchorperson is a channel or conduit that connects your will and thoughts to the mind of the anchor. Feel a connection with the anchor, as though you were seated directly in front of the person, and he or she were reading the news and watching you at the same time. Feel that the anchor is speaking and looking directly at you.

Continue to focus your will strongly through the gateway of the left eye of the anchor, and while maintaining your physical gaze unwaveringly on the eye, reach out with your astral right hand and touch the anchor on some part of the anchor's body that is visible on the screen. It does not matter where you touch the anchor. The back of the hand is a responsive area, as is the neck. Best results will be achieved when you do not move your physical hand.

The way of projecting touch through the will is this—you clearly imagine that you are actually seated or standing immediately in front of the news anchor, and simply reach out and touch his or her skin. Grip the anchor's hand, lay your right hand on the anchor's shoulder, place the palm of your hand flat upon the side of the anchor's neck, or cheek—it does not matter, provided that you make a clear, firm contact that cannot be mistaken for anything other than the touch of a human hand.

Do not stretch or extend your astral touch as though reaching across a great distance—simply touch. Realize that there is no need to stretch out because you are already there. You must be able to actually feel with your subtle perception the texture and curve of the news person's skin against your fingers if this exercise it to be fully effective. The more clearly you feel the touch yourself, the more clearly the anchor will feel it.

As you touch the news anchor, closely observe the emotional response in his or her eyes and face with your peripheral vision, but continue to project your will through the gateway of the anchor's left eye. Do not allow your gaze to waver from the pupil of the eye. The continued projection of the will through the eye serves to maintain a link with the subject of the experiment, in the same way a plugged cord conducts electricity.

The facial or body responses of the subject will let you know whether the projection has been successful. These responses will be subtle because the news anchor will not wish to react in an overtly physical way on live television to an invisible touch. However, when the projection is correctly done, the person reading the news will be unable to prevent an involuntary reaction of surprise, confusion, or fear. Since you are specifically looking for such a response, you will recognize it.

Repeat the projection of touch on different parts of the subject's body over a span of fifteen or twenty minutes whenever the image of the news anchor appears on the screen for more than five seconds, and you are able to make direct eye contact with the anchor. The exercise can prove frustrating when the subject appears on screen for no more than two or three seconds, but usually in the course of a newscast the anchor is on screen half a dozen times for periods of fifteen or twenty seconds. You must learn to work fast to establish a link by eye contact and project a touch in no more than a dozen seconds or so, but after a while this becomes second nature.

At the end of the newscast, or when you sense that you have accomplished the best you can achieve during that practice session, relax, take a deep breath, and close your eyes. Press the heels of your palms gently over your eyes so that you can feel the warmth on your closed eyelids. Draw your hands slowly down as though sliding off a mask. Open your eyes, stretch your body, and go about your usual day.

Commentary

It is possible to achieve a considerable degree of success with this exercise. It should be practiced with restraint. In daily life it would be rude to stare directly into the eyes of another person, and would arouse hostility in the mind of that person that would partially block the projection of your will, but a news anchor is especially vulnerable since he or she cannot look away from the camera, and cannot put on a mask of anger or hostility. On the contrary, a person reading the news live must always maintain an open, neutral expression, and this invites the ray of your will to enter through the gateway of the left eye.

It makes no difference how far away the subject of the experiment may be geographically provided the image is a live image, not an image on tape or digital disk. Make sure the broadcast is live—twenty-four-hour news channels run taped news for most of the day, although it appears to be live. Any person live on the television can be used as a subject provided the person makes prolonged direct eye contact with the camera. This is most common during news broadcasts.

The left eye of the news anchor is used as the gateway because the left side of the body is receptive. Similarly, you should project your will outward from your right eye, although you gaze at the left pupil of the subject on the television screen with both your eyes simultaneously—the right side of the body is projective. The cross that is mentally drawn through the left pupil of the subject, first the vertical beam from top to bottom, then the horizontal beam from left to right, establishes at its intersection the point of focus for your projected ray of will.

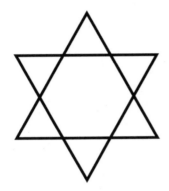

STANDING EXERCISES

Aura Awareness

S TAND IN YOUR practice area facing an undistracting surface with your feet together and your arms at your sides. Keep your back straight. For a few moments, imagine that a string is pulling gently upward on the top of your skull. This will aid you in establishing the correct posture, hereafter referred to as the standing posture. Your weight should be distributed equally on both feet, and equally between your heels and the balls of your feet. Tuck your chin in just a little, push your pelvis forward, and turn your hands slightly outward. There should be no strain, only balance and a slight tone in your muscles to maintain the alignment of your body.

Gaze directly forward at the unseen, distant horizon that lies on the other side of the wall of your practice room. Take several deep, regular breaths.

Direct your inner awareness to the surface of your skin. Slowly, allow your perception to wander over your entire body. Start at the sole of your left foot and move your awareness up your left side, over the top of your head, and down your right side to the sole of your right foot. Repeat this orbit of awareness several times without haste. Shift your focus to the bottoms of your heels and move your awareness up your calves, thighs, and buttocks, up your back and neck, over your head, then down your face and throat, your chest and belly, your groin, thighs, knees, and shins, around the tips of your toes to the underside of the balls of your feet. Complete this orbit several times.

Feel your skin tingling and radiating with subtle energy. The sensation is similar to the static-electric attraction you experience when you rub the surface of a balloon with a silk scarf. Imagine all the tiny hairs on your skin stirring. This tingling on your skin is your aura. With your astral perception see and feel it all around you like a softly glowing second skin that lies within several inches of your physical skin. It is sustained by tiny jets of astral light that stream outward through your pores.

Imagine a bright blue-white star blazing in the heavens directly above the top of your skull, but far away in the distant darkness of space. Raise your point of awareness to the star and enter it. For a minute or so, feel the star all around you, enveloping you within its intense electric whiteness. Deliberately extend a ray of the star's blue-white fire straight downward so that it passes through the roof of your house, the ceiling of your practice room, and the top of your skull, to focus at the center of your chest between your nipples. This place in your body is known as your heart-center.

Allow your awareness to slide down the interior channel of this ray into your chest. Concentrate your will on the focal point of the ray. Visualize inside your torso a spark of light that grows into a shining sphere three inches across. As the spark expands into the sphere, its color dims and changes from blue-white to a softer yellow-white, the color of the sun. Mentally draw energy from the star down the channel of the ray and into the sphere so that the sphere radiates more and more strongly.

When you sense that the sphere at your heart-center cannot hold any more energy from the star, sever the link between the sphere and the ray, and observe with your inner awareness as the ray snaps upward like a contracting rubber band that has been released at one end.

From your point of view within the sphere, project its golden light outward in all directions. Imagine its light spreading throughout the interior of your entire body, up and down your torso, into your head, along your arms and legs, even to the tips of your fingers and toes, until you are filled with light. Feel the radiance press against the inside of your skin, seeking escape.

Allow this light to radiate out through the pores of your skin by deliberately willing your pores to open. Feel it stream through your skin in a million tiny filaments of brightness. The outflow of radiance expands your aura the way air pressure expands a balloon. Continue to expel light from the golden sphere in the center of your chest with your will until your aura has been pushed out from your body into a perfect globe. It extends a foot or so above your head and a foot or so through the floor beneath your feet—physical objects cannot contain it.

Spend at least three minutes contemplating this expanded aura of golden light. Strive to feel its gentle warmth, and to see its glow. It is transparent and exceedingly pale. Its shape ripples and moves in response to your thoughts, like the flame of a candle swaying on faint currents of air. From time to time colors flare across its surface, triggered by different emotions. Keep your emotions calm and balanced, and if you perceive your aura disturbed by color, use the power of your will to make it resume its uniform pale yellow.

After you have contemplated your expanded aura, allow the outward flow of energy from the blazing yellow ball of light in your chest to lessen, so that your aura begins to shrink back in upon itself. Visualize the intensity of the sphere in your heart-center becoming less and less. It reduces to a faint spark and fades completely away.

Your energized aura naturally sustains itself away from the surface of your body at a distance that is between several inches to almost a foot. It is closer where it surrounds your hands and feet, more extended where it envelops your head and chest. Feel its energy continue to stream from the pores in your skin in innumerable tiny invisible jets no thicker than fine hairs. These jets merge together to form a single glowing field of astral force that is always present around your body, but which varies in intensity depending on your mood or state of health.

Hold your entire aura in your awareness. With the force of your will, draw its towards the surface of your skin. The sensation of resistance is similar to what is felt when you try to compress a balloon. The aura has a tendency to seek to expand through any gaps, just as when you squeeze a balloon it will expand between your fingers. Balance the energy of your will over the entire surface of the aura and compress it until it floats less than an inch above the skin of your body.

Maintain this compression for a minute or two, and contemplate the sensation of this concentrated aura as a subtle pressure of energy against your skin, then release it.

Allow your aura to resume its natural shape and distance from your body. Contemplate your natural aura for several minutes by observing the sensations it produces in various places within your body and on the surface of your skin.

Close your eyes for a few seconds and take a deep breath. Press your hands over your face and slide them down. Open your eyes, relax from your standing pose, and continue on with your day.

Commentary

The auras of other individuals are seen as colored, radiant envelopes around their bodies, but seldom felt. You are able to experience your own aura tactually. Active visualization can help you to become aware of its existence. At first you produce the tactile sensations of your aura on the astral level through visualization. With practice it is possible to become sensitive enough to feel your aura without deliberately visualizing it.

It is difficult to see the colors of your own aura from the perspective of your physical sight because it lies so close to your face, but you can perceive them by projecting your point of view out from your body astrally, and looking back upon yourself from a distance. This projection can be physically simulated through the use of a mirror. Try performing this exercise in dim light while standing about six feet away from a floor-length mirror. Imagine that the image in the mirror is your physical body, and that you are watching yourself astrally from a distance. When you perceive colors in your aura, use your will to return it to a pale, transparent gold. This yellow color is so pale that it is almost invisible.

Not everyone can see color in auras, even in the auras of others. Seeing auras at all requires latent psychic ability. However most persons are able to tactually sense their own aura with practice. The ability to expand or contract the aura at will is useful in practical magic. The aura can be expanded around others for healing purposes, or contracted close to the skin to act as a magic barrier against occult attacks from human beings or spirits, or to contain and concentrate esoteric energies.

In my opinion, the aura is not a physical field of energy susceptible to photography or measurement with machines. The electrical field recorded by Kirlian photography is not the aura. Even though it is nonphysical, the aura is a very real astral phenomenon and has many practical uses in magic, including the analysis of the personality and health, both mental and physical, of other individuals.

The distant blue-white star symbolically represents the highest sphere of creation, Kether, and the golden sphere in the heart-center represents the middle sphere of creation, Tiphareth. Kether is the seat of the Source of Being, in Christian terms God the Father; Tiphareth is the seat of the higher self, in Christian terms

Christ, the Messiah. Kether energizes Tiphareth through a direct, vertical descending channel. It is not possible to astrally rise up in awareness to Kether, but by visualizing this ascent, it becomes easier to link Kether with Tiphareth—or more accurately speaking, it becomes easier to gain an awareness of the ever-existing link between these two Sephiroth.

You need not understand these terms from the system of Jewish occultism known as the Kabbalah in order to perform this exercise properly. I merely mention these associations for the interest of those readers familiar with the Tree of the Sephiroth, to show that a basis exists in the Kabbalah for the star and golden sphere, which play so important a part in later exercises.

EXERCISE 24

Grounding and Centering

FACE A BLANK wall, curtain, door, or other surface that has few visual distractions, and assume the standing pose described in the previous exercise, with feet together, arms at sides, back straight, chin tucked in, and pelvis pushed forward. Strive for straightness in your body, but do not strain. Direct your gaze ahead and focus your eyes on the unseen horizon that lies beyond the surface in front of you. Take several slow, deep breaths.

Visualize your body as a rough, natural pillar of gray stone that rises up from the grassy ground in a clearing of the forest. The pillar is of human dimensions, but irregular. Feel the sunlight warming one side of the pillar and the coolness of the other side in shadow. Feel the grass that grows on the top of the stone and the moss in small crevices in its side.

Become aware of the changelessness of the pillar. Allow summer to gradually give way to autumn as you accelerate the time. The days and night flash past, and the sun and moon trace alternating arcs across the sky. Let autumn become winter, and feel the snow cover the browning grass on top of the pillar and pile high around its foot. See the bare gray branches of the forest trees against the grayness of the sky. Let winter give way to spring as the snow melts and the new leaves bud and unfurl. Allow spring to warm and dry into summer, bringing the year full circle before slowing time to its normal rate.

Project your awareness downward under the soil, tracing along the hidden sides at the base of the pillar. Become aware that the pillar is only a finger of stone projecting up from a much larger mass of bedrock. Follow this stone down and down, deep beneath the earth. Feel the fissures in the rocks and the water that wells within them.

Continue ever deeper, until the coolness of the rock gives way to warmth, then heat, and the darkness is replaced by a red glow. Go even lower, and observe the rock turn orange, then yellow as it melts and become liquid magma. Go lower still until you are surrounded by molten iron that glows with dazzling whiteness. Contemplate the center of the planet Earth for thirty seconds or so.

Ascend up the way you descended, passing through the liquid iron into the molten rock. Watch with your inner vision as it becomes orange, then red, then dark, and changes from liquid magma to solid bedrock. Press up past the fissures and pockets of subterranean water until you enter the base of the pillar. Emerge from the ground and fill the pillar of gray stone with your awareness.

Observe that while you were beneath the earth, day has passed into night. In the moonless sky directly overhead is a large star that outshines all the other stars in the black vault of heaven. Draw this star downward in the form of a blazing point of light and cause it to enter the pillar through its rounded, grass-covered top. The star continues to sink until it reaches the heart of the pillar, where it stops. Contemplate the star inside the pillar. Around the star forms a golden sphere three inches in diameter. The intense blue-white radiance from the star energizes the sphere and causes it to shine with bright golden light. Feel its warming rays penetrate every cranny of the stone like sunlight.

Extend three white rays from the blazing star at the heart of the golden sphere. The first shines up through the top of the pillar into the night heavens, and down through its base to pass through the center of the Earth. The second shines outward through the right and left sides of the pillar. The third ray shines outward through the front and back of the pillar. All three rays intersect in the star at right angles, and are infinite in length. Contemplate the three rays for half a minute or so.

Draw the rays back into the star in reverse order—first the ray passing through the front and back of the pillar, then the ray passing through the sides, and finally the ray passing through the top and bottom. Release the star and watch it rise straight up from the golden sphere, exiting the pillar at the top and ascending through the air until once more it shines brilliantly in the night sky. The sphere remains within the pillar, glowing warmly.

Become aware of your own physical body. Raise both your arms horizontally at the sides and turn your palms so that the flat of your hands face forward, and your body forms a great cross. Momentarily feel the column of your body in union with the Earth beneath your feet. Speak the words:

"The cross grounds me."

Bring your hands together in front of your chest palm to palm in the traditional prayer gesture. Momentarily visualize three perpendicular rays of white light extending out from the bright center of a three-inch golden sphere located in the middle of your chest. The ray exiting through the front of your body between your nipples also passes between the joined palms of your hands. Speak the words:

"The star centers me."

Allow your arms to fall to your sides and assume the standing pose. Hold an awareness in your mind that you are both grounded to the Earth, and centered in the universe by the three rays extending from your chest.

Let the rays withdraw into the center of the golden sphere in your chest, and let the sphere contract into a single bright point of light that fades from your awareness. Close your eyes and take several deep breaths. Press your palms over your face and draw them slowly downward as though sliding off a skin-tight mask. Open your eyes, relax from your posture, and go about your day.

Commentary

Many methods of grounding and centering are described by various teachers. The details of the method presented here are original, but the basic purpose of the exercise is always the same regardless of variations in technique.

Grounding establishes a connection with the solidity and density of the Earth. You can use grounding both to draw upon this solidity when creating manifest spirit forms and charging physical objects, as when making talismans, and to channel excess occult energy harmlessly through your body into the ground, as when disposing of the destructive energy of an illness during healing. The stone and soil of the Earth act as a kind of universal storage battery that can be called upon to accept a charge of energy, or release it.

Centering establishes your location at the center of the universe. Location can only be fixed by means of a point, which is why a star is visualized in the middle of the sphere of the heart-center, the traditional center of the human body. A point can only be located in space by means of three intersecting, perpendicular lines. Centering helps spiritual intelligences, such as any angels or deities that you may subsequently invoke, to locate your presence. Centering in one form or another should be done at the opening of most rituals.

The cross is a symbol for the Earth. By making your body into a cross, you momentarily become the Earth. The star within the sphere of the heart-center is a symbol for the creative, empowering Source within the higher self of the individual. By identifying yourself with the star through centering, you momentarily become the spiritual center of the universe.

Each human being resides at the center of his or her own universe, and indeed can never leave it, but this truth is usually veiled by the distractions of material existence. Centering reminds us that we are always at the center of everything, in perfect union with the source of being.

The visualization of the stone pillar at the start of this exercise helps to awaken an intuitive awareness of the energies involved in grounding and centering. Through repeated practice of the entire exercise, you become more and more conditioned, so that after a dozen repetitions the last part of the exercise alone is sufficient to ground and center you during actual ritual work. You need only assume the standing pose and feel yourself an extension of the ground as you spread your arms to form your body into a cross and speak the words "The cross grounds me," then press your hands together palm to palm in front of your chest and speak the words "The star centers me" as you visualize the three rays of light intersecting at your heart-center.

EXERCISE 25

Vibrating
Names of Power

Assume the standing pose in your practice area facing east, with your gaze directed straight ahead and your eyes focused on the distant horizon that lies beyond the walls of your chamber.

Visualize high above your head a blazing blue-white star of pure spiritual energy that is untainted by intention, thought, emotion, or sensation. Let your inner awareness rise up to this white star and enter it so that the brilliance of the star completely surrounds you and blocks out all other perceptions. Feel the cooling, balanced energy of this light.

Extend a ray of white light downward from the star through the top of your skull to your heart-center. Visualize this center as a three-inch transparent sphere of glowing golden radiance, the color of sunlight. The exact focus of the white ray descending from the star is the center of the yellow sphere.

Allow your awareness to slide down the interior channel of this white ray to your heart-center. Continue to draw spiritual energy down the ray until your heart-center turns from yellow to soft radiant white with a slight golden tint.

Visualize the Hebrew letters of the name *IHVH* (I= י, H= ה, V= ו, H= ה) written within the globe of your heart-center from right to left. They blaze with brilliant blue-white light against the softer, slightly yellow background of the sphere, and flicker with electricity around their edges. The letters are blindingly intense, similar to the spark of an arc welder—it is difficult to look upon them, they are so bright.

ה ו ה י

Take a slow, deep breath. Imagine as you inhale that your body is being expanded by the air to gigantic proportions. Your head and shoulders rise through the ceiling of your practice chamber as though passing through a shadow. They continue upward through the roof of the building, further upward into the sky above the level of the clouds, until you find yourself balancing on the sphere of the Earth with almost all of your body projected above the atmosphere into the starry midnight of space.

Retain your breath with your lungs filled for four slow beats. During the retention visualize the warm white light from your heart-center radiating outward to expand the envelope of your aura into a sphere that surrounds your entire gigantic form.

Sound the four Hebrew letters of the name *IHVH* individually so that the resonance of your voice sets every part of your body vibrating in sympathetic response. The letters are vibrated with a regular rhythm, their sounds of equal duration and drawn out upon the breath. The vibration of the name empties most of the air from your lungs but does not leave you gasping.

"Yod-Heh-Vav-Heh"

This resonant sound-force expands to fill your transparent golden aura and sets it vibrating in sympathy. The vibrations of your aura send the air issuing from between your lips outward in all directions, expanding at an exponential rate until the vibration of your voice fills the entire universe to its uttermost limits. Feel with your astral awareness the entire universe humming with this vibration as though it were a giant crystal bell.

Draw several normal breaths and allow the expanded balloon of your aura to contract to its normal shape nearer to the limits of your form. Allow your giant form to shrink back into your physical body within your practice chamber.

Turn one quarter of a revolution clockwise on the spot where you stand and assume the standing pose facing the south. Continue to maintain the awareness of the glowing ball of your heart-center. Look straight ahead and focus your physical eyes on the distant horizon to the south beyond the wall of your practice room.

Visualize written within your heart-center from right to left the four Hebrew letters of the name *Adonai* (A= א, D= ד, N= נ, I= י). These letters blaze with blinding blue-white intensity against the softer yellow-white of the sphere.

$$ \text{א   ד   נ   י} $$

Draw in a deep breath. As you inhale imagine your body enlarging to gigantic proportions so that your upper body leaves the atmosphere of the Earth and projects into space. Hold the breath for four slow beats, and visualize the warm light from your heart-center radiating out through your skin to expand your aura into a complete sphere that surrounds your magnified form.

Voice the name *Adonai* in four separate sounds that correspond with the four individual Hebrew letters of the name, so that the vibrations set your entire body resonating in sympathetic response.

"Ah-doh-en-aye"

This resonance expands outward to fill your transparent golden aura, and sets it vibrating in sympathetic response to your body. The air issuing from your lips is driven outward in all directions by the vibrations of your aura with rapidly increasing force until the vibrations of the name fill every part of the universe, and cause a sympathetic vibration in the universe itself.

Take several normal breaths. Allow your aura to resume its usual shape and your visualized astral body to shrink to it physical size. Turn a quarter-revolution clockwise to face the west. Gaze westward at the distant, unseen horizon beyond the wall of your room and maintain the inner perception of your glowing heart-center.

Visualize written within this golden-white, transparent orb from right to left the four Hebrew letters of the name *Eheieh* (A= א, H= ה, I= י, H= ה). These letters shimmer and almost blind your inner sight with their blue-white intensity.

א י ה ה

Draw in a deep breath and imagine as you do so that your body enlarges through the ceiling of your ritual chamber, past the level of the clouds, until it projects gigantically into the darkness of space. Hold the breath for four slow beats as you visualize the light from your heart-center shining outward in all directions to expand the envelope of your aura into a perfect sphere that is colored a transparent pale gold.

Sound the name *Eheieh* with four separate sounds that correspond with the four individual Hebrew letters in the name, so that your entire physical body vibrates with their force.

"Ah-heh-aye-yah"

The sound energy expands outward from its source in your heart-center and sets the sphere of your aura resonating in sympathy. The breath that issues from between your lips is driven away in all directions by your energized aura so that it fills the entire universe. The universe itself begins to vibrate with the combined sounds of the letters.

Draw in several normal breaths. Allow your aura to contract to its ordinary shape, and your astral body to shrink and fit itself to your physical body. Turn a quarter-revolution clockwise to face the north. Let your physical eyes focus on the distant, unseen horizon beyond the wall of your room, while you maintain your inner concentration on your glowing heart-center.

Visualize written from right to left within this warmly glowing orb in the middle of your chest the four Hebrew letters of the name *AGLA* (A= א, G= ג, L= ל, A= א). These letters scintillate with blazing blue-white intensity against the softer radiance of your heart-center.

א ל ג א

Draw a long, deep inhalation. As you do so, visualize the air filling your body and expanding it to gigantic stature. Hold the breath for four slow beats and visualize the light from your heart-center shining outward to enlarge the envelope of your aura into a perfect transparent sphere of palest gold.

Voice four separate sounds that correspond with the four individual Hebrew letters of the name, so that your entire body tingles with the vibrations resonating within your expanded chest.

"Ah-Geh-Lah-Ah"

The force of the sound expands outward from your heart-center and causes your aura to tremble and vibrate in sympathetic resonance. Simultaneously, the air issuing from your lungs is energized and driven outward in all directions by your aura the way sound expands from the vibrating diaphragm of a stereo speaker. It fills the universe and sets the universe vibrating in harmony.

Take several normal breaths. Allow your aura to slowly fall inward until it has its usual form and distance away from your body. Draw your visualized astral body in upon itself to reduce it to the dimensions of your physical body. Turn a quarter-revolution clockwise to face the east and assume the standing pose.

Continue breathing easily for half a minute or so. Close your eyes for a few seconds to rest them. Press the palms of your hands upon your face and slid them down as though drawing off a skin-tight mask. Relax from the standing pose and stretch gently, then go on with your day.

Commentary

The correct technique for vibrating words of power is essential in ritual magic because it is the most effective way to employ the immense esoteric potential of the human voice. It has an application in mantras, prayers, blessings, curses, invocations, evocations, exhortations, and exorcisms.

The method of vibration I have described in the exercise is that used by the Hermetic Order of the Golden Dawn, with slight modifications. The exercise itself is original, and will not be found elsewhere in exactly this form.

A word of power may be vibrated either by voicing the letters of the word individually, or by voicing its syllables. Generally, I find it is more effective to voice individual letters when working with Hebrew divine names of power with five letters or less. When vibrating English, Latin or Greek words, it is usually better to voice syllables.

The four Hebrew words used in the exercise are the Hebrew names of God assigned in the Golden Dawn system to the four directions of the compass: *IHVH* (east), *Adonai* (south), *Eheieh* (west), *AGLA* (north). It is no accident that all four names have four Hebrew letters. Four is the number of physical manifestation, and applies to the four quarters of the world. Because of this fourfold symmetry I find it best to express each of these names with four sounds, when they are employed together to stand for the four directions and four elements.

IHVH, also known as the *Tetragrammaton,* is written all in capital letters because the name is too powerful and too universal to be spoken as a single word. Its letters should always be voiced individually by vibrating the names of the letters, rather than their sounds. The ancient Jewish pronunciation of this supreme name of God is unknown. In the fourth century before Christ its use was suppressed by the priests of the Temple at Jerusalem, who kept the occult might of the name for their own uses. Sometimes it is pronounced *Yahweh,* but this pronunciation should not be used in ritual magic. *IHVH* is linked in the Golden Dawn system with the east and the element Air, because the east is the first quarter and *IHVH* is the primary name that created the world.

Adonai means "Lord." It is the name of God that Jews customarily substitute for *IHVH* when they encounter the Tetragrammaton while reading the Pentateuch in order to express the name aloud or in their own thoughts, rather than leave a gap in the text (the average Jew does not pronounce *IHVH* by sounding its individual letters—this is an esoteric practice of Kabbalists). The Golden Dawn linked this name with the south and the element Fire, because Fire is the element of will and *Adonai* is a name of command. In the rituals of the original Golden Dawn, this name was sounded in three syllables, but to preserve the fourfold symmetry of the four names of the quarters I prefer to voice it in four sounds that express its four Hebrew letters.

Eheieh is usually translated "I am" or "I will be"—it denotes pure existence, and is the name by which God described himself on Mt. Horeb when Moses asked to know the name of God. It was linked by the Golden Dawn with the west and the element Water, because Water is a formative element and *Eheieh* is a formative name. In the Golden Dawn it was pronounced with three syllables, but for the reasons already given, I prefer to voice it in four distinct sounds in this exercise.

AGLA is written all in capital letters since it is an acronym composed of the first letters from the Hebrew words *Ateh Gibor Le-olam Adonai* that translate "Thou art mighty forever, O Lord." This name was linked to the north and to the element Earth by the Golden Dawn, because it is a composite name and Earth is a composite element. In the Golden Dawn it was usually pronounced in two syllables, but in this exercise I prefer to express it with four sounds.

Note the difference between the voicing of *IHVH* and *AGLA* in the exercise. *IHVH* is expressed by vibrating the actual names of its individual Hebrew letters. *AGLA* is expressed by vibrating individual sounds based on the separate letters. To take as an example the Hebrew letter א, equivalent to the English *A*, it is the difference between vibrating "Aleph" (the name of the letter) and "Aaaah" (the sound of the letter).

If you wish to pronounce the four divine names of the quarters as they were vibrated by the members of the original Golden Dawn, express *IHVH* as "Yod-Hay-Vahv-Hay," *Adonai* as "Ah-doh-nye," *Eheieh* as "Eh-heh-yeh," and *AGLA* as "Ah-glah." Try doing the exercise alternately with both forms for several days, and choose the form you prefer.

Keep your throat and mouth open when vibrating divine names or other words of power, and project the sound from your diaphragm so that your entire chest and nose vibrate. When projected properly, vibrated words have immense carrying power. One sign that you are vibrating the words correctly is a tickling sensation inside your nose.

It is not necessary to shout the sounds—they can be vocalized quietly under the breath. This may be desirable when you wish to conceal your practice from others, or late at night when others are trying to sleep. It is even possible to subvocalize the vibrations, and emit air without sound while voicing the names, provided that you vibrate them resonantly in your imagination.

EXERCISE 26

Charging an Object

PLACE THE OBJECT you wish to charge with occult virtue on a table in the western part of your practice room. Adopt the standing posture in the east about four feet away from the table, facing west, with your gaze directed at the object. Behind the table there should be a blank wall or other featureless surface to minimize distractions.

Stand breathing normally for several minutes to gather your forces. Keep your attention directed at the object without effort— merely look at it unwaveringly and be completely aware of it.

While continuing to regard the object with your physical eyes, direct your inner awareness upward through the top of your head, through the ceiling of the room, to a brilliant white star that shines in the firmament directly above you. Let your point of awareness ascend to the star and enter it, and be aware for a moment of its radiance all around you.

Send down a ray of white light through the top of your head to focus upon your heart-center, where you visualize a three-inch golden sphere of energy. Cause your point of awareness to descend down the hollow channel of this ray of light into your heart-center, and continue drawing energy down the ray to charge the golden sphere until it shines with a pale yellow-white glow, like the sun at noon. Release the ray from the star. Brilliant light radiates out from the sphere at your heart-center and fills your entire body with power as though your body were a battery.

Visualize the name of power that best expresses the force with which you wish to charge the object as written in Hebrew letters upon the sphere of your heart-center. For example, we will assume you are charging a wand with fiery virtue, so that it will thereafter serve as a weapon for the projection of your will. As noted in the previous exercise, the divine name of elemental Fire in the Golden Dawn system is *Adonai*. Visualize the four Hebrew letters of *Adonai* written from right to left upon the bright yellow sphere of your heart-center.

א ד נ י

Exhale deeply while holding this inner visualization and continuing to gaze at the object.

Begin to inhale slowly, and at the same time raise your arms on either side of your body with your elbows straight and your fingers extended stiffly together so that each hand resembles the leaf-shaped blade of a spear. As you lift your arms, gradually rotate your palms forward. When your arms are horizontal on either side of your body so that your body forms a great cross, your palms should be directed forward.

Continue raising your arms on either side in a smooth motion while filling your lungs. As you do so, rotate your palms upward. At the same moment your arms are elevated at a steep angle on either side of your body and your palms are turned up and inward, you lungs reach their full capacity and can take in no more air.

As you raise your arms and inhale, visualize your astral body expanding and rising upward to gigantic proportions, so that it extends through the ceiling of your practice chamber, through the clouds, far above the atmosphere, until you are surrounded by stars. Carry upward along with you the astral form of the object on the table. Visualize it floating before you against the blackness of space. Hold in your mind two realities—your enormous astral body in front of the enlarged astral object, and your physical body in front of the physical object on the table.

Hold this pose and stop your breath for four slow beats. During the retention of air, send the golden-white radiance of your heart-center outward through the opened pores of your skin to expand the envelope of your aura into a perfect globe that completely surrounds you. The object you intend to charge lies beyond the limit of your expanded aura—be aware of it outside this shining balloon of light. Harden the shell of your aura by the power of your will and make its inner surface like transparent glass.

As you step forward with your right foot a distance of twelve inches or so to shift your center of balance toward the object, throw your hands downward toward the object with your elbows locked and your fingers stiff, and begin to vibrate on your exhaled breath the name of power.

Project your will strongly through your eyes and hands at the object while vibrating the name, which in the example is *Adonai*. Since the name is used in an elemental context, each Hebrew letter of the fourfold name is voiced separately, as in the previous exercise.

"Ah-doh-en-aye"

The correct posture for projection is with the right foot advanced in front of the left a little more than the length of the foot itself, both heels pressed firmly to the floor; the body leaning forward at an angle; the arms pointing stiffly to the front with the hands extended palm down and the thumbs and index fingers touching along their lengths; the head inclined forward and down, so that the rays projected from under the lowered eyebrows extend from the eyes along the forearms and over the backs of the hands to focus upon the object.

The resonant sound of the name expands from your lips to fill your aura, and sets it vibrating in sympathy. Your hardened aura acts like a reflector, and concentrates the energy of the sound back into your heart-center, where it rebounds along the ray of your will outward from your body through your eyes and fingertips to the object on the table. Visualize the Hebrew name transferred by the act of projection from your heart-center through your hands and eyes to the object, so that it becomes visible to your astral sight written from right to left upon the object, and causes the object to glow with elemental energy. In the example, the wand would glow with the redness of elemental Fire.

When the vibration of the name of power has exhausted the air in your lungs, pause for a heartbeat in the pose of projection with your lungs held empty, then step back, drawing the right foot beside the left, and straighten your body. As you are in the motion of stepping back, fold your arms across your chest so that your forearms make an *X* over your heart-center, and your hands are angled upward with your palms facing your shoulders. Keep your hands extended stiffly into spear points. Close your eyes, bow your head, and stand motionless.

Draw a slow, deep breath while visualizing inwardly the glowing yellow-white sphere of your heart-center without the Hebrew name of power written upon it. Completely detach your awareness from the charged object. Make your mind tranquil, like the smooth surface of a lake at twilight. Hold your breath with your lungs full for a heartbeat.

Exhale smoothly and lower your arms to your sides so that once again you occupy the basic standing posture. Lift your head so that it is level. Continue to breathe normally for several minutes with eyes closed. Allow the expanded sphere of your aura to soften and contract to its normal shape near your skin. Let your godlike astral form shrink back into your physical body within the practice room.

Press the heels of your palms over your eyes and draw your hands downward as though sliding off a mask. Open your eyes, relax from your standing pose, and wrap the charged object in clean white cloth. Place it where it will remain secure and undisturbed until you are ready to use it. Continue on with your normal day.

Commentary

This exercise employs the technique for projecting occult virtue that was taught in the original Golden Dawn, and used by Aleister Crowley and Israel Regardie, among many others. I have modified the method and expanded its description for the sake both of utility and clarity.

Four distinct Golden Dawn ritual postures are employed in the exercise. When the practitioner stands with arms extended out to the sides like the arms of a great cross, palms forward, his body forms the posture known as the Sign of Osiris Slain. When his arms are raised at a sharp angle, though not quite straight overhead, with the palms turned up and in, the pose is a modified form of the Sign of Apophis and Typhon (in this sign the palms are more usually turned outward). The posture with the right leg extended in a step and the arms held outward in front of the chest is a version of the Sign of the Enterer, also called the Sign of Horus, the Projecting Sign and the Attacking Sign. When the forearms are crossed over the heart-center to form an *X*, the posture is very similar to the Sign of Osiris Risen.

Crowley was especially fond of using the Sign of the Enterer for projecting occult power. He advised that the rays from the eyes be directed along the thumbs. The hand gesture illustrated by Israel Regardie in his *Golden Dawn* shows the extended hands turned inward palm to palm, with the thumbs on top and the fingers inclined upward at a slight angle. The palms do not appear to touch, but this is unclear in the illustration.

I have experimented with various hand positions, and have found that the greatest force is projected when the hands are extended palm downward in the shape of spears, with the index fingers and thumbs touching along their full lengths. This causes the united thumbs to be hidden from sight beneath the plane of the fingers. Good results are also obtained when the thumbs are locked one over the other to keep the hands together.

In the Z3 document of the Golden Dawn, where the Projecting Sign is described at length, it appears that the hands are extended with a space between the thumbs. In my own work I have found that separating the hands weakens the projection of force. Since this matter is so important, I will quote the description, which comes from Regardie's *Golden Dawn* (sixth edition, page 371):

> Let the Adept, in using the Sign of the Enterer, give the step as he commences the Sign and let him imagine himself colossal, clothed with the form of the God or Goddess appropriate to the work—his head reaching to the clouds—his feet resting upon Earth. And let him take the step as if he stamped upon the Earth and the Earth quaked and rocked beneath him. . . .
>
> Standing as before described, in the form of the God, and elevating the mind to the contemplation of Kether, take the step like a stroke with the foot, bring the arms up above the head as if touching the Kether, and as the step is completed bring the hands over the head forwards. Thrust them out direct from the level of the eyes horizontally—arms extended, fingers straight, palms downwards, the hands directed towards the object it is wished to charge or to affect. At the same time, sink the head till the eyes look exactly between the thumbs. In this way, the rays from the eyes, from each finger and from the thumbs, must all converge upon the object attacked. If any of them disperse, it is a weakness.
>
> Thus performed, this Sign is a symbol of tremendous attacking force and of projection of will power, and it should be employed in all cases where

force of attack is required—especially in charging of Talismans and the like. Generally, it is best to have the thumbs and all the fingers extended—but if a particular effect is desired, you may extend only the fingers appropriate thereto, keeping the rest folded back in the hand.

In the Neophyte Ritual of the Golden Dawn, students were taught to make the Sign of the Enterer by advancing their left foot. However, Regardie's illustration shows the right foot advanced in the Sign of the Enterer, and symbolically this is more appropriate for a posture of projection. The right side of the body projects, the left side receives. When the left foot is advanced the sign implies a groping forward to reach something; when the right foot is advanced it implies a thrusting forward of something away from the body. Changing the foot that is put forward changes the fundamental meaning of the sign.

The projection can be made more vigorous if the step taken by the right foot is lengthened to incline the body more sharply forward. The heel of the left foot should remain firmly planted on the floor—when the left heel is raised the stance is much weaker, as any student of the Eastern martial arts will testify. The heels ground the practitioner to the manifest force of the Earth—elevation of the heel symbolically represents spiritualization. The head should be brought forward and lowered between the biceps so that the gaze from the eyes extends along the tops of the forearms and over the fingertips. The eyes, arms, and fingers must all be aligned.

The technique I have described for combining the vibration of names of power with the Projecting Sign is slightly different from that presented in the teachings of the Golden Dawn, where it is called the Vibratory Formula of the Middle Pillar (see *Golden Dawn,* sixth edition, pages 345–46). For purposes of comparison, I will quote the original method:

> Let the Adept, standing upright, his arms stretched out in the form of a Calvary Cross, vibrate a Divine Name, bringing with the formulation thereof a deep inspiration into his lungs. Let him retain the breath, mentally pronouncing the Name in his *Heart,* so as to combine it with the forces he desires to awake thereby; thence sending it downwards through his body past Yesod, but not resting there, but taking his physical life for a material basis, send it on into his feet. There he shall again momentarily formulate the Name—then, bringing it rushing upwards into the lungs, thence shall he breathe it forth strongly, while vibrating that Divine Name. He will send his breath steadily forward into the Universe so as to awake the corresponding

forces of the Name in the Outer World. Standing with arms out in the form of a Cross, when the breath has been imaginatively sent to the feet and back, bring the arms forward in "The Sign of the Enterer" while vibrating the Name out into the Universe. On completing this, make the "Sign of Silence" and remain still, contemplating the Force you have invoked.

Note that in the original Golden Dawn technique the name of power is vibrated mentally in the heart and the feet while the full inhalation of breath is retained in the Sign of Osiris Slain. The purpose of the double mental sounding of the name is to create a resonant pulse that will rebound from the feet out through the lungs on the breath. The Sign of Apophis is not used at all, but the sign of Osiris Slain appears in this description to transition directly into the Projecting Sign as the breath is expelled and the name vibrated aloud. I find that more force of projection is achieved when the arms and hands are flung downward as well as forward from the Sign of Apophis upon exhalation, while the step is taken with the right foot. Another difference is the use by the Golden Dawn of the Sign of Silence to create an inner stillness after the violent act of projection. This posture, also known as the Sign of Harpocrates, is made by standing with the feet together, right arm at the side, left index finger pressed to the lips.

In my own experience, I find the Sign of Osiris Risen more potent in forming a barrier against a reflux of power from the charged object. When charging a physical object, the purpose is to expel as much occult force of the desired kind as strongly and quickly as possible, then to separate yourself from the object, severing all links with it, so that this force cannot rebound and be dissipated, but must remain within the object. The *X* formed by the forearms across the heart-center in the Sign of Osiris Risen constitutes an effective barrier against this reflux of force. It is to further prevent this reflux that the eyes are closed at the end of the exercise.

It is not enough to charge an object, you must charge it with a specific potency suitable to your purpose. Divine names of power should be used when employing this vibratory formula. The four names given in the previous exercise embody the qualities of the four elements. Their Golden Dawn associations are: *IHVH*—Air, *Adonai*—Fire, *Eheieh*—Water, *AGLA*—Earth. Almost any purpose may be categorized under one of the elements, making these four names particularly useful for charging objects and talismans. Practice projecting the energies of the four elements in turn, but project no more than one elemental force in any given day. The power of

Air may be projected into a short dagger; the power of Fire into a short wooden rod; the power of Water into a small vase or goblet; the power of Earth into a flat disk.

This method of projecting force should be used with discretion. Do not employ it against living things. Avoid practicing with electronic or complex mechanical objects, such as a watch or a computer. Years ago, while practicing this projection technique, I directed energy at a new television tuner box. The television immediately began to change channels randomly on its own at irregular intervals ranging from a few seconds to half a minute. Prior to my projection of occult force, the tuner had been working perfectly. This erratic behavior continued even after I removed the remote control from the room. Turning the tuner off and unplugging it to reset it had no effect. Of course, the tuner was completely worthless following the experiment.

The Kabbalistic Cross

ELIMINATE ANY VISUAL distractions from your field of view on the eastern side of your practice chamber. Face east and assume the standing posture, with feet together, arms at your sides, and spine and head erect. Gaze straight ahead and focus your eyes on the distant horizon that lies beyond the wall in front of you. Take several deep, slow breaths and calm your thoughts.

Visualize high over your head in the midnight darkness of space that lies beyond the Earth's atmosphere a blue-white star that blazes with pure spiritual energy. Ascend in your inner awareness to this star and enter it. Allow the brilliance of the star to completely surround you and block out all other perceptions. Feel the balanced power of this cool light saturate your awareness.

Extend a ray of white light from the star straight downward through the top of your skull to your heart-center. Visualize this center as a three-inch transparent sphere of glowing golden radiance. Focus the white ray on the center of the transparent golden sphere.

Allow your awareness to slide down the inner channel of this white ray to your heart-center. Continue to draw spiritual energy down the ray until your heart-center turns from yellow to soft radiant white with a slight golden tint. Sever the link to the star and hold your awareness in your heart-center.

Take a deep breath. As you inhale, your body expands to godlike proportions. Your head and shoulders rise through the ceiling of your practice chamber, continuing upward above the level of the clouds, until your body projects into starry space.

Retain the air in your lungs for four slow beats as you visualize the warm light from your heart-center radiating outward to expand your aura into a sphere.

Touch your right index finger to your forehead between your eyebrows. Using a portion of the air in your lungs, vibrate the syllables of the Hebrew word *ateh* briefly but with power and authority.

"ah-teh"

Feel the resonance in your chest energize your aura, and the vibrations of your aura propel your articulated breath outward to fill the universe.

Touch your right index finger to the end of your breastbone, in the region of your solar plexus. Vibrate the syllables of the Hebrew word *Malkuth* briefly but with authority, using a little more of the air in your lungs.

"Mal-kuth"

Feel the vibrations in your chest energize your aura, and sense that your aura propels your breath outward to fill the universe.

Visualize a white ray extending from the glowing sphere of your heart-center vertically up and down, so that it passes through the top of your skull and between your feet. Conceive this ray to be a laser beam of infinite length.

Touch your right index finger to your right shoulder and with another portion of the air in your lungs vibrate the syllables of the Hebrew words *ve-Geburah* briefly with force.

"veh-Geb-u-rah"

Feel the vibrations in your chest energize your aura, and sense that your aura propels your breath outward to fill the universe.

Touch your right index finger to your left shoulder and vibrate the syllables of the Hebrew words *ve-Gedulah* briefly with force, expelling a bit more of the air you have retained.

"veh-Ged-u-lah"

Feel the vibrations in your chest energize your aura, and sense that your aura propels your breath outward to fill the universe.

Visualize a white ray extending from the glowing sphere of your heart-center horizontally to the left and right so that it passes out the sides of your body. Conceive this ray to be a laser beam of infinite length. This horizontal ray intersects the vertical ray at right angles at the center of your heart-center.

Press the palms of your hands together in front of your heart-center in a prayer gesture so that your extended fingers point directly upward, and cup your palms slightly to create space between them. Vibrate the Hebrew words *le-olam* strongly to create a resonance in your chest.

"leh-oh-lam"

Feel the vibrations in your chest energize your aura, and sense that your aura propels your breath outward to fill the universe. With these words your lungs are nearly empty.

Visualize a white ray extending from the glowing sphere of your heart-center horizontally in front and behind, so that it passes out of your body through the center of your chest between your joined hands and out the center of your back. This horizontal ray intersects the first two rays at right angles in your heart-center.

Raise your joined hands above the level of your head, fingers pointing upward and elbows bent. Vibrate the Hebrew word *amen* strongly to create a resonance in your chest. Extend the final syllable so that the remaining air in your lungs is expelled.

"ah-mennnnn"

Feel the vibrations in your chest energize your aura, and sense that your aura propels your breath outward to fill the universe. Lower your hands to your sides and adopt the standing pose.

Remain motionless in this posture for a minute or so, breathing normally, and contemplate with your inner sight the large golden sphere of your expanded aura, the smaller gold-white sphere of your heart-center, and the three brilliant-white rays that extend at right angles from your gigantic astral body.

Mentally draw the three rays into your heart-center, and let the sphere of your heart-center fade out of your conscious awareness. Allow your aura to contract slowly to its usual elongated shape nearer the surface of your skin, then cause your expanded astral form to shrink down to the dimensions of your physical body.

Close your eyes for several seconds to rest them. Take a deep breath and let it out slowly. Press your hands to your face and draw them down and around your chin as though sliding off a skin-tight mask. Relax from your standing posture to continue with your normal day.

Commentary

The original Kabbalistic Cross or one of its numerous modern variants is commonly employed for centering at the beginning of rituals. It is among the most important techniques of magic, and was created over a century ago for use in the ritual practices of the Golden Dawn. There are differences in the details of this formula from group to group—perhaps inevitable, since it is described only in skeletal form in the original Order papers, and is impossible to reconstruct with perfect assurance using only this description. In my own ritual work I have evolved several variations, all effective.

In addition to the basic gestures and words of the Kabbalistic Cross, visualizations are included in the exercise to empower it and make it more meaningful to beginners. After the exercise has been diligently performed on a regular basis, the amount of visualization can be reduced without lessening the effectiveness of the exercise.

All of the Hebrew words are to be vibrated with a single exhalation of breath. Greater energy can be generated, if desired, by vibrating each word or joined pair of words with its own separate breath, in the manner described in exercise 25.

The Hebrew *ateh* means "thou art." The word *Malkuth* means "Kingdom" and is the title of the tenth sphere on the Tree of the Sephiroth. The words *ve-Geburah* are usually translated "and the Power"—*Geburah* is the common title for the fifth

Sephirah, and is more accurately translated as Strength. The words *ve-Gedulah* are usually translated "and the Glory"—Gedulah is a less common, alternative title for the fourth sphere on the Tree, and translates better as Greatness. The Hebrew words *le-olam* mean "for ever." The word *amen* means "truly."

The complete Hebrew text of the Kabbalistic Cross was translated in the original Golden Dawn documents by the English words: "Thou art the Kingdom, and the Power, and the Glory, for ever. Amen." It is the final part of the Lord's Prayer (refer to Matthew 6:13).

The original Golden Dawn method of forming the Kabbalistic Cross has been presented here because it is important for beginners to have a clear understanding of this procedure, which is the most widely accepted. It should be practiced regularly for several months until it becomes second nature, before trying variations.

As a modification in the gestures that accompany the Hebrew words of the original Golden Dawn formula, instead of pressing the palms together at the words *le-olam* you can, if you wish, lay your hands flat over your chest so that they form an *X* with your left palm pressed directly over your heart-center and your right hand crossed over your left. At the word *amen,* instead of raising your joined hands above your head, bring your palms together in a prayer gesture and raise them to the level of your forehead to momentarily press the lower segments of your two thumbs against the dome at the top of your forehead, then allow your arms to fall to your sides. The word *amen* should be vibrated as your hands touch your forehead. I have found this minor variation in the original Golden Dawn formula to be quite effective.

In my own work I use a modified form of the Kabbalistic Cross more in harmony with my system of magic, described in detail in my book *New Millennium Magic*. This method employs English rather than Hebrew. Instead of the words "Thou art" at the top of the cross I use the words " the Crown" to indicate that the head is the place on the body assigned to the highest Sephirah, Kether—Kether means Crown. I assign the bottom of the cross to the groin rather than the base of the sternum, because the functions of the groin are more in keeping with the nature of Malkuth than the solar plexus. Also, in my method I invert the arms of the cross from left to right, assigning Gedulah to the right shoulder and Geburah to the left shoulder. By this inversion the practitioner symbolically becomes the manifest body of God, rather than a reflection of that body. Instead of the words "for ever" I prefer the words "and the Law everlasting" as the final part of the formula. The word "Law" refers to Tiphareth, the central Sephirah assigned to the Messiah or Christ.

The text and accompanying gestures of my version of the Kabbalistic Cross are as follows: "Thou art" (press hands together in prayer gesture in front of heart-center with fingertips up) "the Crown" (press left palm to center of chest and touch top of brow with right index finger) "and the Kingdom" (touch groin), "the Power" (touch left shoulder) "and the Glory" (touch right shoulder), "and the Law" (touch back of left hand over heart-center with right index finger) "everlasting" (point directly forward with extended right arm and index finger), "Amen" (still gazing forward, raise right arm to point with index finger directly overhead).

The purpose of the hand gestures is to describe physically the vertical and horizontal beams of light that intersect in your heart-center. In the original Golden Dawn formula, the focus is upon the vertical and horizontal beams of a two-dimensional cross and their point of intersection. The vertical beam is described by drawing the column of the cross on the axis of your body, the horizontal beam by drawing the arm of the cross from shoulder to shoulder, and the point of intersection is located by pressing the hands together in front of the chest.

In my opinion, if the Kabbalistic Cross is to be used for centering, it is vital not to overlook the horizontal axis that runs through the body from front to back. This third axis makes the cross three-dimensional rather than two-dimensional. My personal variation of the Kabbalistic Cross emphasizes this third axis. In my description of the original Golden Dawn formula for this exercise, the third axis is visualized as shining between the joined palms when the hands are held in front of the chest. If you use the variation to the original Golden Dawn formula where the hands are laid flat on the chest in an *X,* the third beam should be visualized as shining through the palms of the hands at the location of the stigmata.

The original Golden Dawn text of the formula directs that a steel dagger be used to draw the cross on the body, rather than the right index finger. It is better to become accustomed to performing the Kabbalistic Cross without an instrument, and indeed, no ritual tool is necessary. However, after practicing the Kabbalistic Cross for three or four weeks without an instrument, if you wish you may charge a dagger with the occult virtue of elemental Air, using the technique described in exercise 26, and employ this dagger to draw the beams of the cross on your body. Once you have charged the dagger, it becomes a ritual instrument and thereafter must not be used for common purposes or handled by any other person.

The Middle Pillar

MAKE SURE THERE are no visual distractions in the western end of your practice chamber. Assume the standing posture facing west. Direct your gaze straight ahead and focus on the unseen distant horizon. Take several slow breaths to calm your thoughts.

Visualize a brilliant blue-white star blazing in space directly over your head. Extend your awareness up toward this radiant point of light like an invisible hand and draw it downward until it is just above the top of your head. Expand it into a sphere the size of a dinner plate. It spins and vibrates as though alive. Be aware of the pure spiritual energy radiating from it through your hair, making your scalp tingle and prickle. Allow its soothing coolness to penetrate into your brain and melt downward to spread throughout your body.

Draw a deep breath without enlarging your astral form. Hold it for four slow beats while concentrating your awareness in the blue-white sphere above your head. Do not expand your aura.

Imagine that your consciousness is submerged within the scintillating radiance of the shining sphere.

Vibrate the syllables of the Hebrew name of God *Eheieh* using most of your breath. Draw the sounds of the name out so that they cause a buzzing in your throat and nose. Emphasize each syllable equally and sound them for equal durations.

"Ah-heh-yeh"

Using the power of your will, cause the vibrations in your chest to resonate strongly inside the sphere of light above you. Feel it humming like a bell.

Breathe normally. Visualize the vibration in the shining blue-white sphere becoming stronger, until it extends a white ray vertically downward through your head to the pit of your throat. The white ray does not fade but persists throughout the exercise. Observe with your inner awareness as a second radiant sphere forms at the end of the ray within the base of your neck. It is the diameter of a small saucer and of a light silvery-gray color, like polished lead. Feel it spinning and humming within your neck at the pit of your throat.

Draw a deep breath and hold it four slow beats while concentrating your awareness within the sphere in your neck. Submerge your consciousness in its silvery radiance.

Vibrate the syllables of the compound Hebrew name of God *Yah-Elohim* using most of your breath. Draw the sounds out at length, and give them equal emphasis and duration.

"Yah-Ey-lo-heem"

Using the power of your will, cause the sound vibrations in your chest to resonate strongly within the silver-gray sphere inside your neck. Feel the sphere humming like a bell.

Breathe normally. Visualize the vibration in the shining silvery sphere becoming stronger, until it extends a white ray vertically downward to the center of your chest. Understand that this ray is an extension of the first ray. It persists for the remainder of the exercise. Observe with your inner awareness as a radiant sphere forms in the region of your heart-center. It is the same size as the first sphere, approximately the diameter of a dinner plate, and colored a bright yellow, like sunlight. Feel it spinning and humming within the middle of your chest.

Draw a deep breath and hold it four slow beats while concentrating on the golden glowing sphere inside your chest. Submerge your consciousness in its yellow radiance.

Vibrate the syllables of the Hebrew name of God *Adonai* using most of your breath. Makes the sounds of the name equal in emphasis and duration, and draw each syllable out until you can clearly feel it humming in your body.

"Ah-doh-nye"

As you sound the name, use the power of your will to make the vibrations in your chest resonate inside the yellow sphere, so that the sphere hums like a bell.

Breathe in your normal manner. Visualize the vibration of the pale-golden sphere gaining intensity, until the sphere suddenly extends a white ray of light straight downward to your groin. This ray is an extension of the previous ray, and persists for the remainder of the exercise. With your inner perceptions observe that a sphere forms around your groin and penetrates the bones of your lower pelvis. It is the same size as the first, and of a bright, glowing violet color. Feel it spinning and humming with energy in your groin.

Draw a deep breath and hold it four slow beats while concentrating on the brightly glowing sphere surrounding your genitals. Submerge your consciousness in its violet radiance.

Vibrate the syllables of the Hebrew name of God *Shaddai* using most of your breath. Makes the sounds of the name equal in emphasis and duration, and draw each syllable out until you can clearly feel it humming in your body.

"Shah-dye"

As you sound the name, use the power of your will to make the vibrations in your chest resonate in the violet sphere at your pelvis, so that the sphere hums like a bell.

Breathe normally. Visualize the vibration in the shining violet sphere becoming stronger, until abruptly the sphere extends a white ray vertically downward between your legs to your feet. It is an extension of the previous ray, and persists for the remainder of the exercise. Observe with your inner awareness as a fifth radiant sphere forms around your feet. It is the diameter of the first and bright green in color, like new spring leaves with sunlight shining through them. Feel it spinning and humming around and within your feet.

Draw a deep breath and hold it four slow beats while concentrating on the brightly glowing sphere surrounding your feet. Submerge your consciousness in its green radiance.

Vibrate the syllables of the compound Hebrew name of God *Adonai-ha-Aretz* using most of your breath. Makes the sounds of the name equal in emphasis and duration, and draw each syllable out until you can clearly feel it humming in your body.

"Ah-doh-nye-hah-Ahr-retz"

As you sound the name, use the power of your will to make the vibrations in your chest resonate within the bright green sphere around your feet, so that the sphere hums like a bell.

For several minutes be aware of the vertical column of white light that extends up the axis of your body and emerges out through the top of your skull. Hold all five colored spheres in your field of attention at the same time. Identify with the column of light.

Breathe normally. Visualize the vibrations in the sphere around your feet becoming stronger. Abruptly the sphere emits a pulse of green light that flows up the hollow interior of the white ray like water under pressure up a pipe.

This green pulse enters the violet sphere at your groin, which begins to vibrate more strongly. Abruptly the sphere at your groin emits a pulse of violet light that travels up the hollow interior of the white ray above it.

This violet pulse enters the yellow sphere at your heart-center, causing it to vibrate more strongly. Abruptly the sphere in your chest emits a pulse of golden light that travels up the hollow interior of the white ray above it.

This pale-gold pulse enters the smaller silvery sphere at the base of your throat, causing it to vibrate more strongly. Abruptly the sphere in your throat emits a pulse of silver light that travels up the hollow interior of the white ray above it.

This silver-gray pulse enters the brilliant white sphere above the top of your head, causing it to vibrate more strongly. After a minute or so, the sphere above

MOVING
EXERCISES

Projecting
the Lesser Circle

ASSUME THE STANDING posture in your practice area facing the east, with your gaze level and your eyes focused on the distant horizon that lies beyond the wall in front of you. Take several slow, calming breaths.

Visualize a brilliant white star high in the heavens above your head. Mentally ascend upward toward the star, through the ceiling of your chamber, the roof of the building, the level of the clouds, until you enter the star and are surrounded with dancing, scintillating light that is so dazzlingly intense it has a blue tinge. Remain within the star for a minute or so and feel with your astral senses its cooling brilliance.

Extend a single ray of light straight downward from the star through the top of your head and into your heart-center. With the force of your will, push the radiance of the star down the central channel of this ray into your chest, like electricity flowing down a wire, so that it expands your heart-center into a glowing golden-white sphere three inches in diameter.

121

Allow your awareness to slide down the ray of light into your heart-center, and once you are firmly resident within the golden sphere, allow the ray from the star to withdraw itself back upward, breaking the link between your physical body and the star.

With your awareness still focused in your heart-center, place the palm of your left hand over the slight hollow of your chest just above the base of your sternum. Press your palm firmly into your chest. Extend your right arm in front of your body and point to the east with your right index finger at the level of your heart. Slowly turn a complete circle on your own axis clockwise.

As you turn, draw the white light from your heart-center through the front of your chest into the middle of your left palm and send it in an expanding spiral loop up your left arm, across your shoulders, and down your right arm.

Project this energy as a stream of white flame out the tip of your right index finger a distance of several feet to paint an astral circle of fire upon the air around you. Focus your gaze upon the flaming ring as it forms itself. Begin this circle in the east and carry it around at the level of your heart so that it ends where it began, and links up with its starting point.

Lower your arms to your sides and reassume the standing posture, facing east, with your gaze straight ahead, and your eyes focused on the unseen horizon. Extend your inner senses to feel the lesser circle of fire floating upon the air all around you at the level of your heart. Be aware of the entire unbroken circle. Visualize the flaming band of the circle in your field of view below your line of sight. It is tinged with a slight golden color, like bright sunlight—the same color as your heart-center. Feel the radiance of the flame upon your skin. Contemplate this circle of fire for a minute or so with full awareness of its unbroken circumference around you and your place at its center.

Cause your body and the room around you to become transparent and fade by withdrawing from them the focus of your consciousness, so that you are aware only of the white circle of flame surrounding the radiant white ball that is your heart-center. Contemplate the relationship between the two for a minute.

Once again become conscious of your body and the room, but remain aware of the flaming circle and your heart-center. Lay your right hand over the slight hollow in the middle of your chest, just above the end of your sternum. Press your right palm firmly into this hollow. Extend your left arm and point with your left index finger to the east at the ring of flame. Be strongly aware of the sphere of your heart-center beneath your right palm. Focus your gaze on the flaming circle and will it to break apart at the spot where you point with your finger. Slowly turn on your axis a complete rotation counterclockwise with your left hand extended at heart level.

Visualize as you turn your body the ring of white fire flowing in a thin stream into the tip of your extended left index finger, like air sucked into the end of a vacuum cleaner's nozzle. Feel the occult energy of the fire wind inward in a spiral to your heart-center as it travels up your left arm, across your shoulders, down your right arm, and out the center of your right palm into your chest. As more and more of the lesser circle is absorbed, your heart-center blazes more brightly and vibrates with greater energy.

You end where you began, pointing east with your left index finger, the entire projected circle of white flame drawn back into your heart-center. Lower your arms to your sides and return your gaze to the unseen distant horizon beyond the wall of your practice room. Breathe slowly and deeply for a minute or two as you contemplate with your astral vision your heart-center shining brightly in your chest. Feel its gentle warmth.

Expand the sphere of your heart-center to fill the entire interior of your body so that every part of your physical form is evenly suffused with gentle vitality. Feel it tingle in your fingertips and toes, along your spine and at the back of your neck. Contemplate this diluted light in every part of your body for a minute or so.

Allow the light to shine outward through your skin to gently energize your aura. The more the light expands, the weaker it becomes. As it fills your aura it is felt only as a faint background glow upon your skin. Contemplate this light for a minute.

Close your eyes and press your palms upon your face, then slide them downward and over the edge of your chin as though pulling off a skin-tight mask. Take several deep breaths and open your eyes. Relax and gently stretch your body. Go about the rest of your day.

Commentary

Casting or projecting the circle is an essential part of ritual magic. Evocation, invocation, banishing, consecration, and charging are all best done inside a circle of astral fire. The circle is an extension of the perceived self of the person who projects it, and serves the duel function of a barrier against hostile or disruptive spiritual beings and forces, and a focus where the magic worked during the ritual is concentrated and intensified.

The general rule is to project from the right side of the body, and receive through the left side. Circles are best projected with the right hand and indrawn with the left hand.

The lesser circle is used where workspace is limited. Anywhere you can stand, you can project the lesser circle around yourself by rotating on your own axis. You can project the circle through the furniture and walls of the practice room—inanimate physical objects do not obstruct the astral circle, which passes through them unbroken. A convenient size for the lesser circle is a diameter of seven feet, but if your practice space is too small to allow you to move and work freely within a circle of this size, a smaller circle can be used. The lesser circle is often best for solitary practitioners.

The astral circle may be conceived to define the wall of an invisible cylinder that extends up into the heavens and down into the earth endlessly, so that when looking up or down from within the circle with the astral sight, it appears to narrow in the distance to a point, just as a set of parallel railroad tracks seem to come together on the horizon when viewed from between the rails.

Oftentimes a magician will draw a circle on the floor of the ritual temple, or have one permanently painted. It is vital for beginners to understand that this painted circle is not the actual magic circle, but only a material shadow of it. The circle is always projected in the air at the level of the heart, never on the floor. When a circle is painted or marked on the floor, it merely defines the boundary of the astral circle, which can be projected to any desired diameter.

The circle of the art is projected upon the astral world using vital energy drawn from the heart-center, and is usually visible only to the inner sight. With months and years of practice, this astral circle becomes so clearly perceptible to the magician that it can be seen as a glowing white band in the air. However, those with no training would probably receive only a vague impression of its existence.

During practice, never step through the circle before it has been indrawn with the left hand. The magic circle is as real as the practitioner believes it to be, no more and no less. If you step through the circle, you physically express the fact that you do not regard it as an actual barrier. And if the circle is unreal to you, it cannot be real to the spiritual entities summoned outside its edge during ritual evocations. Strive to convince yourself that the astral circle is an actual band of fire that would burn you if you touched it. Feel its heat and hear the flutter of its flames. In this way it becomes a real barrier to spiritual beings.

EXERCISE 30

Projecting
the Greater Circle

FIND A PRACTICE area with an open floor at least seven by seven feet. Assume the standing posture in the center of the floor facing east, with your gaze level and your eyes focused on the unseen distant horizon beyond the wall in front of you. Draw and exhale several slow, deep breaths.

Visualize a white star in the heavens directly above your head. Rise up toward the star, through the ceiling of your practice room, the roof of the building, beyond the level of the clouds, until you enter the star and are surrounded with dazzling bluish light that dances and scintillates with spiritual energy. Remain within the star for a minute or so and feel with your astral senses its cooling brilliance.

Extend a single ray of light straight downward from the star through the top of your head and into your heart-center. With the force of your will, push the radiance of the star down the central channel of this ray into your chest, like electricity flowing down a wire, so that it expands your heart-center into a glowing golden-white sphere three inches in diameter.

Allow your awareness to slide down the ray of light into your heart-center. Once you are firmly resident within the golden sphere, detach the ray from the star and let it withdraw itself back upward, breaking the link between your physical body and the star. Contemplate the glow of your heart-center for a minute.

With your awareness still focused in your heart-center, walk forward to the eastern side of your practice area. Turn your body a quarter-turn to your right to face south. Place the palm of your left hand over the slight hollow of your chest just above the base of your sternum. Press your palm firmly into the center of your chest. Raise your right arm and bend your elbow so that your right forearm crosses in front of your chest and your right index finger points to the east on your left side at the level of your heart.

Slowly walk in a sunwise or clockwise direction around the circumference of an imaginary circle that fills your practice area. As you walk this circle, draw white light from your heart-center through the front of your chest into the center of your left palm and send it in an expanding spiral loop up your left arm, across your shoulders, and down your right arm. Extend your awareness to comprehend the spiritual force flowing through your arms and chest.

Project this energy as a stream of white flame out the tip of your right index finger a distance of a foot or so to paint an astral circle of fire upon the air in your practice room as you walk. Extend your awareness outward to the flaming ring while it forms itself. Begin this great circle in the east and carry it around the room at the level of your heart so that it ends where it began, and links up with its starting point.

Lower your arms to your sides and reassume the standing posture, facing east, with your gaze straight ahead, and your eyes focused on the unseen horizon. Be aware of the diminished strength of the light in your heart-center. Step backward until you once more stand in the center of the room. Assume the basic standing pose.

Extend your inner senses to feel and see the circle of fire floating upon the air all around the room at the level of your heart. Visualize the flaming band of the circle in your field of view below your line of sight. It is tinged with a slight golden color, like bright sunlight. Feel the radiance of the flame upon your skin. Contemplate this circle of fire for several minutes with full awareness of its unbroken circumference around you, and your place at its center.

Eliminate from your awareness everything except the sphere of your heart-center and the flaming circle of white light. Make your body and the room around you transparent and let them fade away to nothingness. With your inner astral sight, contemplate the white circle and the white dot at its center. Hold this awareness for a minute or so. Throughout the time of this contemplation, maintain the clarity and strength of the astral circle.

Once more allow yourself to become aware of your body and the room around you, while reinforcing the circle upon the air with your will. Walk forward to stand in the eastern part of the room with the band of flame only a foot or so in front of your chest.

Turn your body on its own axis a quarter-turn to your left side so that you stand facing north. Lay your right hand over the slight hollow in the center of your chest, just above the end of your sternum. Press your palm firmly into this hollow at the center of your chest. Raise your left arm and bend your elbow so that your left fore-arm crosses in front of your chest and your left index finger extends to the east and points at the ring of flame. Mentally will the ring of fire to break apart at the place where you point with your finger.

Be aware of the sphere of your heart-center beneath your right palm. Slowly walk around the inner circumference of the great circle widdershins or counter-clockwise so that you return to your starting place in the east. As you walk, visual-ize the ring of white fire flowing in a thin stream into the tip of your extended left index finger, like air sucked into the end of a vacuum cleaner's nozzle. Feel the occult energy of the fire winding inward in a spiral to your heart-center as it travels up your left arm, across your shoulders, down your right arm, and out the center of your right palm into your chest. As more and more of the circle is absorbed, your heart-center blazes more brightly and vibrates with greater energy.

When you complete the circle, and absorb the last of the white flame back into your heart-center, lower your arms to your sides and turn your body on its axis to face the east so that you stand on the eastern side of your practice chamber facing east. Assume the standing posture and return your gaze to the unseen distant hori-zon. Breathe slowly and deeply for a minute or two as you contemplate your heart-center shining brightly in your chest. Feel its gentle warmth.

Step backward to stand in the center of your practice area facing east. Be aware only of the light of your heart-center. Mentally expand its sphere to fill the interior of your entire body so that every part of your physical form is evenly suffused with gentle vitality. Feel it tingling in your fingertips and toes, along your spine, and at the back of your neck. Contemplate this diluted light in every part of your body for a minute or so.

Allow the light to shine outward through your skin to gently energize your aura. The more the light expands, the weaker it becomes. As it fills your aura it is felt only as a faint background glow upon your skin. Contemplate this light for a minute.

Close your eyes and press your palms upon your face, then slide them downward and over the edge of your chin as though pulling off a skin-tight mask. Take several deep breaths and open your eyes. Relax and gently stretch your body. Go about the rest of your day.

Commentary

The lesser circle is often convenient for solitary magic, when the floor area is limited, or when rituals are worked away from the physical ritual temple. The greater circle is best for group magic, or when working in a permanent physical temple where floor space is abundant. A good dimension for the greater circle of an individual is nine feet in diameter, but if there is a group working in the circle, it should be made wide enough to accommodate everyone comfortably.

In the Golden Dawn, all movement around the circle was done in a sunwise or clockwise direction when forming the circle, or working within it. Sunwise means in imitation of the movement of the sun across the sky. We move around the magic circle in the same way the shadow of a sundial moves around the dial, following the sun.

Not all groups project the magic circle sunwise. Some Wiccan covens and ceremonial lodges project the circle by moving counterclockwise or widdershins, and if they absorb the circle, do so by moving clockwise. There is a strong rationale for this practice. Since occult energy is projected from the right side of the body, and absorbed through the left, a more natural posture results when the great circle is projected through the right hand while walking around it counterclockwise, and absorbed through the left hand while walking clockwise.

I have given my own manner of projecting the circle, which follows the path of the sun. The posture of holding the left hand over the heart-center while projecting the circle with the right hand is not universally used, but I find it highly effective to initiate the circle with an expanding spiral that begins at the heart-center and flows through my body. To me, it feels awkward and unnatural to simply allow the left hand to dangle at the side while projecting the circle with the right hand.

It is common for those working magic to omit the re-absorption of the circle at the end of a ritual. In my opinion, this is a serious error. If the circle is habitually allowed to fade out on the air after ritual work, it becomes more difficult to hold a clear awareness of its presence and power throughout the course of the ritual. As mentioned in the commentary to the previous exercise, the ritual circle is only as real as you believe it to be in your own mind. When you simply step through it and forget about it at the end of rituals, you inevitably weaken its efficacy.

In ceremonial magic, the circle is often projected using a tool such as the athame (a dagger used by witches for many functions) or the magic wand. During the evocation of demons or other potentially dangerous spirits, a ritual sword may be used to draw the circle upon the air. Beginners should practice projecting the circle with the right index finger. This technique is frequently used by experienced magicians as well—I seldom employ an instrument when projecting the circle.

Once you have established a permanent temple in a room or part of a room dedicated to ritual work, and have positioned an altar in the middle of its open floor, you can project the greater circle by walking around the altar. While you are still learning the basics, your own body takes the place of the altar. This is why, when practicing how to project the greater circle, you begin and end standing at the center. Those with limited work space often place the altar in the east of the temple, or some other quarter, and work from the center of the open floor—in this case, the altar becomes a part of the band of the greater circle, like a diamond set in a golden ring.

Numerous different ways exist for projecting the greater circle during rituals. What you must understand is that the circle, however it may be traced, always exists on the astral level. Any physical circle drawn on the floor of the ritual chamber or on the ground of a ritual place is merely a template or guide for establishing the dimension of this astral circle, which can be projected to any size and can be modified in shape by the power of will.

EXERCISE 31

Invoking the Guardians of the Quarters

G O TO THE center of the practice area and face the east. Assume the standing posture, with your head erect and your back straight, your feet together, your hands at your sides and slightly opened outward. Gaze straight ahead, your eyes focused on the distant, unseen horizon beyond the wall in front of you.

Visualize a bright star high above your head in the heavens and ascend up to it. Take a minute to contemplate the purity of its white light, which is so intense, it has a slight bluish tinge.

With the scintillating radiance of the star all around you, send a white beam down through the top of your skull to the yellow sphere of your heart-center. Use your will to push spiritual energy down the central channel of this ray and into your heart-center so that your heart-center glows with white light that is tinged with yellow.

Slide down the ray into the golden-white sphere of your heart-center. Detach the ray and let it withdraw itself back upward into the star. Contemplate the warm light that fills the astral sphere in the center of your chest for a minute or two.

Expand your awareness to take in your physical body, but keep its main focus on your heart-center. Press your left palm over your chest just above the end of your sternum, and extend your right arm directly in front of you. Point with your right index finger to the east at the level of your heart.

Use the force of your will to make the golden-white energy fill the sphere of your heart-center fountain through your chest into the palm of your left hand. Guide it in an expanding spiral up your left arm, across your shoulders and down your right arm. Project this spiritual energy in the form of white fire in a stream from the tip of your right index finger.

As you begin projecting the fire, rotate clockwise on your own body axis and trace a circle of brilliant white flame around you at the level of your heart. A good size for this circle is seven feet in diameter, but it may be larger or smaller depending on your workspace. Take care to join the end of the circle to its beginning.

Let your arms fall to your sides as you resume the standing pose. Contemplate the circle around you, and the golden-white sphere in the center of your chest. Hold both of these dynamic astral forms in your consciousness at the same time for at least a full minute. Then shift your attention strongly to your heart-center.

Visualize the Hebrew letters of the name *IHVH* (I= י, H= ה, V= ו, H= ה) written within the shining sphere of your heart-center from right to left. They blaze with brilliant blue-white light against the softer, slightly yellow background of the sphere. The letters are blindingly intense, similar in color to the light of the star.

ה ו ה י

Take a slow, deep breath. Imagine as you inhale that your body is being expanded by the indrawn air to gigantic proportions. Your head and shoulders rise through the ceiling of your practice chamber as though passing through a shadow. They continue upward through the roof of the building, further upward into the sky above the level of the clouds, until you find yourself balancing on the sphere of the Earth with almost all of your body projected above the atmosphere into the starry midnight of space. As you grow larger, the astral circle of fire around your form enlarges at the same rate and remains at the level of your heart.

Retain your breath within your lungs for four slow beats. During the retention, visualize the warm white light from your heart-center radiating outward to expand the envelope of your aura into a sphere that surrounds your entire godlike form.

Pronounce the four Hebrew letters of the name *IHVH* individually so that the resonance of your voice sets every part of your body vibrating in sympathetic response. The letters are vibrated with a regular rhythm, their sounds of equal duration and drawn out upon the breath. The vibration of the name empties most of the air from your lungs but does not leave you gasping.

"Yod-Heh-Vav-Heh"

This resonant sound-force fills your transparent golden aura and sets it vibrating in sympathy. The vibrations of your aura send the air issuing from between your lips outward in all directions, expanding at an exponential rate until the vibration of your voice saturates the entire universe to its uttermost limits. Feel with your astral awareness the entire universe humming with this vibration as though it were a giant crystal bell.

Visualize the energy as the sounds rebound from the outer limits of the universe and return to focus in the east, just beyond the shining ring of the magic circle. The sounds become ever more concentrated, until they assume a vaguely humanoid shape that is bright yellow. As you watch with your astral vision, this shape defines itself into an angel of vast size, taller even than your enlarged astral body. The angel has a human head, golden hair, a beautiful male face, and white feathered wings that hang downward on its back almost to its bare feet. It wears a long robe of a light yellow color.

Extend your consciousness to the angel. As the angel becomes aware of your existence, gaze directly into its pale gray eyes. Visualize the angel nod in acknowledgement and spread its white wings so that they fill the entire region of the east.

Draw several normal breaths and allow the expanded balloon of your aura to contract to its normal shape nearer to the limits of your form. Allow your giant form to shrink back into your physical body within your practice chamber. The astral circle shrinks with you. Maintain an awareness of the angel in the east towering above you like a vast statue.

Turn one quarter of a revolution clockwise on your body axis and assume the standing pose facing the south. Continue to maintain the awareness of the glowing ball of your heart-center and the flaming circle around you. Look straight ahead and focus your physical eyes on the distant southern horizon beyond your chamber.

Visualize written within your heart-center from right to left the four Hebrew letters of the name *Adonai* (A= א, D= ד, N= נ, I= י). These letters blaze with blinding blue-white intensity against the softer yellow-white of the sphere.

$$\text{י נ ד א}$$

Draw in a deep breath. As you inhale imagine your body enlarging to gigantic proportions so that your upper body leaves the atmosphere of the Earth and projects into space. The circle grows with you and remains at the level of your heart. Hold the breath for four slow beats, and visualize the warm light from your heart-center radiating out through your skin to expand your aura into a complete sphere around your enlarged form.

Voice the name *Adonai* in four separate sounds corresponding with the four individual Hebrew letters of the name, so that the vibrations set your entire body resonating.

"Ah-doh-en-aye"

This resonance travels outward to fill your transparent golden aura and set it vibrating in sympathetic response to your body. The air issuing from your lips is driven forth in all directions by the vibrations of your aura with rapidly increasing force until the vibrations of the name fill every part of the universe, and cause a sympathetic vibration in the universe itself.

Visualize the energy as the sounds rebound from the outer limits of the universe and return to focus in the south, just beyond the shining ring of the magic circle. The sounds become ever more concentrated, until they assume a vaguely humanoid shape that is bright red, the color of fresh blood. As you watch with your astral vision, this shape defines itself into an angel of vast size, taller even than your enlarged astral body. The angel has the maned, golden-red head of a male lion, and feathered white wings that hang down on its back almost to its bare feet. It wears a long robe of a bright red color.

Extend your consciousness to the angel. As the angel becomes aware of your existence, gaze directly into its golden eyes. Visualize the angel nod its leonine head in acknowledgement and spread its white wings so that they fill the entire region of the south.

Draw several normal breaths and allow the expanded balloon of your aura to contract to its normal shape nearer to the limits of your projected form. Allow your giant form to shrink back into your physical body within your practice chamber. The magic circle shrinks to remain at the level of your heart. Hold an awareness of the lion-headed angel in the south towering above you like a vast statue.

Turn a quarter revolution clockwise to face the west. Adopt the standing pose. Gaze on the unseen western horizon and maintain the inner perception of your glowing heart-center and the flaming circle that surrounds you.

Visualize written within this golden-white, transparent orb from right to left the four Hebrew letters of the name *Eheieh* (A= א, H= ה, I= י, H= ה). These letters shimmer and almost blind your inner sight with their blue-white intensity.

$$\text{ה י ה א}$$

Draw in a deep breath and imagine as you do so that your body enlarges through the ceiling of your ritual chamber, past the level of the clouds, until it projects gigantically into the darkness of space. Hold the breath for four slow beats as you visualize the light from your heart-center shining outward in all directions to expand the envelope of your aura into a perfect sphere that is colored a transparent pale gold.

Vocalize the name *Eheieh* in four separate sounds that correspond with the four individual Hebrew letters of the name, so that your entire physical body vibrates with the force of the sound.

"Ah-heh-aye-yah"

The sound energy expands outward from its source in your heart-center and sets the sphere of your aura resonating in sympathy. The breath that issues from between your lips is driven away in all directions by your energized aura so that it fills the entire universe. The universe itself begins to vibrate with the combined sounds of the letters.

Visualize the energy as the sounds rebound from the outer limits of the universe and return to focus in the west, just beyond the shining ring of the magic circle. The sounds become ever more concentrated, until they assume a vaguely humanoid shape that is a beautiful dark blue, the color of the sea. As you watch with your astral vision, this shape defines itself into an angel of vast size, taller even than your enlarged astral body. The angel has the light-brown, feathered head and hooked beak of a golden eagle, and white feathered wings that hang downward on its back almost to its bare feet. It wears a long robe of a rich, dark-blue color.

Extend your conscious to the angel. As the angel becomes aware of your existence, gaze directly into its bronze-colored eyes. Visualize the angel nod its beaked head in acknowledgement and spread its white wings so that they fill the entire region of the west.

Draw several normal breaths and allow the expanded balloon of your aura to contract to its normal shape nearer to the limits of your form. Allow your giant form to shrink back into your physical body within your practice chamber. Maintain an awareness of the angel in the west towering above you like a vast statue.

Turn a quarter-revolution clockwise to face the north and assume the standing posture. Let your physical eyes focus on the distant, unseen horizon, while you maintain your inner concentration on your glowing heart-center and the astral circle that surrounds you.

Visualize written from right to left within the warmly glowing orb in the middle of your chest the four Hebrew letters of the name *AGLA* (A= א, G= ג, L= ל, A= א). These letters scintillate with blazing blue-white intensity against the softer radiance of your heart-center.

$$\text{א ל ג א}$$

Draw a long, deep inhalation. As you do so, visualize the air filling your body and expanding it to gigantic stature. The astral circle expands at the same rate and continues to float at the level of your heart. Hold the breath for four slow beats and visualize the light from your heart-center shining outward to enlarge the envelope of your aura into a perfect transparent sphere of palest gold.

Voice the name *AGLA* with four separate sounds that correspond with the four individual Hebrew letters of the name, so that your entire body tingles with the vibrations resonating within your expanded chest.

"Ah-Geh-Lah-Ah"

The force of the sounds expanding outward from your heart-center causes your aura to tremble and vibrate in sympathetic resonance. Simultaneously, the air issuing from your lungs is energized and driven outward in all directions by your aura the way sound expands from the vibrating diaphragm of a stereo speaker. It fills the universe and sets the universe vibrating in harmony.

Visualize the energy as the sounds rebound from the outer limits of the universe and return to focus in the north, just beyond the shining ring of the magic circle. The sounds become ever more concentrated, until they assume a vaguely humanoid shape that is a beautiful dark green, the color of evergreen trees. As you watch with your astral vision, this shape defines itself into an angel of vast size, taller even than your enlarged astral body. The angel has the dark-brown, horned head of a bull, and white-feathered wings that hang down its back almost to its bare feet. It wears a long robe of a deep evergreen color.

Extend your consciousness to the angel. As the angel becomes aware of your existence, gaze directly into its dark-brown eyes. Visualize the angel nod its horned head in acknowledgement and spread its white wings so that they fill the entire region of the north.

Draw several normal breaths and allow the expanded balloon of your aura to contract to its normal shape nearer to the limits of your form. Allow your giant form to shrink back into your physical body within your practice chamber, and along with it the surrounding circle of astral fire. Maintain an awareness of the angel in the north towering above you like a vast statue.

Turn a quarter-revolution clockwise to face the east and assume the standing pose. Be aware of all four angels towering above you like mighty carven pillars, their wings completely enclosing the magic circle as they touch tip to tip.

Spread your arms wide so that your body imitates the shape of a cross. Draw a long, deep inhalation. As you do so, visualize the air filling your body and expanding it to gigantic stature. The magic circle grows in proportion to your body. The angels are now closer to your own dimension, but you are still like a child in comparison with their greatness. Hold the breath for four slow beats and visualize the light from your heart-center shining outward to enlarge the envelope of your aura into a perfect transparent sphere of palest gold.

Vibrate upon your breath the following words so that your chest, throat, and nose resonate inwardly:

"Be-fore me, Raph-a-el."

Visualize the yellow-robed angel Raphael in the east glowing with the energy of your vibrated words. Exhale the remainder of your breath and draw in another deep inhalation while maintaining your enlarged stature and your expanded aura. Hold it for four slow beats as you focus your awareness in your heart-center.

Vibrate upon your breath the following words:

"Be-hind me, Gab-ri-el."

Visualize the blue-robed angel Gabriel behind you in the west, glowing with the energy of your vibrated words. Exhale the remainder of your breath and draw another deep inhalation while maintaining your enlarged stature and your expanded aura. Hold the breath for four slow beats as you focus your awareness in your heart-center.

Vibrate upon your breath the following words:

"At my right hand, Mich-a-el."

Visualize the red-robed angel Michael on your right side in the south, glowing with the energy of your vibrated words. Exhale the remainder of your breath and draw in another deep inhalation while continuing to maintain your enlarged stature and expanded aura. Hold the breath for four slow beats as you focus your awareness in your heart-center.

Vibrate upon your breath the following words:

"At my left hand, Aur-i-el."

Visualize the green-robed angel Auriel on your left side in the north, glowing with the energy of your vibrated words. Let the rest of your breath leave your lungs silently.

Drop your arms to your sides and adopt the standing posture. Draw several normal breaths and contract the pale-golden sphere of your aura to its usual shape nearer to the limits of your form. Allow your giant astral body to shrink back into your physical body within your practice chamber. As your astral form reduces in size, the circle of fire shrinks in proportion to remain at the level of your heart.

Hold the awareness of the four angels of the quarters towering above you with the tips of their expanded wings touching. They gaze down on you with serious, intense awareness. Feel their strength both shielding you and protecting your circle.

Visualize the bodies of the angels become paler and brighter. As you watch them with your inner awareness, they lengthen and narrow into four identical pillars of white light. These pillars come together high above your head to focus upon the distant white star. Mentally release the angels and watch astrally as their pillars are drawn upward into the star.

Turn your attention inward and contemplate the warm light of your heart-center for a minute or two. Expand your awareness so that you are conscious of your physical body, but keep the main focus of your attention on the golden-white sphere in the center of your chest.

Press your right palm over your chest just above the end of your sternum, and extend your left arm directly in front of you. Point with your left index finger to the circle of fire in the eastern quarter and will the circle to break apart at that place. Begin to draw the golden-white flame of the circle into the tip of your left index finger, up your left arm, across your chest, down your right arm, and out your right palm into your heart-center. As you do so, rotate counterclockwise on your own body axis a full turn so that the circle is completely absorbed.

Let your arms fall to your sides as you resume the standing pose. Continue breathing easily for half a minute or so. Close your eyes for a few seconds to rest them. Press the palms of your hands upon your face and slide them down as though drawing off a skin-tight mask. Relax and stretch gently, then go on with your day.

Commentary

The guardians of the quarters represent the genii or daemons of the four elemental forces that play so vital a role in modern magic. The archangelic names and kerubic visages of the guardians described in this exercise were those used by the original Golden Dawn.

I have specified dark green for the color of the robe on Auriel, the angel of the north, because this seems the most appropriate of the four Golden Dawn Earth colors, which are citrine, olive, russet, and sable. Dark brown or black would also be acceptable.

These angels are visualized in various ways by different offshoot traditions of Golden Dawn magic—sometimes as four human figures, sometimes as four living creatures that express the elements (man—Air, lion—Fire, eagle—Water, bull—Earth), sometimes as four heads without bodies, sometimes as four pillars of stone or four pillars of elementally colored light.

Once you gain skill in visualizing the guardians of the quarters, they may be summoned more quickly with no reduction in their authority or weakening of their power as protectors of the circle. This exercise is designed to prepare you to effectively perform the Lesser Invoking Ritual of the Pentagram, described in exercise 33.

Exercise 32

Projecting
the Pentagram

POSITION YOURSELF IN the middle of your practice chamber and
face east. Adopt the standing posture. Look straight ahead
and focus your eyes on the distant, unseen horizon beyond the
limits of the room. Take several slow, deep breaths to calm your
thoughts and focus your intention.

Extend your awareness upward to the blazing white star high
in the heavens above your head. Rise up to the star and contemplate its radiance surrounding you for a minute or so.

Project a white ray of light straight downward through the top
of your head to your heart-center, and with the power of your
will, cause the spiritual energy of the star to flow down the ray to
fill your heart-center with energy until it vibrates and rotates
with power.

When you feel that your heart-center has absorbed all the
occult energy it can hold, slide your point of consciousness down
the interior channel of the white ray to your heart-center and
detach the ray from your body, allowing it to withdraw upward

into the star. Contemplate the golden-white glory all around your awareness for a minute or so.

Take a step forward toward the east. Become aware of the wall in front of you. Press your left palm to your chest just above the base of your sternum. Raise your right arm and extend your right index finger. Cause spiritual energy to flow out of your heart-center into your left palm, up your left arm, across your shoulders, and down your right arm, so that it exits out the tip of your right index finger as a stream of bright yellow astral fire. Use the projected flame to draw a large pentagram on the air to the east with one continuous line. Make it approximately four feet across. Begin the yellow star from its upper-right point and proceed counterclockwise, finally linking the end of its flaming line with its beginning. Using the power of your will, cause the pentagram to move away from you until it touches the eastern wall of the practice room.

Drop your hands to your sides and resume the standing pose. Contemplate the yellow pentagram flaming on the surface of the eastern wall. It is known in the Golden Dawn system as the Invoking Pentagram of Air.

Place your left hand on the center of your chest and from your right index finger project a second yellow pentagram upon the air to the east, beginning at the upper-left point and proceeding clockwise. This form of the pentagram is known in the Golden Dawn system as the Banishing Pentagram of Air. With the power of your

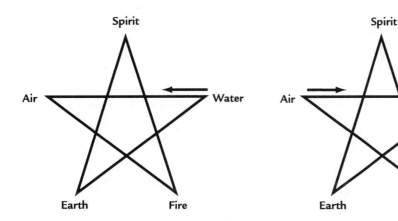

Figure 32-1.
Invoking Pentagram of Air

Figure 32-2.
Banishing Pentagram of Air

will project it onto the eastern wall over the first yellow pentagram so that the two are exactly superimposed.

Stand with your arms at your sides and contemplate the two yellow pentagrams as they begin to flicker and neutralize each other. Watch them fade to nothingness with your astral vision.

Take a step backward to return to the middle of the room and rotate on your body axis a quarter-turn clockwise to face the south. Extend your awareness to the southern wall. Step forward and stand with feet together and arms at your sides in front of the wall, facing south. Adopt the posture of projection with your left hand pressed over your heart-center and your right index finger extended in front of you. Project a red pentagram on the air, beginning at the uppermost point and proceeding clockwise.

Sustain the ruby-colored pentagram upon the air in your awareness for a few moments, then with the power of your will send it away from you onto the southern wall of your practice room. Resume the standing posture and contemplate the red pentagram burning on the wall. In the magical system of the Golden Dawn, this form is known as the Invoking Pentagram of Fire.

Adopt the pose of projection and draw a second red pentagram upon the air in the south. Begin at the lower-right point of the star and move your index finger in a counterclockwise direction. Contemplate this pentagram for a few moments. In the Golden Dawn system it is known as the Banishing Pentagram of Fire. Project it

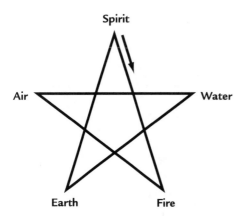

Figure 32-3.
Invoking Pentagram of Fire

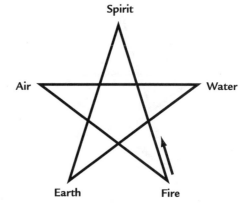

Figure 32-4.
Banishing Pentagram of Fire

onto the wall with the force of your will so that it stands superimposed over the first fiery pentagram.

Resume the standing posture. Hold the two overlapping red pentagrams in your astral awareness for a minute or so. Watch them gradually flicker and fade as their contrary energies neutralize each other.

Step backward to return to the center of the room. Rotate a quarter-turn clockwise to face the west, and become aware of the western wall. Step forward toward the western wall of your practice chamber and adopt the standing pose, with your feet together and arms at your sides. For a minute or so, gaze through the wall at the unseen western horizon. Adopt the posture of projection and draw on the air to the west a pentagram of blue fire from the tip of your right index finger, beginning at the upper-left point of the pentagram and proceeding clockwise. Project the pentagram away from you onto the western wall.

Stand with arms at your sides and contemplate the bright blue flaming lines of this pentagram. In the system of the Golden Dawn, this form is known as the Invoking Pentagram of Water.

Adopt the projecting posture and draw another fiery blue pentagram on the air to the west, beginning at the upper-right point and proceeding counterclockwise. This form is known in the Golden Dawn as the Banishing Pentagram of Water. Using the force of your will, project it away from you and superimpose it on top of the first blue pentagram.

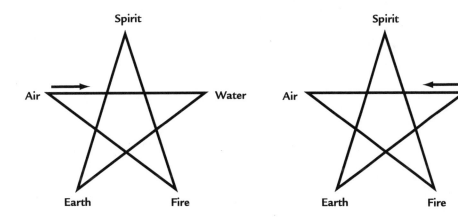

Figure 32-5.
Invoking Pentagram of Water

Figure 32-6.
Banishing Pentagram of Water

In the standing pose, watch the flaming lines of these two overlapping blue pentagrams become unstable and fade from the wall.

Take a step backward to once more stand in the middle of the room. Rotate a quarter turn clockwise and become aware of the northern wall. Step forward toward the northern side of your practice room and adopt the standing posture with your arms at your sides, gazing through the wall at the unseen distant northern horizon. Assume the pose of projection, with your left palm pressed to the center of your chest just above the end of your sternum and your right arm and index finger extended in front of your body.

Use the fire flowing from the tip of your index finger like a stream of ink and your finger like a pen to draw in the north upon the air in front of you a green five-pointed star with a single line that reflects from point to point, and ends where it began. Start at the uppermost point of the star and proceed in a counterclockwise direction. When the green pentagram is complete, use the force of your will to project it away from you onto the surface of the northern wall of your practice room.

Allow your hands to fall to your sides and assume the standing pose. Contemplate the pentagram for a minute or so. Actually see it flaming with evergreen fire on the surface of the north wall with your inner perception. It should be regular in shape, four feet across, formed of a single unbroken line. In the system of the Golden Dawn this pentagram is known as the Invoking Pentagram of Earth.

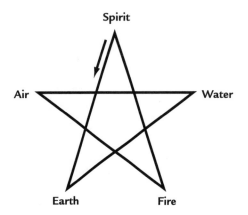

Figure 32-7.
Invoking Pentagram of Earth

Figure 32-8.
Banishing Pentagram of Earth

Press your left palm over your heart-center and extend your right index finger. Draw upon the air a second pentagram in dark green fire. Start at the lower-left point of the star, and extend the line of fire in a clockwise direction. This pentagram is known in the system of the Golden Dawn as the Banishing Pentagram of Earth. With the force of your will, project it away from you onto the northern wall, so that it is exactly on top of the first green pentagram.

Resume the standing posture with your arms at your sides and contemplate the two pentagrams superimposed one on top of the other. They flicker and dance as their energies conflict and begin to neutralize each other. Continue regarding the green pentagrams with your astral sight until they have completely faded from existence, and the northern wall is blank once again.

Step back to the center of the room. Turn a quarter rotation clockwise to face the east and assume the standing posture. Look up at the ceiling. Place your left palm over your heart-center and extend your right index finger straight over your head. Drawing upon the energy in the sphere of your heart-center, use your right index finger to inscribe a horizontal pentagram in white fire upon the air overhead. Begin at the lower-right point of the star and proceed clockwise. Immediately, with your right index finger draw on top of this white star a second pentagram also using white fire, but begin the second pentagram at the lower-left point and proceed counterclockwise. Watch with your astral vision as these two white pentagrams merge and reinforce each other, so that they become a single brilliantly flaming star.

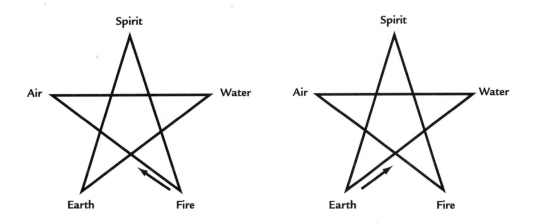

Figure 32-9. Active and passive invoking pentagrams of Spirit

Project the united pentagrams upward onto the surface of the ceiling with the force of your will. Allow your arms to fall to your sides and spend a minute or so contemplating the conjoined pentagrams flaming upon the ceiling overhead. When drawn together in this order, the first pentagram is known as the Active Invoking Pentagram of Spirit, and the second pentagram is known as the Passive Invoking Pentagram of Spirit.

Place your left palm over your heart-center and raise your right index finger above your head to draw with white astral fire in the air above you a pentagram that begins at its upper-left point and proceeds counterclockwise. Immediately draw a second pentagram of white fire that overlaps it, beginning at the upper-right point and proceeding clockwise. Watch with your inner vision as these two pentagrams merge and reinforce each other. When drawn in this order together, the first member of this pair is known in the Golden Dawn system as the Active Banishing Pentagram of Spirit, and the second pentagram is known as the Passive Banishing Pentagram of Spirit.

Use the force of your will to project this second double pentagram of white fire on top of the double pentagram already burning upon the ceiling. Let your arms fall to your sides and watch as these two pairs of pentagrams neutralize each other and gradually fade from your inner perception.

Lower your gaze and focus your eyes on the distant eastern horizon beyond the wall in front of you. Remain in silent contemplation for several minutes, aware of

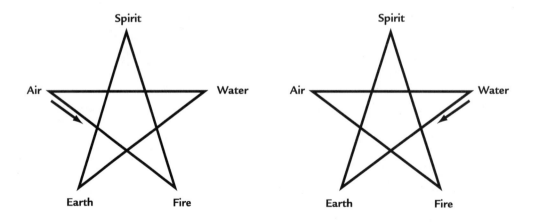

Figure 32-10. Active and passive banishing pentagrams of Spirit

the glowing sphere of your heart-center. Breathe slowly and deeply. Allow the golden-white light in your heart-center to expand and diffuse itself throughout your entire body, so that you can feel it tingling in your fingertips and toes. Cause it to continue to expand through your skin to fill your aura. As it does so, it dims and is no longer visible to your astral sight.

Close your eyes and relax from your standing pose. Press your hands to your face and draw them downward. Open your eyes and go about your day.

Commentary

The ability to project the pentagram is central in Western magic. Through the pentagram are controlled the four elements of ancient philosophy, and also the spiritual radiance that underlies them, know as the fifth element (quintessence), that modern magicians call Spirit or Light.

In the system of the Golden Dawn, the top point of the pentagram is assigned to Spirit, the upper-left point to Air, the upper-right point to Water, the lower-left point to Earth, and the lower-right point to Fire. These elemental forces are summoned and banished by projecting the pentagram in various ways.

It is essential that you are able to draw the pentagram upon the air from any point in both clockwise and counterclockwise directions. You should practice using paper and a pen until you can form the pentagram in all ten possible ways without hesitation. Your pentagrams must be regular, all of the points equally separated around the circumference of an invisible circle, and all of the rays or beams of the figure of equal size and length. This requires practice.

To avoid confusion, I will emphasize that the pentagram is drawn with a single uninterrupted line that crosses in straight segments from point to point, and ends on the same point where it began. Do not make the mistake of outlining the star, or confuse it with the pentagon, which is a completely different geometric figure of five points and five sides that do not intersect. There is only one form of the pentagram, but it may be made in ten different ways, by beginning it at any of its five points and proceeding either clockwise or counterclockwise.

The most common error in projecting the pentagram, from a purely mechanical point of view, is to make it too small. It should be drawn with broad, sweeping strokes of the extended right arm on the air in front of you. Keep your arm straight and your elbow locked. Once inscribed upon the air, the pentagram can be projected away from you to any distance—it is unnecessary for you to physically touch the surface on which you project the figure, or even to be near it. The pentagram can also be mentally enlarged or reduced in size as needed.

In this exercise I have described the Golden Dawn method for drawing the pentagrams because it is a system every ceremonial magician should know, even if it is never used. Its faults are complexity and duplication. It is not obvious to students at first impression why two pentagrams are required to invoke Spirit, and two to banish Spirit, but only one to invoke and one to banish each of the lower four elements. Nor is it immediately apparent why the pentagrams to invoke or banish different elements are not formed in the same general way. Note that in the Golden Dawn method, the Invoking Pentagram of Water is the same as the Banishing Pentagram of Air, and the Banishing Pentagram of Water the same as the Invoking Pentagram of Air, making confusion of these forms inevitable.

I might mention that the Active Invoking Pentagram of Spirit is called active because its initial line segment extends from the point of Fire to Air, and both these are active elements; the Passive Invoking Pentagram of Spirit likewise derives its passive designation from its initial line segment, which extends from Earth to Water, both passive elements. Similarly, the initial line segment of the Active Banishing Pentagram of Spirit runs from Air to Fire, both active elements; and the initial line segment of the Passive Banishing Pentagram of Spirit runs from Water to Earth, both passive elements. These relationships are not at all obvious to beginners and are nowhere explained in the Golden Dawn documents.

Whether or not the pentagram of an element is invoking or banishing is generally determined by the first line segment. If the first segment extends toward the point of the element, the pentagram invokes that element; if the first line segment extends away from the point of the element, the pentagram banishes the element. Unfortunately, there are exceptions to this general rule. The first line segments of the invoking pentagrams of Spirit, both active and passive, do not extend directly to the point of Spirit, but only in the general direction upward; the first line segments of the banishing pentagrams of Spirit do not extend directly away from the point of Spirit, but only in the general direction downward.

Happily, there is a much simpler way to invoke and banish the forces of the elements by pentagrams. I developed this method independently in the course of my own practice, and was later surprised to learn that it had been used for some years by the occult organization known as Aurum Solis.

The method is simplicity itself. To invoke an element, begin the pentagram from the point assigned to that element and proceed clockwise; to banish an element, began at the point of that element and proceed counterclockwise.

That is all there is to it—elemental Spirit is invoked by a single pentagram, and banished by a single pentagram, in the Aurum Solis method. This modern method makes so much good sense, and is so easy to remember and use, it has been years since I have bothered to employ the Golden Dawn technique for invoking or banishing the elements. However, no one can claim to understand Western magic without a perfect knowledge of the Golden Dawn method. The invoking and banishing forms of the pentagram should be practiced in pairs in the directions assigned to the elements by the Golden Dawn. Spirit is linked to the heights, and for this reason the pentagrams of Spirit are best projected onto the ceiling during practice.

Lesser Invoking Ritual of the Pentagram

FIND AN OPEN floor where you have room to walk around the inner circumference of a circle seven feet or so in diameter. If necessary due to lack of space, the ritual can be done by standing in one spot and rotating on your own axis to form a lesser circle, but it is better to use a greater circle.

Stand in the middle of the floor facing east. Adopt the standing pose, with your feet together, arms at your sides, back straight and head erect. Direct your gaze straight ahead and look through the wall at the unseen, distant horizon. Take several long, deep breaths to focus your resolve and prepare for what you are about to do.

Visualize high over your head a blue-white star that blazes with pure spiritual energy. Ascend in your inner awareness to this star and enter it. Allow the star's brilliant rays to completely surround you and saturate your awareness with cooling light.

Extend a ray of white light from the star straight downward through the top of your skull to your heart-center. Visualize this center as a three-inch transparent sphere of glowing golden radiance, the color of sunlight. Focus the white ray from the star on the center of the transparent golden sphere.

Allow your awareness to slide down the interior channel of this white ray to your heart-center. Continue to draw spiritual energy down the ray until your heart-center turns from yellow to soft radiant white with a slight golden tint. Hold your awareness in your heart-center.

Take a deep breath. As you inhale, your body expands to godlike proportions. Your head and shoulders rise through the ceiling of your practice chamber, continuing upward above the level of the clouds, until your body projects into starry space.

Hold the air in your lungs for four slow beats as you visualize the warm light from your heart-center radiate outward to expand your aura into a sphere.

Touch your right index finger to your forehead between your eyebrows. Vibrate the syllables of the Hebrew word *ateh* briefly but with power and authority.

"ah-teh"

Feel the resonance in your chest energize your aura, and the vibrations of your aura propel your articulated breath outward to fill the universe.

Touch your right index finger to the end of your sternum, just above your solar plexus. Vibrate the syllables of the Hebrew word *Malkuth* briefly but with authority.

"Mal-kuth"

Feel the vibrations in your chest energize your aura, and sense that your aura propels your breath outward to fill the universe.

Visualize a white ray extending from the glowing sphere of your heart-center vertically up and down, so that it passes through the top of your skull and between your feet. Conceive this ray to be a laser beam of infinite length.

Touch your right index finger to your right shoulder and vibrate the syllables of the Hebrew words *ve-Geburah* briefly with force.

"veh-Geb-u-rah"

Feel the vibrations in your chest energize your aura, and sense that your aura propels your breath outward to fill the universe.

Touch your right index finger to your left shoulder and vibrate the syllables of the Hebrew words *ve-Gedulah* briefly with force.

"veh-Ged-u-lah"

Feel the vibrations in your chest energize your aura, and sense that your aura propels your breath outward to fill the universe.

Visualize a white ray extending from the glowing sphere of your heart-center horizontally to the left and right so that it passes out the sides of your body below the level of your armpits. Conceive this ray to be a laser beam of infinite length. This horizontal ray intersects the vertical ray at right angles at the center of your heart-center.

Press the palms of your hands together in front of your solar plexus so that your extended fingers point directly upward, and cup your hands slightly to create space between them. Vibrate the Hebrew words *le-olam* strongly to create a resonance in your chest.

"leh-oh-lam"

Feel the vibrations in your chest energize your aura, and sense that your aura propels your breath outward to fill the universe.

Visualize a white ray extending from the glowing sphere of your heart-center horizontally in front and behind, so that it passes out of your body through the center of your chest between your joined hands and out the center of your back. This horizontal ray intersects the first two rays at right angles in your heart-center.

Raise your joined hands above the level of your head, fingers pointing upward and elbows bent. Vibrate the Hebrew word *amen* strongly to create a resonance in your chest. Extend the final syllable so that the remaining air in your lungs is expelled.

"ah-mennnnn"

Feel the vibrations in your chest energize your aura, and sense that your aura propels your breath outward to fill the universe. Lower your hands to your sides and adopt the standing pose.

Stand motionless in this posture for a minute or so, breathing normally, and contemplate with your inner sight the large golden sphere of your expanded aura, the smaller gold-white sphere of your heart-center, and the three brilliant white rays that extend from the three axes of your gigantic astral body. Mentally draw the three rays into your heart-center, but continue to be aware of its radiance. Allow your aura to contract slowly to its usual elongated shape nearer the surface of your skin, and cause your expanded astral form to shrink down to the dimensions of your physical body.

Step forward and stand in the eastern quarter of your practice area still facing east. Assume a posture of projection with your left hand over your heart-center and your right arm extended. Project a large yellow pentagram upon the air in the east, beginning it from the upper point and drawing its line counterclockwise. Visualize it glowing brightly with rich yellow flame.

Draw a deep breath, hold it four beats while visualizing the Hebrew letters of the name *IHVH* (I = י, H = ה, V = ו, H = ה) written from right to left within the sphere of your heart-center. The letters flame brilliantly with a dazzling blue-white radiance.

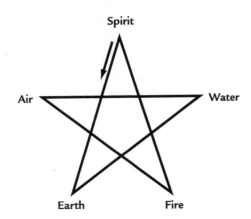

Figure 33-1.
Invoking Pentagram of Earth

יהוה

Stab the center of the pentagram with your right index finger and vibrate the letters of the divine name so that the sound resonates in your chest, throat, and nose, and expands outward to the limits of the universe.

"Yud-Heh-Vav-Heh"

Continue pointing to the center of the pentagram with your right index finger. The vibrations of the holy name cause a pillar of white light to extend downward from the star beyond the yellow pentagram in the east. Contemplate this pillar of light.

Turn your body to the right to face south while continuing to point at the center of the eastern pentagram, so that your right forearm crosses in front of your chest. Keep your left palm pressed to your heart-center. Walk along the quarter arc of an imaginary seven-foot circle to the south, projecting a line of golden-white fire upon the air as you go. Feel the vital energy that fills your heart-center spiral outward through your chest into your left palm, up your left arm, across your shoulders, and down your right arm to exit in a flaming stream from your right index finger. The expanding spiral it follows as it circulates through your body increases its force. Continue to sustain in the back of your awareness the pentagram in the east.

Stand in the pose of projection in the southern quarter of the practice area facing south. Project a pentagram of bright red fire on the air to the south so that the termination of the quarter circle you have previously drawn at heart level from east to south is in the exact center of the pentagram. The size and shape of the pentagram are identical to the one in the east. It begins from the upper point and proceeds counterclockwise.

Take a deep breath and hold it four beats as you intensify the radiance of your heart-center. While your breath is stopped, visualize the Hebrew letters of the divine name *Adonai* (A = א, D = ד, N = נ, I = י) written in brilliant blue-white flame from right to left within the sphere of your heart-center.

אדני

Stab the center of the pentagram with your right index finger and vibrate the letters of the divine name so that the sound resonates within your body and expands to fill the universe.

"Ah-doh-en-aye"

Continue pointing to the center of the pentagram with your right index finger. The vibrations of the holy name cause a pillar of white light to extend downward from the star beyond the red pentagram in the south. Contemplate this pillar of light.

Turn your body to the right while continuing to point south, so that your right forearm crosses in front of your chest. Keep your left palm pressed over your heart-center. Walk along the quarter circumference of an imaginary circle to the west, projecting a line of golden-white fire upon the air at heart level as you go. Feel the vital energy that fills your heart-center spiral through your chest into your left palm, up your left arm, across your shoulders, and down your right arm to exit in a flaming stream from your right index finger. The expanding spiral it follows as it circulates through your body increases its force. Continue to sustain in the back of your awareness the pentagrams in the east and south.

Stand in the pose of projection in the western quarter of the practice area facing west. Project a pentagram of dark blue fire on the air to the west so that the termination of the quarter circle you have previously drawn is in the exact center of the pentagram. The pentagram is identical in size and shape to the ones in the east and south. It begins from the upper point and proceeds counterclockwise.

Take a deep breath and hold it four beats as you intensify the radiance of your heart-center. While your breath is stopped, visualize the Hebrew letters of the divine name *Eheieh* (A = א, H = ה, I = י, H = ה) written in brilliant blue-white flame from right to left within the sphere of your heart-center.

$$\text{ה י ה א}$$

Stab the center of the pentagram with your right index finger and vibrate the letters of the divine name so that the sound resonates within your body and expands to fill the universe.

"Ah-heh-aye-yah"

Continue pointing to the center of the pentagram with your right index finger. The vibrations of the holy name cause a pillar of white light to extend downward from the star beyond the blue pentagram in the west. Contemplate this pillar of light.

Turn your body to the right while continuing to point west, so that your right forearm crosses in front of your chest. Keep your left palm pressed over your heart-center. Walk along the quarter-circumference of an imaginary circle to the north, projecting a line of golden-white fire upon the air at heart level as you go. Feel the vital energy that fills your heart-center spiral through your chest into your left palm, up your left arm, across your shoulders, and down your right arm to exit in a flaming stream from your right index finger. The expanding spiral it follows as it circulates through your body increases its force. Continue to sustain in the back of your awareness the pentagrams in the east, south and west.

Stand in the pose of projection in the northern quarter of the practice area facing north. Project a pentagram of dark green fire on the air to the north so that the termination of the quarter-circle you have previously drawn is in the exact center of the pentagram. The pentagram is identical in size and shape to the ones in the east, south, and west. It begins from the upper point and proceeds counterclockwise.

Take a deep breath and hold it for four beats as you intensify the radiance of your heart-center. While your breath is stopped, visualize the Hebrew letters of the divine acronym name *AGLA* (A = א, G = ג, L = ל, A = א) written in brilliant blue-white flame from right to left within the sphere of your heart-center.

$$\text{א ל ג א}$$

Stab the center of the pentagram with your right index finger and vibrate the letters of the divine name so that the sound resonates within your body and expands to fill the universe.

"Ah-Geh-Lah-Ah"

Continue pointing to the center of the pentagram with your right index finger. The vibrations of the holy name cause a pillar of white light to extend downward from the star beyond the green pentagram in the north. Contemplate this pillar of light.

Turn your body to the right while continuing to point north, so that your right forearm crosses in front of your chest. Keep your left palm pressed to your heart-center. Walk along the quarter circumference of an imaginary circle to the east, projecting a line of golden-white fire upon the air at heart level as you go. Feel the vital energy that fills your heart-center spiral through your chest into your left palm, up your left arm, across your shoulders, and down your right arm to exit in a flaming stream from your right index finger. The expanding spiral it follows as it circulates through your body increases its force. Continue to sustain in your awareness the pentagrams in the east, south, west, and north.

Join the end of the line of golden fire to its beginning in the center of the eastern pentagram. Drop your arms to your sides and step backward to the center of the flaming astral circle. Assume the standing pose. Gaze straight ahead, and focus your eyes on the distant eastern horizon that lies in front of you beyond the wall and other intervening obstructions. Extend your astral awareness to the circle and the four invoking pentagrams of Earth that are set in its golden-white band. Contemplate the circle and the different colors of the pentagrams for several minutes. Strive to hold the complete, unbroken circle in your mind. Be aware of the four white pillars beyond the circle.

Spread your arms wide so that your body forms the shape of a cross. Draw a long, deep inhalation. As you do so, visualize the air filling your body and expanding it to gigantic stature. The circle of fire and its four pentagrams expand with you. Hold the breath four slow beats and visualize the light from your heart-center shining outward to enlarge the outer surface of your aura into a perfect transparent sphere of palest gold.

Vibrate upon your breath the following words so that your chest, throat, and nose resonate inwardly:

"Be-fore me, Raph-a-el."

Exhale the remainder of your breath while maintaining your enlarged stature and your expanded aura. Visualize the yellow of the eastern pentagram transfer into the pillar behind it. As the pillar turns yellow, the pentagram fades to a clear golden-white.

The yellow pillar thickens and solidifies into the towering, yellow-robed angel Raphael. The angel stands barefoot beyond the circle, gazing down at you with vigilant awareness in its pale gray eyes. Its golden hair is the same color as its robe. The human face of the angel glows with the residual energy of your vibrated words. Watch with your astral awareness as the angel opens wide its white wings to fill the eastern quarter.

Draw a deep breath and hold it four slow beats as you focus your awareness in your heart-center.

Vibrate upon your breath the following words.

"Be-hind me, Gab-ri-el."

Exhale the remainder of your breath while maintaining your enlarged stature and your expanded aura. Without turning your head, visualize behind your back the blue of the western pentagram transfer into the pillar beyond it. As the pillar turns deep blue, the western pentagram fades to a clear golden-white.

The blue pillar thickens and solidifies into the towering, blue-robed angel Gabriel. The angel stands barefoot beyond the circle, gazing down at you with vigilant awareness in its eyes. The golden-brown eagle's head of the angel glows with the residual energy of your vibrated words. Watch with your astral awareness as the angel opens wide its white wings to fill the western quarter.

Vibrate upon your breath the following words.

"At my right hand, Mich-a-el."

Exhale the remainder of your breath while maintaining your enlarged stature and your expanded aura. While still facing east, visualize the bright red of the southern pentagram transfer into the pillar beyond it. As the pillar in the south turns red, the pentagram fades to a clear golden-white.

The red pillar thickens and solidifies into the towering, scarlet-robed angel Michael. The angel stands barefoot beyond the circle, gazing down at you with vigilant awareness in its golden eyes. The maned lion's head of the angel glows with the residual energy of your vibrated words. Watch with your astral awareness as the angel opens wide its white wings to fill the southern quarter.

Draw a deep breath and hold it four slow beats as you focus your awareness in your heart-center.

Vibrate upon your breath the following words.

"At my left hand, Aur-i-el."

Exhale the remainder of your breath while maintaining your enlarged stature and your expanded aura. While continuing to gaze eastward, visualize the dark green of the northern pentagram transfer into the pillar beyond it. As the northern pillar turns green, the pentagram fades to a clear golden-white.

The green pillar thickens and solidifies into the towering, green-robed angel Auriel. The angel stands barefoot beyond the circle, gazing down at you with vigilant awareness in its dark eyes. The brown bull's head of the angel glows with the residual energy of your vibrated words. Watch with your astral awareness as the angel opens wide its white wings to fill the northern quarter.

Contemplate the four angels standing outside the circle. Hold simultaneously in your awareness the circle, the pentagrams, and the angels as you continue to stand facing east with your arms spread into a cross.

Visualize your heart-center. Use its energy to expand forward through the center of your chest a white pentagram that hangs upon the air inside the circle about two feet in front of your chest. At the same time expand backward from your heart-center a white hexagram that hangs upon the air inside the circle about two feet behind your back. Make both the pentagram and hexagram three feet across.

Draw a deep breath. Hold it four slow beats while focusing your awareness upon the pentagram before you and the hexagram behind you. Vibrate the following words.

"Before me flames the pentagram— behind me shines the six-rayed star."

Lower your arms and adopt the standing pose. For several minutes hold in your mind the white pentagram in front, the white hexagram behind, the golden-white circle with its four inset pentagrams around you, and the four angels at the quarters who surround the circle with their opened wings.

Allow your expanded aura to contract to its normal shape, and reduce your enlarged astral form so that it fits within your physical body. The astral forms around you also diminish in size, save for the angels which remain gigantic.

Turn your attention to the pentagram and hexagram and draw them into your heart-center through your chest and back.

Focus awareness on the four guardian angels beyond the circle and elongate them into pillars of colored light that stretch upward to the star high overhead. When the pillars touch the star, they immediately turn blue-white and scintillate with brilliant radiance. Let them withdraw themselves upward into the star.

Become aware of the four white pentagrams on the magic circle. Mentally reduce them in size until they merge with the circle and disappear.

Step forward to the eastern part of the circle and stand facing east. Place your right hand upon your chest over your heart-center, and extend your left arm in front of you. Concentrate on your heart-center, and begin to draw the energy of the circle into your body through the tip of your left index finger as though sucking air in through the nozzle of a vacuum cleaner. This breaks the band of the circle in the east at the spot where you point.

Turn your body a quarter-turn to the left while still pointing east with your left index finger, so that your left forearm crosses your chest. Slowly walk counter-clockwise around the inside of the circle, drawing in its flaming white band with your left hand as you go, until you have returned to the eastern quarter, and the circle has been completely reabsorbed into your heart-center. The energy from the circle causes your heart-center to shine more brightly.

Turn to face east and let your arms fall to your sides. Step backward to the center of your practice area and adopt the standing posture. Draw several normal breaths. Focus your attention inward and contemplate the warm light of your heart-center for a minute or two. Expand your awareness so that you are conscious of your physical body, but keep the main focus of your attention on the golden-white sphere in the center of your chest.

Take a deep breath. As you inhale, your body expands to an immense height, sending your head and shoulders through the ceiling of the practice room as though it were a shadow. You rise up above the level of the clouds, beyond the atmosphere of the Earth, until you are surrounded by glittering stars set against the blackness of space.

Retain the air in your lungs four slow beats, and visualize the light from your heart-center radiating outward through your pores to expand your aura into a sphere.

Touch your right index finger to your forehead between your eyebrows. Using part of the air in your lungs, vibrate the syllables of the Hebrew word *ateh* briefly but with power and authority.

"ah-teh"

Feel the resonance in your chest energize your aura, and the vibrations of your aura propel your articulated breath outward to fill the universe.

Touch your right index finger to the end of your sternum, just above your solar plexus. With a bit more of the retained breath, vibrate the syllables of the Hebrew word *Malkuth* briefly but with authority.

"Mal-kuth"

Feel the vibrations in your chest energize your aura, and sense that your aura propels your breath outward to fill the universe.

Visualize a white ray extending from the glowing sphere of your heart-center vertically up and down, so that it passes through the top of your skull and between your feet. Conceive this ray to be a laser beam of infinite length.

Touch your right index finger to your right shoulder and with another small portion of the breath vibrate the syllables of the Hebrew words *ve-Geburah* briefly with force.

"veh-Geb-u-rah"

Feel the vibrations in your chest energize your aura, and sense that your aura propels your breath outward to fill the universe.

Touch your right index finger to your left shoulder and vibrate the syllables of the Hebrew words *ve-Gedulah* briefly with force.

"veh-Ged-u-lah"

Feel the vibrations in your chest energize your aura, and sense that your aura propels your breath outward to fill the universe.

Visualize a white ray extending from the glowing sphere of your heart-center horizontally to the left and right so that it passes out the sides of your body below the level of your armpits. Conceive this ray to be a laser beam of infinite length. This horizontal ray intersects the vertical ray at right angles at the center of your heart-center.

Press the palms of your hands together in front of your solar plexus so that your extended fingers point upward, and cup your palms slightly to create a space between them. Vibrate the Hebrew words *le-olam* briefly but strongly with another small part of your breath to create a resonance in your chest.

"leh-oh-lam"

Feel the vibrations in your chest energize your aura, and sense that your aura propels your breath outward to fill the universe.

Visualize a white ray extending from the glowing sphere of your heart-center horizontally in front and behind, so that it passes out of your body through the center of your chest between your joined hands and the out-center of your back. This horizontal ray intersects the first two rays at right angles in your heart-center.

Raise your united hands above the level of your head so that your fingertips point upward. Vibrate the Hebrew word *amen* strongly to create a resonance in your chest. Extend the final syllable so that the remaining air in your lungs is expelled.

"ah-mennnn"

Feel the vibrations in your chest energize your aura, and sense that your aura propels your breath outward to fill the universe.

Separate your hands and lower your arms to your sides. Remain in the standing posture for a minute or so, breathing normally, and contemplate with your inner sight the large golden sphere of your expanded aura, the smaller gold-white sphere of your heart-center, and the three brilliant-white rays that extend from the three axes of your gigantic astral body. Mentally draw the three rays to a bright point in the center of your heart-center and allow this spark to fade away, but continue to be aware of the warm radiance of the golden-white sphere. Allow your aura to contract slowly to its usual elongated shape nearer the surface of your skin, and cause your expanded astral form to shrink down to the dimensions of your physical body.

Close your eyes for a few seconds to rest them. Press your hands upon your face so that the heels of your palms fit into the hollows of your eyes, and slide down your hands as though drawing off a skin-tight mask. Open your eyes, relax, and stretch your body gently, then go on with your day.

Commentary

The combined ritual of the Kabbalistic Cross and the Lesser Invoking Ritual of the Pentagram was the first ritual technique taught to beginners shortly after their initiation into the Golden Dawn. It is presented in the form of a brief and disordered outline (the illustration of the pentagram is out of its proper place) in the Golden Dawn documents, making it necessary for anyone performing the ritual to fill in the details. I have added visualization to the ritual, which is necessary for the ritual to be worked effectively. Some details have been reinterpreted to integrate the ritual more organically with the previous exercises.

The attributions of elements, divine names, and angels to the four quarters are those used by the Golden Dawn. It is best for beginners to learn the Golden Dawn correspondences, since these are the most widely used in modern magic. Once the system of the Golden Dawn is understood, it is possible to modify the occult associations to develop a more personalized system of magic, but to attempt this personalization too early results only in confusion.

This ritual invokes the forces and spirits connected with elemental Earth. Among these spirits are the four archangels who rule the four quarters of the material world—Raphael, Michael, Gabriel, and Auriel. In the Golden Dawn system, the pentagram that begins at the upper point and proceeds counterclockwise is the invoking pentagram of Earth. To banish the forces and spirits of Earth, it is only necessary to draw the four pentagrams set in the magic circle clockwise, beginning each pentagram from the lower-left point. The ritual then becomes the Lesser Banishing Ritual of the Pentagram.

If you wish to change this ritual into the Lesser Banishing Ritual, draw banishing pentagrams of Earth at the quarters instead of invoking pentagrams, and visualize the four angels facing outward rather than inward. When the angels face inward, they attract and concentrate the elemental powers of the four quarters— when they face outward, they repel and dissipate these powers.

It may be wondered how a single form of the pentagram can represent all four lower elements. Earth is a compound element that contains all four elements within itself in their heavier, more tangible aspects. For this reason the pentagram of Earth can be used to express the lower, material qualities of Air, Fire, and Water, as well as of Earth itself. I find it useful to distinguish by means of elemental colors the application of the Earth pentagram to other elements, making the Earth pentagram of the airy east yellow, that of the fiery south red, that of the watery west blue, and that of the earthy north green, but this distinction was not made in the Golden Dawn documents.

When the pentagram of Earth is employed alone to invoke the four archangels, it should be understood that it invokes the guardians of the quarters in their lower, more material guise, not in their higher, more spiritual nature. The higher elemental energies of the archangels are invoked by the Supreme Invoking Ritual of the Pentagram (see exercise 39).

The founders of the Golden Dawn provided this ritual of invocation and banishing to new initiates in the Order because the simple act of going through the steps, even when there is little or no understanding of their meaning, awakens awareness of occult forces. In the beginning of magic study, it is important to open your consciousness to the presence of subtle currents and spiritual entities. These exist all around you, and have always existed, but the study of magic allows you to perceive them for the first time. I have described the Lesser Invoking Ritual of the Pentagram rather than the Lesser Banishing Ritual in order to attract these forces, not drive them away. The beginner seldom needs to worry about too much contact with spirits, but often is vexed by a complete lack of contact.

Regular practice of the Lesser Pentagram Ritual is the best way to activate occult perceptions and latent abilities in magic. This deceptively simple ritual has no equal. It is the single most valuable thing you can do when seeking to learn Western ceremonial magic.

EXERCISE 34

Ritual of
the Rose Cross

FIND AN EMPTY room or open floor where you can move around freely. It is best if the practice area is square or roughly square. Procure a stick of rose incense and light it. Place a holder for the incense stick in the southeast corner. Stand in the southeast corner of the place of practice facing southeast, with the burning incense stick at your side in your right hand, and adopt the standing posture. Take several slow, normal breaths to calm and focus your thoughts.

Become aware of the ever-present white star that blazes in the heavens high above you. Ascend up to it with your point of consciousness and let its radiance surround you. Extend a ray downward through the top of your skull to focus at your heart-center, and channel energy from the star along the interior of this ray to expand your heart-center into a three-inch sphere of pale golden light. Will your consciousness to descend down the ray into your heart-center and allow the ray to withdraw upward into the star.

Visualize the golden-white sphere in your chest spinning and vibrating with power. Assume the posture of projection, with your left hand pressed over your chest in the hollow above the point of your sternum and your right arm extended to the southeast at the level of your heart.

With the extended, smoking tip of the incense stick, project from your heart-center a large, upright Christian cross in the air in front of you to the southeast, and inscribe a circle around its point of intersection. Pull energy from your heart-center into your left hand and send it racing up your left arm, across your shoulders, and down your right arm to exit through the incense stick. First inscribe the vertical beam of the cross from top to bottom; then the horizontal beam of the cross from left to right; then the circle clockwise beginning midway along the right arm of the cross. Take care to connect the end of the circle with its beginning. Its center is on the same level as your heart. Visualize this cross and circle sustained on the air of the practice room in glowing lines of white light. This light is an extremely subtle astral fire.

Transfer your awareness to the transparent sphere inside your chest. See within it the five Hebrew letters of the divine name *Yeheshuah* (I = י, H = ה, Sh = ש, V = ו, H = ה), written from right to left in lines of brilliant white fire edged with electric blue.

י ה ש ו ה

Draw a deep breath and visualize the inrush of air filling your entire body from the soles of your feet to the top of your skull, even to the ends of your fingers and toes. Hold the inhalation four slow beats and cause the sphere of your heart-center to rotate more rapidly, sending its energy streaming outward through every pore of your body to enlarge your aura into a perfect transparent sphere of pallid yellow-white.

Stab with the glowing point of the incense stick at the intersection of the cross and vibrate the four syllables of the divine Hebrew name *Yeheshuah*.

"Yah-hesh-shu-ah"

As you sound the name, contract your aura like a bellows, driving the vibrations inward back to their source in your heart-center. The compression of your aura forces the power of the vibrations into the palm of your left hand and drives them with incredible force in an expanding spiral up your left arm, across your shoulders, down your right arm, and out through the shaft of the incense stick to the astral cross, which glows with intense whiteness. Contemplate the bright light of the circle-cross for ten seconds or so while maintaining the projection pose.

Turn your body to the right to face west, but continue to point with the incense stick at the center of the circle-cross, so that your right forearm now crosses in front of your chest and points slightly behind you. Walk west in a straight line to the southwest corner of the practice area while projecting a stream of white light from the tip of the incense stick along the southern side of the room at the level of your heart.

Stand in the southwest corner, facing southwest. Inscribe a similar cross and circle on the air to the southwest by drawing energy from your heart-center into your left hand and sending it in an expanding spiral across your body that exits from the incense stick in your right hand. First trace the vertical beam, then the horizontal beam, then the circle.

Visualize the cross glowing with white light. The horizontal beams of these circle-crosses are somewhat thicker than the line of light connecting the crosses—even though they are the same color, this extra thickness makes the arms of the crosses stand out against the line of light. The end of the line traced from the first cross terminates at the intersection of the second cross.

Visualize the Hebrew letters of the name *Yeheshuah* written from right to left within your heart-center. Slowly inhale to fill your body from head to toe. Hold the breath four beats while energizing your heart-center by making it rotate more quickly. Watch with your subtle vision as the outward shining light of your heart-center expands your aura into a transparent sphere.

Stab the glowing point of the incense stick at the intersection of the cross in the southwest. Vibrate the four syllables of the divine Hebrew name *Yeheshuah*.

"Yah-hesh-shu-ah"

As you vibrate the name, contract your aura and send the expanding vibrations rebounding back upon their source in your heart-center. The compression of your aura acts like a pump to drive the vibrations in a high-pressure stream out through the palm of your left hand, up your left arm, across your shoulders, and down your right arm to exit through the shaft of the incense stick. The vibrations strike the astral cross, causing it to glow with intense whiteness. For ten seconds or so, contemplate with your inner vision the cross glowing with white light.

Continue to point with the incense stick at the center of the circle-cross as you turn your body to your right so that you face north. Your right arm now extends across your chest and points slightly behind you. Walk northward to the northwest corner of the practice area while projecting a line of white light from the tip of the incense stick along the western side of the room at heart level.

Stand in the northwest corner of the room, facing northwest. Draw energy out of your heart-center with your left hand and project from the incense stick in your right hand a circle-cross similar to the others on the air to the northwest. Contemplate the cross for ten seconds. The band of white light you traced across the western side of the room terminates exactly in the center of the cross.

Visualize the Hebrew letters of the name *Yeheshuah* written from right to left within your heart-center. Take a deep breath and hold it four beats while energizing your heart-center by increasing its rate of spin. Watch with your subtle vision as the outward shining light of your heart-center expands your aura into a transparent sphere.

Stab with the incense stick at the center of the cross and vibrate the holy name *Yeheshuah*.

"Yah-hesh-shu-ah"

As you vibrate the name, contract your aura strongly. The vibrations rebound from the inner surface of your aura and focus back upon their source. The extreme compression of the name drive its power in an expanding spiral into your left hand, across your body, and out through the shaft of the incense stick. The stream of vibrations strike the astral cross and makes it glow with intense whiteness. Contemplate the energized cross for ten seconds or so.

Continue pointing at the center of the cross with the incense stick as you turn your body to face east. Walk eastward to the northeast corner while projecting a white line of light along the northern side of the practice area from the glowing tip of the incense stick.

Stand in the northeast corner facing northeast. Draw energy from your heart-center into your left hand and send it out through the incense stick in your right hand to project a white circle-cross upon the air to the northeast. Contemplate this cross briefly. The end of the line you drew along the northern side of the room terminates in the center of this cross.

Visualize the Hebrew letters of the name *Yeheshuah* written from right to left within your heart-center. Take a deep breath to fill your body with air and hold it four beats as you energize your heart-center. The outward shining light of your spinning heart-center expands your aura into a transparent sphere.

Stab the glowing point of the incense stick at the intersection of the cross in the northeast. Vibrate the four syllables of the divine Hebrew name *Yeheshuah*.

"Yah-hesh-shu-ah"

Contract your aura strongly as you vibrate the name. The sounds expanding outward from your heart-center reflect from your shrinking aura and rebound upon their source, greatly magnified in strength. The compressed power of the name releases itself into the palm of your left hand and is driven in an expanding spiral up your left arm, across your shoulders, down your right arm, to fountain out through the shaft of the incense stick upon the astral cross, which glows with intense whiteness. Contemplate the cross for ten seconds or so.

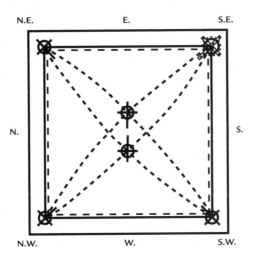

Figure 34-1. Ritual of the Rose Cross, from Israel Regardie's *Golden Dawn*

Continue pointing with the incense stick at the center of the cross as you turn to face the south. Walk straight toward the south while projecting a line of white light along the eastern side of the room with the glowing tip of the stick. Join this line to the center of the first cross you made in the southeast corner. It is unnecessary to repeat the holy name for this cross.

While standing in the southeast corner, facing southeast, take a minute to contemplate with your astral perception the four circle-crosses glowing in the corners of the practice room, and the lines of white light along the sides of the room that connect the centers of the crosses.

Point at the center of the cross in the southeast with the incense stick and raise it in an arc above your head, projecting a line of white light in the air above you. As you raise the stick, turn your body to face the northwest. Holding the stick high in your right hand, walk diagonally across the room toward the northwest corner.

When you reach the center of the room, stop and project a circle-cross upon the ceiling that is the same size and shape as the other four crosses. First draw its pillar from southeast to northwest. Then draw its beam from southwest to northeast. Then make a clockwise circle around its intersection that begins midway along its right arm.

Contemplate the cross, and note that the line of white light you drew diagonally on the ceiling from the first cross in the southeast enters the top of the cross on the ceiling and terminates in its center. The pillar and beam of the cross are the same brilliant white color as this line, but thicker.

Visualize the Hebrew letters of the name *Yeheshuah* written from right to left within your heart-center. Take a deep breath to fill your body with air, and retain it four beats while energizing your heart-center by making its sphere rotate more rapidly. Watch with your subtle vision as the outward shining light from your heart-center expands your aura into a transparent sphere.

Stab the incense stick directly overhead at the intersection of the cross while looking upward, and vibrate the divine name *Yeheshuah*.

"Yah-hesh-shu-ah"

Contract your aura as you vibrate the name. The sounds expanding outward from your heart-center reverberate against your contracting aura and rebound back upon their source with increased energy. The inner surface of the auric shell acts as an amplifier, compressing the power of the name ever more tightly until it escapes into your left palm and is driven in an expanding spiral along your left arm, across your shoulders, up your right arm, and out through the shaft of the incense stick to the astral cross, which glows with intense whiteness. Contemplate the circle-cross on the ceiling for ten seconds or so.

Point at the center of the cross. With the incense stick held high in your extended right hand and your left palm pressed upon your heart-center, walk to the northwest. As you go, project a line of white astral fire from your heart-center that begins in the center of the cross on the ceiling and proceeds diagonally to the northwest corner, where it connects with the intersection of the cross at heart level in the northwest. Contemplate this cross for ten seconds or so as you stand in the northwest corner facing northwest. It is not necessary to repeat the holy name for this cross, which has already been spoken.

Pointing the incense stick at the center of the northwest cross, project a line of astral fire downward as you turn your body to face the southeast. With the incense stick held straight down in front of you, walk toward the southeast, tracing a thin, glowing line of white light across the floor.

Stop near the center of the room facing southeast, and project a circle-cross upon the floor just in front of your feet. From your perspective, the cross is inverted, with its head nearest your feet. First draw its pillar from northwest to southeast; then its arm from northeast to southwest; and then its circle clockwise beginning midway along the arm on your left side.

Visualize the Hebrew letters of the name *Yeheshuah* written from right to left within your heart-center. Take a deep breath to fill your body with air, and retain the breath four beats while energizing your heart-center by increasing its rate of rotation. Watch with your subtle vision as the outward shining light of your heart-center inflates your aura into a transparent sphere.

Stab at the center of the cross on the floor with the incense stick, and vibrate the holy name *Yeheshuah*.

"Yah-hesh-shu-ah"

Contract your aura as you vibrate the name. The sounds expanding outward in all directions rebound from your contracting auric sphere back upon your heart-center with greatly magnified force. The compressed power of the divine name seeks release from your heart-center and erupts into the palm of your left hand. It is driven in an expanding spiral across your body and out through the shaft of the incense stick in your right hand upon the astral cross, which glows with intense whiteness. Contemplate the cross for ten seconds or so as you point at its center with the incense stick.

Continue walking diagonally to the southeast corner of the room, projecting in front of you on the floor a thin line of white light from the center of the cross on the floor to the center of the cross that is at heart level in the southeast. As you near the southeast, raise the incense stick to point directly at the intersection of the southeast cross. It is not necessary to vibrate the name a second time for this cross.

Turn to face the west but continue to point at the center of the southeast cross with the incense stick, so that your right forearm extends across your chest and points slightly behind you. Walk to the southwest corner, retracing the line of light that already exists at heart level across the southern side of the room. It is not necessary to project this line a second time—merely follow it with the glowing point of the incense.

Facing southwest, point to the center of the southwest cross, raise the incense stick above your head, and project a line of white light upward from the southwest cross as you turn your body to face the northeast. Walk toward the northeast with the incense stick held in your right hand high over your head, drawing a line of light diagonally across the ceiling as you go.

When you reach the center of the room, visualize the diagonal cross that has already been formed on the ceiling. Draw the line of light along its arm to terminate at its intersection.

Visualize the Hebrew letters of the name *Yeheshuah* written from right to left within your heart-center. Take a deep breath to inflate your body with air, and hold the breath four beats while energizing your heart-center. Watch with your subtle vision as the shining light of your rapidly whirling heart-center expands your aura into a transparent sphere.

Point at the center of the cross on the ceiling and vibrate the divine name *Yeheshuah*.

"Yah-hesh-shu-ah"

As you vibrate the name, contract your aura strongly. The sounds reverberate against your aura, causing it to resonate in sympathy, and rebound from its shrinking, reflective surface to focus back upon your heart-center with greatly magnified force. The concentrated vibrations are compressed ever more tightly until they release themselves into the palm of your left hand and are driven in an expanding spiral up your left arm, across your shoulders, down your right arm, and out through the shaft of the incense stick. The power of the name strikes the center of the astral cross and causes it to glow with intense whiteness. Contemplate the cross for ten seconds or so as you continue pointing at its intersection.

Walk toward the northeast corner of the room with your right arm held up slightly in front of you, drawing the line of white radiance along the ceiling as you go, and connect the line with the center of the cross in the northeast. Contemplate this cross for ten seconds. It is not necessary to vibrate the name again in the northeast.

Point to the center of the cross in the northeast and project a line of white light downward as you turn your body to face the southwest. Walk toward the southwest, continuing to project this radiant line downward in front of you.

Pause in the center of the room to link the line of light with the intersection of the cross already drawn on the floor. Contemplate this cross.

Visualize the Hebrew letters of the name *Yeheshuah* written from right to left within your heart-center. Take a deep breath to fill your body with air, and retain the breath four beats while making your heart-center spin more rapidly. The outward shining light of your heart-center expands your aura into a transparent sphere.

Stab with the incense stick at the center of the cross in front of you on the floor. As you do so, vibrate the divine name *Yeheshuah*.

"Yah-hesh-shu-ah"

As you vibrate the name, contract your aura. The vibrations rebound from the inner surface of your aura and focus back upon your heart-center with magnified potency, compressing the name until it fountains into the palm of your left hand and is driven in an expanding spiral across your body and out the shaft of the incense stick. It strikes the astral cross, making it glow with intense whiteness. Contemplate the cross at your feet for ten seconds while continuing to point to its center.

Walk diagonally to the southwest as you project downward in front of you a glowing line of radiance across the floor. Link up this thin line of subtle fire with the intersection of the cross in the southwest, so that you end by pointing directly ahead at heart level to the middle of this cross.

Contemplate the cross in the southwest for ten seconds or so. Point at its center and turn your body to face north so that your right forearm is angled across your chest and slightly behind you. Walk northward to the northwest corner of the room while trailing the tip of the incense stick on the glowing white line previously projected along the western side of the room. Pause in the northwest corner, facing northwest, and point at the center of the cross. Contemplate the cross in the northwest. It is not necessary to vibrate the name.

Turn to face the east while continuing to point at the intersection of the cross in the northwest. Walk east while trailing the point of the incense stick along the line of light already established on the northern side of the room. Pause in the northeast corner, facing northeast, and point at the center of the cross. Contemplate the cross in the northeast. It is not necessary to vibrate the name.

Turn to face the south while continuing to point at the intersection of the cross in the northeast. Walk south while trailing the point of the incense stick along the line of light already established on the eastern side of the room. Pause in the southeast, facing southeast, and point at the center of the first cross. Contemplate the cross in the southeast for ten seconds or so.

With the incense stick, draw a second circle-cross directly over the first, but make this second cross larger, with a larger circle. First project its vertical beam from top to bottom, then its horizontal beam from right to left.

Before beginning the circle of this larger cross, visualize the Hebrew letters of the name *Yeheshuah* written from right to left within your heart-center. Take a deep breath and hold it four beats while energizing your heart-center. The radiance of your heart-center expands your aura into a transparent sphere.

As you trace the lower arc of the circle from midway on the right arm across the lower segment of the column to midway on the left arm, use half of your breath to vibrate the holy name *Yeheshuah*.

"Yah-hesh-shu-ah"

As you vibrate the name, contract your aura. The vibrations expanding outward from your heart-center reflect from your contracting aura and concentrate within your heart-center with greatly magnified energy. The compressed power of the name releases itself into the palm of your left hand and is driven in an expanding spiral up your left arm, across your shoulders, down your right arm, and out through the shaft of the incense stick as you inscribe upon the large astral cross the lower arc of its circle, which glows with intense whiteness.

Visualize the divine name of five Hebrew letters *Yehovashah* (I = י, H = ה, V = ו, Sh = ש, H = ה), written from right to left within your heart-center. Retain the second half of your breath four beats to energizing your heart-center, so that its radiating light expands your aura into a sphere.

ה ש ו ה י

As you continue tracing the upper arc of the circle from midway on the left arm across the upper segment of the column to midway on the right arm, vibrate the divine name *Yehovashah* with what is left of your breath.

"Yah-ho-vah-shah"

Contract your aura as you vibrate the name. The expanding sounds reverberate and rebound from the inner surface of your shrinking aura and focus back upon your heart-center with greatly magnified force, compressing ever more tightly until their power fountains into the palm of your left hand and is driven in an expanding spiral up your left arm, across your shoulders, down your right arm, and out through the shaft of the incense stick. Use this stream of subtle astral fire to inscribe the upper arc of the circle upon the cross. The arc glows with intense whiteness.

Contemplate the large circle-cross in the southeast. It glows brightly from the combined vibrations of the two holy names.

Place the incense stick in its holder in the southeast. Walk to the center of the room and face east. Assume the standing pose with your feet together, arms at your sides, back straight, and head erect. Take a few moments to inwardly visualize the three bands of light that surround you, and the crosses set in the intersections of those bands.

Draw in a slow, deep breath and retain it four beats as you energize your heart-center and send its radiance flying out in all directions through the pores of your skin to inflate the envelope of your aura into a pale golden sphere.

Spread your arms to the sides with your fingers extended stiffly and your palms facing forward, so that your body forms a great cross. Vibrate the four Latin letters I. N. R. I. with one breath and send the force of the sounds outward from your resonating aura to fill the universe. Do not contract your aura.

"Eye-En-Are-Eye"

As you continue to sustain the sphere of your aura with your will, take a another deep breath, hold it four beats, and energize your heart-center. Vibrate the names of the four Hebrew letters: *Yod-Nun-Resh-Yod* (I = י, N = נ, R = ר, I = י). The vibrations are driven outward by your resonating aura to fill the universe.

"Yod-Nun-Resh-Yod"

Take another breath while maintaining your expanded aura, hold it four beats while energizing your heart-center, and vibrate the syllables of the words: *The Sign of Osiris Slain.* The vibrations are driven outward in all directions by your aura.

"The Sign of Oh-si-ris Slain"

Raise your right arm straight upward with your left arm still extended horizontally to the left. Bow your head toward your left shoulder. The open palms of both your hands continue to face east. Draw another breath and hold it four beats while charging your heart-center. Vibrate the following letter and words: *L—The Sign of the Mourning of Isis.* The harmonic resonance of your aura sends these vibrations outward to fill the universe.

"El—The Sign of the Mourn-ing of I-sis"

Let your right arm fall part way to the side and raise your left arm, keeping both straight, so that your arms form a V-shape. Hold both hands flat with your palms turned outward to the sides. Straighten your head, and tilt it back slightly to gaze upward. Take another breath and hold it four slow beats while charging your heart-center. Vibrate the following letter and words: *V—The Sign of Typhon and Apophis*. Your aura sends these vibrations outward to fill the universe.

"Vee—The Sign of Ty-phon and Ah-po-phis"

Cross your forearms on your chest to form an X-shape that has its intersection over your heart-center. Keep your hands flat so that your fingertips rest on the fronts of your shoulders. Bow your head forward. Take another breath and hold it four beats while charging your heart-center. Vibrate the following letter and words: *X—The Sign of Osiris Risen*. Your aura drives these vibrations outward to fill the universe.

"Ex—The Sign of Oh-si-ris Ris-en"

Once more make the Sign of the Mourning of Isis by raising your right arm straight overhead and extending your left arm horizontally to your left side, while bowing your head to the left. Take another breath, hold it to charge your heart-center, and with the first portion of the breath vibrate the letter *L:*

"El"

Straighten your neck, raise your left arm, and lower your right arm to equal angles above your head to once again form the V-shaped Sign of Typhon and Apophis. Tilt your head back slightly to gaze upward. With the second part of the retained breath vibrate the letter *V:*

"Vee"

Cross your forearms on your chest with your hands flat and bow your head to once more form the Sign of Osiris Risen. With the third part of the breath vibrate the letter *X:*

"Ex"

Keep your head bowed, and with the last part of the breath vibrate the Latin word *Lux:*

"Lux"

Maintain the Sign of Osiris Risen. Draw another breath, hold it four beats to charge your heart-center, and vibrate the words *The Light of the Cross:*

"The Light of the Cross"

Remain still for a minute or so, holding this pose. Breath normally. Then raise your head and extend your arms out to the sides with your hands flat and your palms facing forward so that your body forms a great cross. This is the same Sign of Osiris Slain done earlier.

Take a deep breath and hold it four beats while charging your heart-center. Vibrate the words *Virgo—Isis—Mighty Mother.*

"Vir-go, I-sis, Might-ty Moth-ther"

Take another breath, hold it four beats while charging your heart-center, and vibrate the words *Scorpio—Apophis—Destroyer.*

"Scor-pi-oh, Ah-po-phis, Des-troy-er"

Take another breath, hold it four beats while charging your heart-center, and vibrate the words *Sol—Osiris—Slain and Risen.*

"Sol, Oh-si-ris, Slain and Ris-en"

Draw another breath, hold it four beats, and slowly raise your arms higher, keeping them straight and turning your palms upward, as you vibrate the three names *Isis—Apophis—Osiris*. As you do so, gradually turn your face upward.

"I-sis, Ah-po-phis, Oh-sir-is"

Maintain this pose of aspiration to the light and take another breath, hold it four beats, then vibrate the three Latin letters of the Gnostic divine name *I. A. O.*

"Eye-Ay-Oh"

Maintain the pose of aspiration, take another breath, hold it four beats, and vibrate the four names of the Enochian Tablet of Union: *Exarp, Hcoma, Nanta, Bitom.*

"Ex-ar-pay, Hey-com-ah, En-an-tah, Be-it-om"

Concentrate upon the light of the blue-white star high above your head. Extend your desire and pull a beam of light from the star downward to shine upon your upturned face. Feel the cooling radiance of the light on your forehead, cheeks, and lips. Take another deep breath, hold it four beats while charging your heart-center, and vibrate the words: *Let the Divine Light Descend.*

"Let the Di-vine Light De-scend"

With the force of your will draw the spiritual radiance from the star down over the outside of your body from your head to your feet, and feel it covering your entire form like a soft cloak of silk. Open yourself to the light and allow it to penetrate into your body through your skin so that it fills every part of you. Contemplate the light that surrounds and penetrates your entire body for several minutes. Sever your link with the beam of light from the star and allow it to return heavenward.

Lower your hands to your sides and adopt the standing pose facing east. Allow your expanded aura to contract to its normal shape. Be aware of the interlocked network of lines and crosses of light that surround your practice area gleaming brightly on the astral plane. Allow them to fade from your awareness without actively destroying them, so that their diffused energy brightens the ambient light in the room.

Close your eyes momentarily to rest them, and press your palms to your face. Slide your hands downward and over your chin as though pulling off a skin-tight mask. Relax from your standing pose and go about your day.

Commentary

The Ritual of the Rose Cross is one of the most important Golden Dawn rituals, but it is not nearly so popular among practitioners of magic as the Lesser Banishing Ritual of the Pentagram. It is excellent for purifying the atmosphere of a room and keeping it free from unwanted psychic or spirit intrusions. The interlocking framework of lines and crosses acts as a protective barrier without being as obtrusive on the astral level as the pentagrams.

There are two parts to the ritual, the formation of the interlocking framework of circle-crosses, and the invocation of LVX. Both parts can be performed as separate rituals in their own right. The grid of lines and crosses is excellent for cleansing a space. The LVX formula elevates the spirit and opens it to higher influences and communications.

As is the case with most Golden Dawn rituals, the original description in the Order papers is scarcely more than an outline. I have expanded the details and added visualization to make the ritual more effective for beginners. In the illustration supplied by Israel Regardie in his book *The Golden Dawn*, the crosses inscribed on the ceiling and floor of the ritual chamber are aligned parallel to the sides of the room. I believe this to be an error in judgment. In the exercise I direct that these central crosses be aligned with the diagonal lines of astral fire intersecting on the ceiling and floor, since this facilitates the flow of energies during the exercise. The astral loops must pass through the beams and pillars of all the crosses.

The divine name *Yeheshuah* is vibrated twice for the cross on the ceiling and twice for the cross on the floor in order to balance the four vibrations at the corners of the room.

The Hebrew names *Yeheshuah* (I = י, H = ה, Sh = ש, V = ו, H = ה) and *Yehovashah* (I = י, H = ה, V = ו, Sh = ש, H = ה) are associated in the Christian Kabbalism of the Renaissance with Jesus Christ—they are two magic forms of the name Jesus. Osiris, Isis, and Apophis are Egyptian deities. Typhon is the Greek name for Apophis. Isis is the giver of life who resurrects Osiris, Apophis is the giver of death who kills Osiris, and Osiris is the god of rebirth, having died and been restored to life. *Lux* is a Latin word meaning light; *IAO* is a Gnostic name of god that is probably related to Yahweh. The Latin letters I. N. R. I. refer to the crucifixion of Christ—they are the first letters of the words *Iesus Nazarenus Rex Iudaeorum* (Jesus of Nazareth, King of the Jews), and are supposed to have been written on a placard affixed to Jesus by the Romans at the time of his execution. The Hebrew letters *Yod-Nun-Resh-Yod* are merely their transliterations.

The Enochian words *Exarp, Hcoma, Nanta, Bitom* appear on a small magic square used by the Golden Dawn in its version of Enochian magic—a subject far too complex to describe here. In the Golden Dawn, *Exarp* is attributed to elemental Air and the quarter of the east. *Hcoma* is attributed to Water and the west. *Nanta* is attributed to Earth and the north. *Bitom* is attributed to Fire and the south.

The letters of Enochian words were sometimes vibrated individually in the Golden Dawn. For example, *Exarp* might be sounded "Ee-ex-ay-ar-pay," with equal weight given each letter sound. This practice of sounding each letter originated with the Golden Dawn, and as I have indicated earlier, may be applied to Hebrew words as well. However, it is not how Enochian words were intended by the Enochian angels to be pronounced. I have made the vibration of all four words consist of three sounds each, which works very well for this ritual. The technique of vibrating the individual letters of these Enochian words is used in exercise 39.

In his book *Ceremonial Magic,* Israel Regardie provided the following ritual pronunciations for these four Enochian words: "Ex-ar-pay, Heh-coh-mah, En-ah-en-tah, Bay-ee-toh-em." Since Regardie studied under Crowley, who was a member of the original Golden Dawn, and was himself a member of an offshoot branch of the Golden Dawn, this may be the original Order pronunciation. Feel free to use this styling when you vibrate these words, if you prefer it. The best course is to practice vibrating the words both ways to determine which seems to result in the greatest amount of force.

When the aura is expanded into a sphere but left in a natural condition, it remains permeable and transmits by means of harmonic sympathy the vibrations of the divine names outward in all directions to the ends of the universe. If it is contracted slightly and hardened by an act of will, it becomes impermeable and reflective, and sends the vibrations of the names rebounding back upon their source in the center of the chest with increased energy. If the expanded aura is gradually contracted close to the body during the vibration of names, it not only increases the strength of the vibrations by reflection, but can be used like a pump or bellows to drive the enhanced vibrations out of the heart-center in an spiral of explosive release through the chest wall into the left palm, up the left arm, across the shoulders, and down the right arm to exit from the right hand.

This method of contracting the aura to reflect and concentrate vibrations within the sphere of the heart-center is not a part of the Golden Dawn system, but originated in my own work. I find it quite useful. It is somewhat similar to the intensification of a beam of light within the crystal of a laser by repeatedly reflecting the light back and forth between the two polished ends of the crystal, until at last it is emitted explosively from the less reflective end. The left hand pressed to the heart-center provides an avenue of release for the compressed vibrations in the heart-center, and the extended right hand unbalances the aura and allows the stream of energy to be directed through this weak spot on any desired place or object.

The Rose Cross Ritual can be done without expanding your aura into a sphere. Indeed, this is the usual way it is performed. The manipulation of the aura to enhance the effectiveness of the vibrated names is not even mentioned in the outline of the ritual that exists in the Order documents. However, I find the vibration of names to be more effective when the interaction of the aura with the expanding vibrations is visualized. With practice the aura can be expanded or contracted in moments. Experiment by doing the Rose Cross Ritual without paying any attention to your aura, and then performing it as it is presented above, to determine if these techniques for manipulating the aura are beneficial for you.

Ideally, the room in which you practice this ritual should be perfectly aligned to the four directions of the compass. This is almost never the case. Find the wall that is most nearly in the east and regard it as due east for the purposes of the exercise. Adjust the other directions accordingly, treating the wall on the right of the nominally eastern wall as south, the wall on the left as north, and the wall opposite as west. When you perform the exercise in an irregular enclosed space, or outdoors where no walls exist, determine beforehand the approximate direction of east by means of the rising sun or a magnetic compass, and use this as your reference point for the exercise.

EXERCISE 35

Creating a Vortex

Go TO THE center of your practice area and face the east. Assume the standing pose with your back straight, head erect, shoulders relaxed, arms at your sides, and feet together. Gaze straight ahead and focus your eyes on the unseen, distant horizon beyond the wall in front of you. Take several slow, normal breaths to calm your thoughts and prepare your intention.

Ascend upward in your astral awareness to the brilliant blue-white star that should always be visualized as high in the heavens directly above your head. Feel its scintillating, dancing light surround you. Send down a ray of this light through the top of your skull to your heart-center. Descend down the interior channel of this ray into your energized heart-center and release the ray to withdraw back upward into the star.

Assume the posture of projection, with your left palm pressed to the center of your chest and your right arm extended in front of you at an upward angle of forty-five degrees. Be aware of the glowing golden-white light and vibrating power in the sphere of your heart-center.

Draw spiritual energy from your heart-center through your left palm, up your left arm, across our shoulders, along your right arm, and send it out the tip of your extended right index finger in the form of astral fire. Project this stream of fire in the form of a clockwise-inward spiral of three and one-half turns on the air in front of you. Circle your index finger inward three full turns and then loop to the center of this astral spiral.

As you project the spiral upon the air, visualize its line glowing with bright golden-white fire. With the power of your will, draw additional energy downward from the heavens directly into the upper end of the spiral, and channel the energy inward along its clockwise course in the form of spiraling rays of light that revolve around its center point, like the vanes of a great pinwheel. The shining, rotating vortex grows larger, until it fills the entire eastern side of your practice room.

Focus your awareness on the center of the great turning spiral, while continuing to point at its center with your right index finger. The tiny stationary center glows more and more brightly, like a white star. As it accumulates radiant energy from the heavens, it blazes like a tiny sun with countless rays. Project over it from the tip of your right index finger an equal-armed cross of white light. Draw the vertical beam of the cross from top to bottom, then the horizontal beam from left to right. The white cross stops the turning of the spiral.

Figure 35-1.
Clockwise-inward spiral
of three and one-half turns

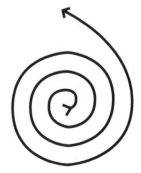

Figure 35-2.
Counterclockwise-outward spiral
of three and one-half turns

Allow your arms to fall to your sides and assume the standing posture. Observe the contracting spiral wind itself inward into the star of light until only the central star remains, shining like a brilliant white diamond at the intersection of the cross. Watch the arms of the cross contract into the star. Contemplate the solitary star for a minute or so.

Assume the projecting posture. Feel the energy vibrating in your heart-center, and allow it to flow into your left palm, up your left arm, across your shoulders, and down your right arm to exit out your right index finger as you draw a cross of white astral fire over the white star, first the vertical beam, then the horizontal beam. Point at the center of the cross with your right index finger. With your inner perception, observe the arms of the cross withdraw themselves into the star.

Project a counterclockwise-outward spiral of three and one-half turns upon the air. It loops outward a half-turn from the center of the white star and winds three full turns, each larger than the last, so that at the end of its tail your extended right arm is elevated at an angle of forty-five degrees. Let your arms fall to your sides and adopt the standing pose.

Visualize this spiral begin to rotate counterclockwise and throw off spiral rays of light from the white star at its center, which energizes the spiral. It expands to fill the entire eastern side of your practice room. The more it expands, the dimmer the star at its center becomes, until at last the star cannot be seen. Continue to observe with your astral perception the expanding vortex grow paler and spin more and more slowly, until it also fades from view.

Adopt the projecting posture with your left palm pressed to the center of your chest, and your right arm extended in front of you at a downward angle of forty-five degrees. Be aware of the glowing golden-white light and vibrating power in the rotating sphere of your heart-center.

Draw spiritual energy from your heart-center through your left palm, up your left arm, across your shoulders, along your right arm, and send it out the tip of your extended right index finger as astral fire. Project this stream of golden-white flame in an inward-counterclockwise spiral of three and one-half turns on the air in front of you. Circle your index finger inward three full turns and then loop to the center of this astral spiral.

As you project the spiral upon the air, visualize its line glowing brightly. Continue to point at the center of the spiral. With the force of your will, draw additional energy upward from beneath the ground and channel it inward along the counterclockwise course of the spiral in the form of turning rays of black that are edged with brightness, and revolve around the center point of the spiral like the vanes of a great pinwheel. The shining, black, inwardly rotating vortex grows larger until it fills the entire eastern side of your practice room.

Focus your awareness on the center of the dark turning spiral. The tiny black central point glows more and more brightly around its edges, like a distant eclipsed sun. As it accumulates radiant energy, it blazes with countless dark rays that seem to absorb the light from the room. Project over it from the tip of your right index finger an equal-armed cross of white light. Draw the vertical beam of the cross from top to bottom, then the horizontal beam from left to right. The white cross stops the turning of the spiral.

Allow your arms to fall to your sides and assume the standing posture. Observe the contracting dark spiral wind itself inward into the black star until only the star remains, shining like a brilliant black diamond at the intersection of the white cross. The arms of the cross contract into the star. Contemplate the solitary black star for a minute or so.

Assume the projecting posture. Feel the energy vibrating in your heart-center, and allow it to flow into your left palm, up your left arm, across your shoulders, down your right arm, and out your right index finger as you draw a white cross over the black star, first the vertical beam, then the horizontal beam. Point at the center of the cross with your right index finger. After a few seconds the arms of the cross contract into the star.

Figure 35-3.
Counterclockwise-inward spiral
of three and one-half turns

Figure 35-4.
Clockwise-outward spiral
of three and one-half turns

Project a clockwise-outward spiral of three and one-half turns upon the air. It loops outward a half-turn from the center of the black star and winds three full turns, each larger than the last, so that at the end of its tail your extended right arm is angled downward at forty-five degrees. Let your arms fall to your sides and adopt the standing pose.

Visualize this white spiral begin to rotate clockwise and throw off shadowy spiral rays that are energized from the black star at its center. Each ray is edged with white fire. The vortex expands to fill the eastern side of your practice room. The more it expands, the dimmer the halo of light around the black star at its center becomes, until at last the star cannot be seen. Continue to observe with your astral perception the expanding vortex grow paler and spin more and more slowly, until it also fades from view.

Take several slow breaths and close your eyes. Press your palms to your face and draw them downward as though pulling off a skin-tight mask. Open your eyes and relax from the standing pose. Go about the rest of your day.

Commentary

The projection of a vortex is one of the most important skills needed for successful magic, but it is seldom adequately described. The vortex concentrates or releases occult energy, depending on its direction of rotation, either inward or outward. A vortex based on the clockwise-inward spiral attracts and focuses the spiritual energies of the Light; a vortex based on the counterclockwise-inward spiral attracts and focuses the compound physical energies of the Earth element. Matter is a shadow of spirit, so the counterclockwise-inward vortex is best visualized as a black whirlpool. The spiral of light is used for works of a spiritual or constructive kind; the spiral of shadow is used for works of an overtly physical or destructive kind.

Opposite outward spirals release these occult energies. For example, when a clockwise-inward spiral is used to focus upon a point and open it into a gateway through which a ray of will can be sent for a desired purpose, a counterclockwise-outward spiral closes the gateway. This is very useful when opening and closing a scrying instrument, such as a crystal or a black mirror. All magic gateways are opened and closed by means of spiral vortices. This is true even when those who work magic are not consciously aware that they are forming vortices.

The cross is used to locate a single point in space that acts as the focus of the spiral, and also to halt the rotation of a spiral vortex. It is drawn after the projection of an inward spiral to fix the center of the vortex, and also to still the turning of the vortex. When drawn before the projection of an outward spiral, the cross locates the point of origin from which the expanding whirl emanates. A spiral drawn on top of a cross replaces the static, balanced force of the cross with dynamic spiral energy; a cross drawn on top of a spiral replaces the dynamic turning energy of the whirl with the static, balanced force of the cross.

By beginning a spiral with the right index finger elevated, energy is drawn down from the heavens and focused upon its center. When a spiral ends with the right index finger elevated, energy is dispersed upward from the focal point of the spiral. Conversely, by beginning a spiral with the right index finger lowered, energy is drawn upward from the depths of the Earth and focused upon its center. When a spiral ends with the right index finger lowered, energy is dispersed downward from the focal point of the spiral. The symbolic nature of these directions—up for spirit and down for matter—makes them no less effective when employed in practical magic.

A clockwise-inward spiral should begin with the right arm elevated, since this spiral is in harmony with the Light. Its opposite whirl, a counterclockwise-outward spiral, ends with the right arm elevated.

A counterclockwise-inward spiral should begin with the right arm lowered, since this spiral is in harmony with the Earth. Its opposite whirl, a clockwise-outward spiral, ends with the right arm lowered.

The outward spiral does not negate or erase the effect of a previously drawn opposite inward spiral. Rather, it complements it. A clockwise-inward spiral is used to open a point doorway through which a particular desire or purpose of a constructive nature is sent along a ray of will. The corresponding counterclockwise-outward spiral allows the desire to fulfill itself. The second is like an echo of the first, or a reply. It completes the circuit.

Whenever occult potency has already been concentrated, like electrical potential in a battery, through an opened point at a place or within an object, an outward spiral may be used to release it, since the initial concentration of the force employed an inward spiral that was created either deliberately or unconsciously. Most occult vortices are made unconsciously, both in the art of magic and in everyday life.

E X E R C I S E 3 6

Invoking the Light

PERFORM THIS RITUAL in a room with ample floor space, so that you can walk around the inner circumference of a circle at least nine feet in diameter. If you do not have such a large room, you can still work the ritual, but you must project your astral circle larger than your actual physical space. In the center of the floor, place a small table such as a bedside table or plant stand to act as an altar. Put a white candle in a candle holder in the middle of the table and light the candle.

Position yourself on the western side of the altar facing east, so that the altar is immediately in front of you. Adopt the standing pose, with your feet together, arms at your sides, back straight, and head erect. Direct your gaze straight ahead and look through the wall at the unseen, distant horizon. Take several long, deep breaths to focus your resolve and prepare for what you are about to do.

Visualize high over your head a blue-white star that blazes with pure spiritual energy. Ascend in your inner awareness to this star and enter it. Allow the brilliant rays from the star to completely surround you and saturate your awareness with cooling light.

Extend a ray of white light from the star straight downward through the top of your skull to your heart-center. Visualize this center expand into a three-inch transparent sphere of glowing golden radiance, the color of sunlight. Focus the white ray from the star on the center of the transparent golden sphere.

Allow your awareness to slide down this white ray to your heart-center. Continue to draw spiritual energy down the ray until your heart-center turns from yellow to soft radiant white with only the slightest golden tint. Hold your awareness in your heart-center.

Visualize yourself standing inside the white circle painted on the hardwood floor of the astral temple described in exercise 19. The altar of polished black marble is immediately in front of you in the center of the circle. A white candle burns on its top in a plain brass holder. You stand in the western quarter of the circle facing the eastern wall of the astral temple. See painted on the mist-gray wall in front of you the upright solid yellow triangle that forms the key feature of the eastern part of your astral temple.

Take a deep breath and hold the air in your lungs for four slow beats as you visualize the warm light from your heart-center radiate outward to expand your aura into a sphere. The sphere of your aura surrounds the altar directly in front of you but does not extend beyond the painted circle of the astral temple.

Touch your right index finger to your forehead between your eyebrows. Vibrate the syllables of the Hebrew word *ateh* briefly but with power and authority.

"ah-teh"

Feel the resonance in your chest energize your aura, and the vibrations of your aura propel your articulated breath outward to fill the universe.

Touch your right index finger to the region of your solar plexus. Vibrate the syllables of the Hebrew word *Malkuth* briefly but with authority.

"Mal-kuth"

Feel the vibrations in your chest energize your aura, and sense that your aura propels your breath outward to fill the universe.

Visualize a white ray extending from the glowing sphere of your heart-center vertically up and down, so that it passes through the top of your skull and between your feet. Conceive this ray to be a laser beam of infinite length.

Touch your right index finger to your right shoulder and vibrate the syllables of the Hebrew words *ve-Geburah* briefly with force.

"veh-Geb-u-rah"

Feel the vibrations in your chest energize your aura, and sense that your aura propels your breath outward to fill the universe.

Touch your right index finger to your left shoulder and vibrate the syllables of the Hebrew words *ve-Gedulah* briefly with force.

"veh-Ged-u-lah"

Feel the vibrations in your chest energize your aura, and sense that your aura propels your breath outward to fill the universe.

Visualize a white ray extending from the glowing sphere of your heart-center horizontally to the left and right so that it passes out the sides of your body below the level of your armpits. Conceive this ray to be a laser beam of infinite length. This horizontal ray intersects the vertical ray at right angles at the center of your heart-center.

Press the palms of your hands together in front of your solar plexus with your extended fingers pointing upward. Vibrate the Hebrew words *le-olam* strongly to create a resonance in your chest.

"leh-oh-lam"

Feel the vibrations in your chest energize your aura, and sense that your aura propels your breath outward to fill the universe.

Visualize a white ray extending from the glowing sphere of your heart-center horizontally in front and behind, so that it passes out of your body through the center of your chest between your joined hands, and out the center of your back. This horizontal ray intersects the first two rays at right angles in your heart-center.

Raise your united hands above your head while continuing to gaze forward. Vibrate the Hebrew word *amen* strongly to create a resonance in your chest. Extend the final syllable so that the remaining air in your lungs is expelled.

"ah-mennnnn"

Feel the vibrations in your chest energize your aura, and sense that your aura propels your breath outward to fill the universe. Lower your joined hands to their former place in front of your solar plexus, and allow them to separate and fall to your sides as you adopt the standing pose.

Remain motionless in this posture for a minute or so, breathing normally, and contemplate with your inner sight the large golden sphere of your expanded aura, the smaller gold-white sphere of your heart-center, and the three brilliant-white rays that extend from the three axes of your body. Mentally draw the three rays back into your heart-center, but continue to be aware of its radiance. Allow your aura to contract slowly to its usual elongated shape nearer the surface of your skin.

Walk around the altar in a clockwise direction and stand in the east facing east. Assume a posture of projection with your left hand over your heart-center and your right arm extended. Project a yellow banishing pentagram of Earth upon the air in

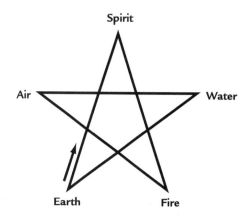

**Figure 36-1.
Golden Dawn
banishing pentagram of Earth**

the east. Begin it from the lower-left point and draw its line clockwise. Visualize its interlocking segments glowing brightly with yellow flame.

Draw a deep breath, hold it four beats while visualizing the Hebrew letters of the name *IHVH* (I = י, H = ה, V = ו, H = ה) written from right to left within the sphere of your heart-center. The letters flame brilliantly with a dazzling blue-white radiance.

$$\text{הוהי}$$

Stab at the center of the pentagram with your right index finger and vibrate the letters of the divine name so that the sound resonates in your chest, throat, and nose, and expands outward to the limits of the universe.

"Yud-Heh-Vav-Heh"

Continue pointing to the center of the pentagram with your right index finger. Breathe normally. The vibrations of the holy name cause a pillar of white light to extend downward from the radiant white star in the heavens. Contemplate this pillar of light, which stands outside the circle behind the yellow pentagram like an infinitely long column of glowing white marble.

While pointing to the center of the pentagram with your right index finger, turn your body to the right so that your right forearm crosses in front of your chest. Walk along the quarter circumference of an imaginary circle to the south, projecting a line of golden-white fire upon the air at heart level as you go. This circle must be at least nine feet across, even if your work area is smaller—walls are no barrier to astral forms. Feel the vital energy that fills your heart-center flow through your chest into your left palm, up your left arm, across your shoulders, and down your right arm to exit in a flaming stream from your right index finger. The expanding spiral it follows as it circulates through your body increases its force. Continue to sustain in your awareness the banishing pentagram of Earth in the east. As you project the line of astral fire upon the air in your practice room, be aware that you are also projecting it above the painted circle on the floor of your astral chamber.

Stand in the pose of projection in the southern quarter of the practice area facing south. Project a fiery red banishing pentagram of Earth upon the air to the south so that the termination of the quarter circle you have previously drawn is in the exact center of the pentagram. The size and formation of the pentagram are identical to the one in the east. It begins from the lower-left point and proceeds clockwise. Visualize its interlocking segments glowing brightly with red flames.

Take a deep breath and hold it four beats as you intensify the radiance of your heart-center. While your breath is stopped, visualize the Hebrew letters of the divine name *Adonai* (A = א, D = ד, N = נ, I = י) written from right to left within the sphere of your heart-center in brilliant white flame that is edged with electric blue.

א ד נ י

Stab at the center of the pentagram with your right index finger and vibrate the letters of the divine name so that the sound resonates within your body and expands to fill the universe.

"Ah-doh-en-aye"

Continue pointing to the center of the pentagram with your right index finger. Breathe normally. The vibrations of the holy name cause a pillar of white light to extend downward from the star beyond the red pentagram in the south. Contemplate this pillar of light.

Turn your body to the right so that your right forearm crosses in front of your chest. Walk along the circumference of the imaginary circle to the west, projecting a line of golden-white fire upon the air at heart level as you go. Be aware that you are also projecting this line above the painted circle on the floor of your astral chamber.

Stand in the pose of projection in the western quarter of the practice area facing west. Project a pentagram of deep blue fire on the air to the west so that the termination of the quarter circle you have previously drawn is in the exact center of the pentagram. The pentagram is identical in formation to the ones in the east and south. It begins from the lower-left point and proceeds clockwise.

Take a deep breath and hold it four beats as you intensify the radiance of your heart-center. While your breath is stopped, visualize the Hebrew letters of the divine name *Eheieh* (A = א, H = ה, I = י, H = ה) written in brilliant blue-white flame from right to left within the sphere of your heart-center.

א י ה ה

Stab the center of the pentagram with your right index finger and vibrate sounds corresponding with the letters of the divine name so that the vibration resonates within your body and expands to fill the universe.

"Ah-heh-aye-yah"

Continue pointing to the center of the pentagram with your right index finger. Breathe normally. The vibrations of the holy name cause a pillar of white light to extend downward from the star beyond the blue pentagram in the west. Contemplate this pillar of light.

Turn your body to the right so that your right forearm crosses in front of your chest. Walk along the circumference of the imaginary circle to the north, projecting a line of golden-white fire upon the air at heart level as you go. Continue to sustain in your awareness the pentagrams in the east, south, and west. As you project this line of fire upon the air of your practice room, visualize yourself projecting it above the painted circle on the floor of your astral temple.

Stand in the pose of projection in the northern quarter of the practice area facing north. Project a pentagram of dark green fire on the air to the north so that the termination of the quarter circle you have previously drawn is in the exact center of the pentagram. The pentagram is identical in formation to the ones in the east, south and west. It begins from the lower-left point and proceeds clockwise.

Take a deep breath and hold it four beats as you intensify the radiance of your heart-center. While your breath is stopped, visualize the Hebrew letters of the divine name *AGLA* (A = א, G = ג, L = ל, A = א) written in brilliant blue-white flame from right to left within the sphere of your heart-center.

א ל ג א

Stab the center of the pentagram with your right index finger and vibrate the letters of the divine name so that the sound resonates within your body and expands to fill the universe.

"Ah-Geh-Lah-Ah"

Continue pointing to the center of the pentagram with your right index finger. Breathe normally. The vibrations of the holy name cause a pillar of white light to extend downward from the star beyond the green pentagram in the north. Contemplate this pillar of light.

Turn your body to the right so that your right forearm crosses in front of your chest. Walk along the circumference of the imaginary circle to the east, projecting a line of golden-white fire upon the air at heart level as you go. Continue to sustain in your awareness the pentagrams in the east, south, west, and north. As you walk along the imaginary circle in the practice room, you also walk around the inside of the painted circle on the floor of the astral chamber.

Join the end of the line of golden fire to its beginning in the center of the eastern pentagram. Drop your arms to your sides and maintain the standing pose for half a minute or so, breathing normally. Walk around the altar clockwise to stand in the west facing east with the altar directly in front of you. At the same time, with your inner vision be aware that you are standing in the western part of your astral temple facing east with the altar of black stone in front of you almost touching your legs.

Adopt the formal standing pose. Gaze straight ahead, and focus your eyes on the distant eastern horizon that lies in front of you beyond the wall and other intervening obstructions. Extend your astral awareness in all directions to the circle and the four banishing pentagrams of Earth that are set in its golden-white band. Contemplate the circle and the different colors of the pentagrams for several minutes. Strive to hold the complete, unbroken circle in your mind. Be aware of the four white pillars beyond the circle.

Spread your arms wide so that your body forms the shape of a cross. Draw a long, deep inhalation. Hold the breath for four slow beats and visualize the light from your heart-center shining outward to enlarge the outer surface of your aura into a perfect transparent sphere of palest gold. Your aura encloses the altar but does not extend outside the limits of the circle. Be sure to keep your physical gaze directed eastward.

Vibrate upon your breath the following words so that your chest, throat, and nose resonate inwardly.

"Be-fore me, Raph-a-el."

Exhale the remainder of your breath while maintaining your expanded aura. Visualize the yellow color of the eastern pentagram transfer itself into the pillar. As the pillar turns yellow, the pentagram fades to a clear golden-white.

The yellow pillar thickens and solidifies into the towering, yellow-robed angel Raphael. The angel stands barefoot beyond the circle, gazing down at you with vigilant awareness in its pale gray eyes. Its golden hair is the same color as its robe. The human face of the angel glows with the residual energy of your vibrated words. Watch with your astral awareness as the angel turns its back upon the circle to face the east, and opens wide its white wings to fill the eastern quarter.

Draw a deep breath and hold it for four slow beats as you focus your awareness in your heart-center.

Vibrate upon your breath the following words.

"Be-hind me, Gab-ri-el."

Exhale the remainder of your breath while maintaining your expanded aura. Visualize the blue of the western pentagram transfer itself into the pillar behind you. As the pillar turns deep blue, the western pentagram fades to a clear golden-white.

The blue pillar thickens and solidifies into the towering, blue-robed angel Gabriel. The angel stands barefoot beyond the circle, gazing down at you with vigilant awareness in its bronze-colored eyes. The golden-brown eagle's head of the angel glows with the residual energy of your vibrated words. Without shifting your physical gaze from the east, watch with your astral awareness as the angel turns its back upon the circle to face west, and opens wide its white wings to fill the western quarter.

Draw a deep breath and hold it for four slow beats as you focus your awareness in your heart-center.

Vibrate upon your breath the following words.

"At my right hand, Mich-a-el."

Exhale the remainder of your breath while maintaining your expanded aura. Visualize the bright red of the southern pentagram transfer itself into the pillar. As the pillar turns red, the pentagram fades to a clear golden-white.

The red pillar thickens and solidifies into the towering, scarlet-robed angel Michael. The angel stands barefoot beyond the circle, gazing down at you with vigilant awareness in its golden eyes. The maned lion's head of the angel glows with the residual energy of your vibrated words. Watch with your astral awareness as the angel turns its back upon the circle to face south, and opens wide its white wings to fill the southern quarter.

Draw a deep breath and hold it for four slow beats as you focus your awareness in your heart-center.

Vibrate upon your breath the following words.

"At my left hand, Aur-i-el."

Exhale the remainder of your breath while maintaining your expanded aura. Visualize the dark green of the northern pentagram transfer itself into the pillar. As the pillar turns green, the pentagram fades to a clear golden-white.

The green pillar thickens and solidifies into the towering, green-robed angel Auriel. The angel stands barefoot beyond the circle, gazing down at you with vigilant awareness in its dark eyes. The bull's head of the angel glows with the residual energy of your vibrated words. Watch with your astral awareness as the angel turns its back to the circle to face north, and opens wide its white wings to fill the northern quarter.

Contemplate the four angels standing outside the circle with their faces turned outward to the four quarters and their wings spread so that the tips of their wings touch and overlap. Hold simultaneously in your awareness the circle, the pentagrams, and the backs of the angels as you continue to stand facing east with your arms spread so that your body forms a cross.

Visualize your heart-center. Use its energy to expand forward and upward through the center of your chest a white pentagram that hangs upon the air just inside the eastern edge of the circle above the level of your head. At the same time expand backward and upward from your heart-center a white hexagram that hangs upon the air just inside the western edge of the circle above the level of your head. Make in your imagination both the pentagram and hexagram approximately three feet across.

Draw a deep breath. Hold it four slow beats while focusing your awareness upon the pentagram before you and the hexagram behind you. Vibrate the following words.

"Before me flames the pentagram— behind me shines the six-rayed star."

Lower your arms and adopt the standing pose. Allow your expanded aura to contract to its usual shape near your body. For several minutes hold in your mind the white pentagram in front, the white hexagram behind, the golden-white circle with its four inset gold-white pentagrams around you, and the four angels at the quarters.

Walk around the altar clockwise to stand in the east facing south. Visualize with your astral perception that you stand within the astral temple. Be aware of the candle burning on top of the black marble altar, the flaming astral circle that floats upon the air at heart level above the painted white circle on the floor, and the four guardians of the quarters who stand just outside the limit of the astral circle, facing outward with their wings spread.

Walk in a complete circle clockwise around the altar, speaking the following in a clear voice so that your words resonate inwardly in the astral temple.

"See that holy and formless fire, which darts and flashes through the hidden depths of the universe."

As you walk, visualize a swirling vortex of light form in the air above the altar. It is shaped like the inverted funnel of a tornado, but bright instead of gray, and it turns clockwise. The funnel of the vortex of light has its focus in the blue-white star high overhead and opens wider as it extends downward to surround the altar. Within the center of the spinning funnel, a column of white light gradually forms, linking the flame of the candle with the white star high above in the heavens. With your astral perceptions, hear the rushing sound of the light as it swirls down from the star into the circle.

When you reach the eastern quarter once again, continue walking clockwise in a second circle around the altar. Speak the following words clearly so that they resound in the astral temple.

"Such a fire existeth, extending through the rushings of air, a fire formless whence cometh the image of a voice."

Visualize the light of the vortex above the candle intensify, and the column of light linking the candle with the star become thicker and brighter. The spiritual radiance drawn down the inside of its inverted funnel cascades over the candle and spreads outward to fill the entire circle with light. Visualize light flooding into the circle from above. The sound of the swirling vortex becomes louder.

When you return to the eastern quarter, continue walking in a third clockwise circle around the altar. Speak the following words so that they resound in the astral temple.

"A flashing light, abounding, revolving, whirling forth, crying aloud. Hear the voice of Fire!"

Visualize the whirling vortex above the altar intensify and brighten, drawing down a flood of light that fills the entire circle. This light shining from the beam above the candle is so concentrated, it makes the astral temple glow, and can even be seen on the air of the physical temple. Hear the rushing of the light as it descends. It sounds similar to roaring fire caught in a powerful downdraft.

When you complete the third circle, adopt the standing pose in the eastern quarter facing west with the altar immediately in front of you, so that you can observe the intensely flaming candle on the altar with your physical sight. At the same time that you are regarding the physical candle, see with your astral vision the astral candle in the astral temple, and the inverted, funnel-shaped astral vortex or tourbillion that surrounds it. Listen with your inner hearing to the rustling and roaring of this vortex.

Begin to perform the fourfold breath with pore breathing while keeping your gaze focused upon the candle flame. Draw in a deep breath for four silent beats, and as you inhale, visualize the light that swirls inside the ritual circle flowing in the form of countless tiny threads into your body through the pores of your skin.

Hold your breath with your lungs comfortably filled with air for the same four silent beats, and visualize the light that now fills your entire body circulating along every vein and nerve channel.

Exhale for four silent beats, and visualize the air flowing from your nostrils to be silver-gray in color. All of its astral light has been absorbed and retained within your body.

Hold your breath with your lungs comfortably empty of air for four beats, and visualize the light that circulates throughout your body concentrate itself in the golden-white sphere of your heart-center.

Repeat this cycle of the fourfold breath four times. As you perform the breath, visualize the inverted vortex above the candle gradually lose its whirling energy and fade from your astral perceptions, leaving the vertical beam of light that links the candle with the star. Visualize the light the fills the circle become fainter as more and more of it is drawn into your body through the pores of your skin.

Breathe normally. For a minute or two, contemplate the flame of the candle on the altar, the beam of light extending upward from its tip, and the air within the circle. At the same time remain aware of the brightness of your heart-center.

Spread your arms wide in the posture of Osiris Slain so that your body forms a great cross. While gazing at the flame of the candle, draw a deep breath and hold it four beats as you energize your heart-center by making it vibrate and spin more intensely. Expand your aura into a sphere that surrounds the altar. Vibrate the word *LVX* on your breath.

"Lux!"

Raise your right arm straight overhead and bow your head slightly to the left in the Sign of the Mourning of Isis. Draw another deep breath and hold it four beats to charge your heart-center, then vibrate the following words.

"I come in the Power of the Light."

Lower your right arm slightly and raise your left arm so that your arms form a V-shape above your head. Straighten your neck. Stand in the Sign of Typhon and Apophis while continuing to gaze at the flame of the candle. Draw a deep breath and hold it four beats to energize your heart-center. Vibrate the following words.

"I come in the Light of Wisdom."

Cross your forearms upon your chest in the Sign of Osiris Risen, with your hands flat and your fingertips at the fronts of your shoulders. Continue to regard the candle. Draw a deep breath and hold it four beats while energizing your heart-center. Vibrate the following words.

"I come in the Mercy of the Light."

Spread wide your arms so that your body forms a great cross, and stand in the Sign of Osiris Slain once again. Visualize that your arms have become white, feathered wings. Regard the flame on the candle. Draw a deep breath, hold it four beats while energizing your heart-center, then vibrate the following words.

"The Light hath healing in its Wings."

Slowly raise your extended arms, and your visualized astral wings, at an angle and at the same time elevate your gaze upward to the white star that is high overhead. Speak in a clear voice the following Adoration of the Light so that the words resonate within your body, and within the astral temple.

"Holy Art Thou, Lord of the Universe,
Holy Art Thou, Whom Nature hath not Formed,
Holy Art Thou, the Vast and the Mighty One,
Lord of the Light and of the Darkness."

Lower your arms to your sides. Make the Sign of Harpocrates by pressing the tip of your left index finger against the little hollow just above your upper lip, so that the first segment of your finger crosses both lips. Take a few moments to listen to the silence as you hold this pose. Even if there is noise coming from the street or another room, concentrate on the stillness within the astral temple as you gaze inwardly at the candle burning on the top of the black marble altar. At the same time, the eyes of your body of flesh are directed at the actual flame of the candle on top of your physical altar. You see both, superimposed one on top of the other, but the astral image is clearer.

Lower your left arm and assume the standing posture. Allow your expanded aura to contract to its normal shape close to your skin. Take a step backward to the eastern edge of the circle and turn to the north. Walk around the altar in a counterclockwise direction while speaking the following in a strong voice that vibrates within your body and resounds in the astral temple.

"Hear the voice of fire! A flashing light abounding, revolving, whirling forth, crying aloud."

As you walk, visualize a counterclockwise vortex of silver-gray begin at the top of the candle flame and extend upward into a funnel, expanding as it rises. This vortex completely surrounds the beam of white light that connects the candle flame with the white star in the heavens. It is wider at its top, narrower at its base.

When you return to the east, keep walking a second circle counterclockwise around the altar. Speak these words so that they vibrate in your chest and resound in the astral temple.

"Such a fire existeth, extending through the rushings of air, a fire formless whence cometh the image of a voice."

Visualize the counterclockwise vortex strengthening and extending upward above the candle. Hear with your astral senses the rushing of its rotation. See it begin to absorb the radiance of the white ray connecting the candle flame with the star, so that the vortex slowly turns from silver-gray to a golden white.

After completing the second circuit around the altar, continue walking counterclockwise for a third circuit. Speak these words so that they vibrate in your chest and resound in the astral temple.

"See that holy and formless fire, which darts and flashes through the hidden depths of the universe."

Complete the third circling of the altar and stand in the east, facing west. For a few moments contemplate the counterclockwise vortex, which has turned completely white and whirls furiously around the beam linking the candle with the star. The beam has become pale and flickers along its length.

Focus your will upon the place where this beam touches the candle flame, and lift your arms upward with your hands turned up and your fingers extended and spread. As you make this gesture, mentally sever the connection between the star and the candle flame and see inwardly the beam withdraw itself upward like a stretched rubber band that has suddenly been released. See the counterclockwise vortex fly apart and scatter sparks of golden-white light throughout the circle. These slowly fade to nothingness.

Walk around the altar in a clockwise direction to stand in the west facing east with the altar directly in front of you. Spread your arms wide so that your body forms the shape of a cross. Draw a long, deep inhalation. Hold the breath for four slow beats and visualize the light from your heart-center shining outward to enlarge the outer surface of your aura into a perfect transparent sphere of palest gold. Your aura encompasses the altar but does not extend beyond the limit of the circle behind you.

Visualize the white pentagram that hangs upon the air above the level of your head in the eastern quarter of the circle. At the same time extend your awareness backward and be aware of the white hexagram that hangs upon the air above the level of your head in the western quarter of the circle. Focus your awareness strongly upon the pentagram before you and the hexagram behind you while vibrating the following words.

"Behind me shines the six-rayed star— before me flames the pentagram."

Visualize the hexagram behind you shrink and descend as it is absorbed into your heart-center through your back. At the same time see with your astral perceptions the pentagram in front of you shrink and descend as it is absorbed through your chest into your heart-center. Contemplate the increase of energy in your heart-center for a minute or so while maintaining your posture.

Draw a deep breath and hold it four slow beats as you focus your awareness in your heart-center.

Vibrate upon your breath the following words.

"At my left hand, Aur-i-el."

Exhale the remainder of your breath while maintaining your expanded aura. Without turning your head, visualize the green-robed angel in the north lower its wings and turn around to face the circle. The bull-headed angel gazes down upon you with an alert but emotionless expression. Its body wavers and lengthens into a dark green pillar. The green color of the pillar transfers itself into the white pentagram that is set in the ring of the astral circle in the north. As the pillar fades to a clear golden-white, the pentagram turns dark green.

Draw a deep breath and hold it for four slow beats as you focus your awareness in your heart-center.

Vibrate upon your breath the following words.

"At my right hand, Mich-a-el."

Exhale the remainder of your breath while maintaining your expanded aura. Visualize the red-robed angel in the south lower its wings and turn around to face the circle. The lion-headed angel gazes down upon you with an alert but emotionless expression. Its body wavers and lengthens into a bright red pillar. The red color of the pillar transfers itself into the white pentagram that is set in the ring of the astral circle in the south. As the pillar fades to a clear golden-white, the pentagram turns bright red.

Draw a deep breath and hold it four slow beats as you focus your awareness in your heart-center.

Vibrate upon your breath the following words.

"Be-hind me, Gab-ri-el."

Exhale the remainder of your breath while maintaining your expanded aura. Visualize the blue-robed angel in the west lower its wings and turn around to face the circle. The eagle-headed angel gazes down upon you with an alert but emotionless expression. Its body wavers and lengthens into a deep-blue pillar. The color of the pillar transfers itself into the white pentagram that is set in the ring of the astral circle in the west. As the pillar fades to a clear golden-white, the pentagram turns blue.

Draw a deep breath and hold it four slow beats as you focus your awareness in your heart-center.

Vibrate upon your breath the following words so that your chest, throat, and nose resonate inwardly.

"Be-fore me, Raph-a-el."

Exhale the remainder of your breath while maintaining your expanded aura. Visualize the yellow-robed angel in the east lower its wings and turn around to face the circle. The human-headed angel gazes down upon you with an alert but emotionless expression. Its body wavers and lengthens into a yellow pillar. The yellow color of the pillar transfers itself into the white pentagram that is set in the ring of the astral circle in the east. As the pillar fades to a clear golden-white, the pentagram turns bright yellow.

Lower your arms and assume the standing pose. Allow your expanded aura to contract to its normal shape close to your skin. Without turning your head, contemplate inwardly the four white pillars at the four sides of the astral temple, beyond the limit of the ritual circle. They extend upward to converge in the blazing white star high overhead. Hold simultaneously in your awareness the circle, the colored pentagrams, and the four white pillars.

Walk clockwise around the altar and stand in the eastern side of the circle, facing east. Assume a posture of absorption with your right palm pressed over your heart-center and your left arm extended.

With your left index finger, trace a banishing pentagram of Earth on top of the yellow pentagram that already hangs upon the air in the east. Begin it from the lower-left point and draw its line clockwise. As you retrace the interlocking segments of the yellow pentagram, visualize its yellow color flowing in a stream of fire into the tip of your left index finger, up your left arm, across your shoulders, down your right arm, and through your right palm into your heart-center. The pentagram that remains upon the air in the east is golden-white. For a moment the sphere of your heart-center glows bright yellow—then it resumes its golden-white color.

Draw a deep breath, hold it four beats while visualizing the Hebrew letters of the name *IHVH* written from right to left within the sphere of your heart-center. The letters flame brilliantly with a dazzling blue-white radiance.

$$\text{ה ו ה י}$$

Stab at the center of the pale white pentagram in the east with your left index finger and vibrate the letters of the divine name so that the sound resonates in your chest, throat, and nose, and expands outward to the limits of the universe.

"Yud-Heh-Vav-Heh"

Continue to point at the center of the pentagram as you breathe normally. The vibrations of the holy name cause the pillar of white light in the east to retract upward into the radiant white star in the heavens. At the same instant, the pale white pentagram contracts to a point and is absorbed into the tip of your left index finger. Its energy travels through the spiral of your upper body into your heart-center. Will the circle to break apart in the east at the place you point.

Turn your body to the left so that your left forearm crosses in front of your chest. Walk along the inner circumference of the ritual circle to the north, absorbing its line of golden-white fire into your left index finger as you go.

Stand in the pose of absorption in the northern quarter of the ritual circle facing north. With your left index finger, trace a banishing pentagram of Earth on top of the green pentagram that already hangs upon the air in the north. Begin it from the lower-left point and draw its line clockwise. As you retrace the interlocking segments of the green pentagram, visualize the dark-green color flowing in a stream of fire into the tip of your left index finger, up your left arm, across your shoulders, down your right arm, and through your right palm into your heart-center. For a moment the sphere of your heart-center glows dark green—then it resumes its golden-white color.

Take a deep breath and hold it four beats as you intensify the radiance of your heart-center. While your breath is stopped, visualize the Hebrew letters of the divine name *AGLA* written from right to left within the sphere of your heart-center in brilliant white flame that is edged with electric blue.

$$\text{א ל ג א}$$

Stab the center of the pale-white pentagram with your left index finger and vibrate sounds corresponding with the letters of the divine name so that the vibration resonates within your body and expands to fill the universe.

"Ah-Geh-Lah-Ah"

Continue to point at the center of the pentagram as you breathe normally. The vibrations of the holy name cause the pillar of white light in the north to retract upward into the radiant white star in the heavens. At the same instant, the pale white pentagram contracts to a point and is absorbed into the tip of your left index finger. Its energy travels through the spiral of your upper body into your heart-center.

Turn your body to the left so that your left forearm crosses in front of your chest. Walk along the circumference of the ritual circle to the west, absorbing its line of golden-white fire into your left index finger as you go.

Stand in the pose of absorption in the western quarter of the ritual circle facing west. With your left index finger, trace a banishing pentagram of Earth on top of the blue pentagram that already hangs upon the air in the west. Begin it from the lower-left point and draw its line clockwise. As you retrace the interlocking segments of the blue pentagram, visualize the deep-blue color flowing in a stream of fire into the tip of your left index finger, up your left arm, across your shoulders, down your right arm, and through your right palm into your heart-center. For a moment the sphere of your heart-center glows deep blue—then it resumes its golden-white color.

Take a deep breath and hold it four beats as you intensify the radiance of your heart-center. While your breath is stopped, visualize the Hebrew letters of the divine name *Eheieh* written in brilliant blue-white flame from right to left within the sphere of your heart-center.

$$\text{א י ה ה}$$

Stab the center of the pentagram with your left index finger and vibrate the letters of the divine name so that the sound resonates within your body and expands to fill the universe.

"Ah-heh-aye-yah"

Continue to point at the center of the pentagram as you breathe normally. The vibrations of the holy name cause the pillar of white light in the west to retract upward into the radiant white star in the heavens. At the same instant, the pale white pentagram shrinks to a point and is absorbed into the tip of your left index finger. Its energy travels through the spiral of your upper body into your heart-center.

Turn your body to the left so that your left forearm crosses in front of your chest. Walk along the circumference of the ritual circle to the south, absorbing its line of golden-white fire into your left index finger as you go.

Stand in the pose of absorption in the southern quarter of the ritual circle facing south. With your left index finger, trace a banishing pentagram of Earth on top of the red pentagram that already hangs upon the air in the south. Begin it from the lower-left point and draw its line clockwise. As you retrace the interlocking segments of the red pentagram, visualize the bright red color flowing in a stream of fire into the tip of your left index finger, up your left arm, across your shoulders, down your right arm, and through your right palm into your heart-center. For a moment the sphere of your heart-center glows bright red—then it resumes its golden-white color.

Take a deep breath and hold it four beats as you intensify the radiance of your heart-center. While your breath is stopped, visualize the Hebrew letters of the divine name *Adonai* written in brilliant blue-white flame from right to left within the sphere of your heart-center.

א ד נ י

Stab the center of the pentagram with your left index finger and vibrate the letters of the divine name so that the sound resonates within your body and expands to fill the universe.

"Ah-doh-en-aye"

Continue to point at the center of the pentagram as you breathe normally. The vibrations of the holy name cause the pillar of white light in the south to retract upward into the radiant white star in the heavens. At the same instant, the pale white pentagram shrinks to a point and is absorbed into the tip of your left index finger. Its energy travels through the spiral of your upper body into your heart-center.

Turn your body to the left so that your left forearm crosses in front of your chest. Walk along the circumference of the ritual circle to the east, absorbing its line of golden-white fire into your left index finger as you go.

Drop your hands to your sides and walk around the altar clockwise to stand in the west facing east, with the altar directly in front of you. Gaze straight ahead, and focus your eyes on the distant eastern horizon that lies beyond the wall and other intervening obstructions.

Take a deep breath and hold the air in your lungs for four slow beats as you visualize the warm light from your heart-center radiate outward to expand your aura into a sphere. Your aura encloses the altar.

Touch your right index finger to your forehead between your eyebrows. Vibrate the syllables of the Hebrew word *ateh* briefly but with power and authority.

"ah-teh"

Feel the resonance in your chest energize your aura, and the vibrations of your aura propel your articulated breath outward to fill the universe.

Touch your right index finger to the end of your breastbone, in the area of your solar plexus. Vibrate the syllables of the Hebrew word *Malkuth* briefly but with authority.

"Mal-kuth"

Feel the vibrations in your chest energize your aura, and sense that your aura propels your breath outward to fill the universe.

Visualize a white ray extending from the glowing sphere of your heart-center vertically up and down, so that it passes through the top of your skull and between your feet. Conceive this ray to be a laser beam of infinite length.

Touch your right index finger to your right shoulder and vibrate the syllables of the Hebrew words *ve-Geburah* briefly with force.

"veh-Geb-u-rah"

Feel the vibrations in your chest energize your aura, and sense that your aura propels your breath outward to fill the universe.

Touch your right index finger to your left shoulder and vibrate the syllables of the Hebrew words *ve-Gedulah* briefly with force.

"veh-Ged-u-lah"

Feel the vibrations in your chest energize your aura, and sense that your aura propels your breath outward to fill the universe.

Visualize a white ray extending from the glowing sphere of your heart-center horizontally to the left and right so that it passes out the sides of your body below the level of your armpits. Conceive this ray to be a laser beam of infinite length. This horizontal ray intersects the vertical ray at right angles at the center of your heart-center.

Press your hands together in front of your solar plexus in the common gesture of prayer so that your extended fingers point upward, and cup your hands slightly to separate your palms. Vibrate the Hebrew words *le-olam* strongly to create a resonance in your chest.

"leh-oh-lam"

Feel the vibrations in your chest energize your aura, and sense that your aura propels your breath outward to fill the universe.

Visualize a white ray extending from the glowing sphere of your heart-center horizontally in front and behind, so that it passes out of your body through the center of your chest between the palms of your joined hands and the out-center of your back. This horizontal ray intersects the first two rays at right angles in your heart-center.

Raise your united hands over your head with your fingers pointing upward. Vibrate the Hebrew word *amen* strongly to create a resonance in your chest. Extend the final syllable so that the remaining air in your lungs is expelled.

"ah-mennnnn"

Feel the vibrations in your chest energize your aura, and sense that your aura propels your breath outward to fill the universe.

Lower your hands to your sides. Stand motionless in this posture for a minute or so, breathing normally, and contemplate with your inner sight the large golden sphere of your expanded aura, the smaller gold-white sphere of your heart-center, and the three brilliant-white rays that extend from the three axes of your body. Mentally draw the three rays into your heart-center, but continue to be aware of its radiance. Allow your aura to contract slowly to its usual elongated shape nearer the surface of your skin.

Close your eyes. Press the heels of your palms into the hollows of your eyes and draw your hands downward slowly as though slipping off a skin-tight mask. Open your eyes, relax from your standing posture, and go about your day.

Commentary

In this ritual I have adhered to the traditional Golden Dawn associations for the four quarters, and have employed the Golden Dawn banishing pentagram of elemental Earth. In spite of its length, the ritual is fairly simple. It is described with an uncommon degree of detail for the benefit of beginners. Writers frequently abbreviate parts of rituals they have previously described to save space, but as I pointed out in the introduction, this can lead to confusion when these elements are not perfectly understood or clearly present in the memory. The basic parts of this ritual are:

- Kabbalistic Cross
- Lesser Banishing Ritual of the Pentagram
- Establishment of the four Guardian angels
- Triple circumambulation to draw down the Light
- Adoration of the Light
- Reverse triple circumambulation to release the Light
- Release of the four Guardian angels
- Reversal of the Lesser Banishing Ritual
- Kabbalistic Cross

In modern magic, it is uncommon to deliberately unmake the ritual circle at the end of a ritual. Usually the astral circle is simply ignored and stepped through as though it did not exist once the ritual has been completed. However, in my opinion, if the circle it to attain its fullest potency during rituals, it must be consciously unmade at the end of rituals rather than simply forgotten. There are numerous possible ways to unmake the circle. I have unmade it in this ritual by reversing the steps by which it was projected during the Lesser Banishing Ritual of the Pentagram.

It should be pointed out that frequently smaller rituals form the components of larger rituals. The Kabbalistic Cross is a ritual in its own right. So is the Lesser Banishing Ritual of the Pentagram, which normally incorporates within itself the Kabbalistic Cross. It was the practice of the Golden Dawn to teach simple rituals, and then compound these into more complicated rituals at higher levels of proficiency. I have followed this excellent precept in the present work.

This exercise for invoking the Light can be used for a wide variety of ritual purposes merely by inserting ritual actions and text designed to accomplish desired purposes directly after the adoration of the Light. It is a valid ritual in its own right, but also the framework upon which an infinite number of other rituals can be based.

Although the ritual is original, it uses elements from more complex Golden Dawn ceremonies, such as the Golden Dawn method of evocation. The various texts quoted play a prominent role in Golden Dawn magic. The invocation pronounced during the triple circumambulation to draw down the Light, which begins "See that holy and formless fire . . ." was modified somewhat from its Golden Dawn model. This was not a sacrilegious act on my part. The text was derived by the founders of the Golden Dawn from the *Chaldean Oracles of Zoroaster* and was modified by them from that older source to suit their purposes. I have merely carried on this traditional practice in magic of taking what you need and making it your own.

It is important for beginners to shake off the superstition that rituals are inviolable patterns that must never be altered. Rituals are created by individuals to accomplish specific purposes when worked under an existing set of circumstances. If the goals of a ritual or the conditions under which it is worked change, it may become useful or necessary to change the ritual, in order to renew its full effectiveness.

It is perfectly permissible to take parts of existing rituals and combine them in original ways to accomplish original goals. Many of the components of Golden Dawn rituals lend themselves extremely well to incorporation into new rituals. Once you have acquired the basic skills of magic, you should not hesitate to construct your own rituals tailored to meet your personal needs. One way to do this is to mix and match parts of traditional rituals such as those worked by the original Golden Dawn, or those described in the medieval grimoires.

EXERCISE 37

Cleansing Prayer

I T IS BEST to perform this exercise directly following a bath or shower. If it is done at other times, first wash your hands and face and brush your teeth. It is also best to do the exercise naked—otherwise, wear comfortable, loose clothing and remove your shoes.

Assume the standing pose facing east. Direct your gaze straight ahead and focus your eyes on the unseen distant horizon. Take several deep breaths to calm your thoughts and prepare for what will follow.

Visualize yourself standing in the western quarter of your astral temple, facing the upright yellow triangle on the east wall, with the altar of black marble in front of you.

Raise your arms slowly out to your sides with your elbows locked until they are angled slightly above your head. Turn your palms up and spread your fingers. At the same time tilt your head back and elevate your gaze so that it is directed upward at the white star high in the heavens. See this star shining in the darkness of space with your astral sight. Take care not to hunch your shoulders or lock your neck—keep your shoulders relaxed and stretch upward with your face.

Speak the cleansing prayer in a clear voice that vibrates within you and makes the astral temple resonate. As you speak the words of the prayer, visualize cooling streams of silvery water fall down from the heavens upon your upturned face and hands, and cascade along your arms and down the length of your body.

> **"Have mercy upon me, O Lord,**
> **Blot out my transgressions.**
> **Wash me thoroughly from my iniquities**
> **And cleanse me from my sins.**
> **Asperge me with hyssop, and I shall be clean;**
> **Wash me, and I shall be whiter than snow.**
> **Create in me a clean heart, O Lord,**
> **And renew a right spirit within me."**

Feel the astral rain from the star penetrate through your skin to wash clean the interior of both your body and soul. Feel the rain wash through your brain and sweep away the chaos of your thoughts, leaving only a quiet clarity. Feel it wash through your heart and carry away fear, anger, sorrow, and other hurtful emotions. Feel it wash through your bowels and genitals and carry away all destructive urges and harmful sexual impulses. Feel it wash down the insides of your legs to your feet and carry out through the soles of your feet all diseases and infirmities of your flesh. As the words of the prayer end, the silvery rain from the star ceases.

Assume the standing posture with your hands at your sides and your gaze directed straight ahead. Take a deep breath and hold the air in your lungs for four slow beats as you visualize the warm light from your heart-center radiate outward to expand your aura into a sphere.

Touch your right index finger to your forehead between your eyebrows. Vibrate the syllables of the Hebrew word *ateh* briefly but with power and authority.

"ah-teh"

Feel the resonance in your chest energize your aura, and the vibrations of your aura propel your articulated breath outward to fill the universe.

Touch your right index finger to the end of your sternum, in the region of your solar plexus. Vibrate the syllables of the Hebrew word *Malkuth* briefly but with authority.

"Mal-kuth"

Feel the vibrations in your chest energize your aura, and sense that your aura propels your breath outward to fill the universe.

Visualize a white ray extending from the glowing sphere of your heart-center vertically up and down, so that it passes through the top of your skull and between your feet. Conceive this ray to be a laser beam of infinite length.

Touch your right index finger to your right shoulder and vibrate the syllables of the Hebrew words *ve-Geburah* briefly with force.

"veh-Geb-u-rah"

Feel the vibrations in your chest energize your aura, and sense that your aura propels your breath outward to fill the universe.

Touch your right index finger to your left shoulder and vibrate the syllables of the Hebrew words *ve-Gedulah* briefly with force.

"veh-Ged-u-lah"

Feel the vibrations in your chest energize your aura, and sense that your aura propels your breath outward to fill the universe.

Visualize a white ray extending from the glowing sphere of your heart-center horizontally to the left and right so that it passes out the sides of your body below the level of your armpits. Conceive this ray to be a laser beam of infinite length. This horizontal ray intersects the vertical ray at right angles at the center of your heart-center.

Press your hands together in front of your solar plexus so that your extended fingers point upward, and cup your palms slightly to create a space between them. Vibrate the Hebrew words *le-olam* strongly to create a resonance in your chest.

"leh-oh-lam"

Feel the vibrations in your chest energize your aura, and sense that your aura propels your breath outward to fill the universe.

Visualize a white ray extending from the glowing sphere of your heart-center horizontally in front and behind, so that it passes out of your body through the center of your chest between the palms of your joined hands and out the center of your back. This horizontal ray intersects the first two rays at right angles in your heart-center.

Raise your united hands above the level of your head with your fingertips pointed upward. Vibrate the Hebrew word *amen* strongly to create a resonance in your chest. Extend the final syllable so that the remaining air in your lungs is expelled.

"ah-mennnnn"

Feel the vibrations in your chest energize your aura, and sense that your aura propels your breath outward to fill the universe. Lower your joined hands to the region of your solar plexus, then allow them to separate and drop to your sides.

Resume the standing pose. Stand motionless in this posture for a minute or so, breathing normally, and contemplate with your inner sight the large golden sphere of your expanded aura, the smaller gold-white sphere of your heart-center, and the three brilliant-white rays that extend from the three axes of your astral body. Mentally draw the three rays into your heart-center, but continue to be aware of its radiance. Allow your aura to contract slowly to its usual elongated shape nearer the surface of your skin.

Be aware of the freshness and cleanness of your body, the clarity and simplicity of your thoughts. Contemplate your condition for several minutes.

Close your eyes and press your hands to your face. Draw them down slowly as though sliding off a skin-tight mask. Open your eyes and relax from your standing posture. Go about your day.

Commentary

The Cleansing Prayer is an excellent exercise to perform each day immediately following your shower. It is based on a much briefer cleansing formula used in Western magic: "Purge me with hyssop and I shall be clean, wash me and I shall be whiter than snow" (Psalms 51:7). I extracted the longer prayer from Psalms 51. The words of the prayer are embedded in the psalm.

The prayer can also be used as a preliminary to ritual work. It frees the mind from the distractions and common concerns of the day and prepares it to concentrate solely on the work at hand. It is best to follow the Cleansing Prayer with the Kabbalistic Cross. The two are in harmony, since both are based on traditional Judeo-Christian texts.

Wiccans and other worshippers of the Goddess will prefer to change the wording of the prayer slightly to reflect their beliefs. Instead of the words "Have mercy upon me, O Lord" they should use "Have mercy upon me, O Lady" or "O Goddess." Instead of the words "Create in me a clean heart, O Lord," the words "Create in me a clean heart, O Lady" or "O Goddess" may be substituted. Those who conceive the highest creative power in an abstract way may wish to use "O Light" or "O Source" in place of "O Lord." Although the prayer originates in Judeo-Christian scripture, its effectiveness is not limited to the conventional Jewish or Christian concept of God. It is simply a request for cleansing and renewal from the highest active expression of deity.

The cleansing prayer can be employed to purify substances and instruments for ritual use. It is especially good as a quick purification method for water, salt, candles, incense sticks, paper, pens, and other common things used in ritual work. To purify an object or material, hold it between your two hands in front of your heart-center while speaking the words of the prayer, and visualize the water from the star falling over and penetrating both your body and the thing in your hands. As the prayer cleanses you, it also cleanses what you hold. When you finish the prayer, set the purified substance on the floor at your feet and trace the Kabbalistic Cross upon your body. Wrap the purified substance in white linen or some other white cloth, and put it away for future use.

Cleansing a Space

I N THE MIDDLE of the room or area you wish to cleanse, place a small table so that you are able to walk completely around the table. The table serves as the ritual altar.

Place a white candle in a holder on the center of the table. On the eastern side of the table put an unlit stick of rose incense (or some other light, pleasant incense) upright in a holder. On the southern side put an unlit red candle in a holder. On the western side of the table put an empty wine goblet and a small decanter or vase filled with plain water. On the northern side put an empty, flat dish and a small container filled with salt.

Light the white candle. Take up the standing posture on the west side of the altar facing east, with your gaze directed straight ahead and your eyes focused on the distant unseen horizon that lies beyond the wall or other obstructions in front of you. Breathe slowly and deeply as you clear your mind and prepare yourself for the ritual.

Visualize yourself standing in the western quarter of your astral temple with the altar of black marble in front of you, facing the upright yellow triangle on the east wall. Inwardly see the white candle and the other materials upon the altar in the astral temple.

Raise your arms slowly out to your sides with your elbows locked so that your body forms a great cross. Continues to elevate your arms until they are angled slightly above your head and turn your palms up with your fingers spread. At the same time, tilt your head back and elevate your gaze so that it is directed upward at the white star high in the heavens. See this star shining in the darkness of space with your astral sight. Keep your shoulders relaxed and extend your neck.

Speak the cleansing prayer in a clear voice that vibrates within you and makes the astral temple resonate. As you speak the words of the prayer, visualize cooling streams of silvery water fall down from the star upon your upturned face and hands, and cascade along your arms and down the length of your body.

**"Have mercy upon me, O Lord,
Blot out my transgressions.
Wash me thoroughly from my iniquities
And cleanse me from my sins.
Asperge me with hyssop, and I shall be clean;
Wash me, and I shall be whiter than snow.
Create in me a clean heart, O Lord,
And renew a right spirit within me."**

Feel the astral rain from the star penetrate through your skin and wash away all the detritus of your daily life, leaving only a quiet clarity. As the words of the prayer end, the silvery rain from the star ceases.

Assume the standing posture with your hands at your sides and your gaze straight ahead. Take a deep breath and hold the air in your lungs for four slow beats as you visualize the warm light from your heart-center radiate outward to expand your aura into a sphere. Your expanded aura encompasses the table, and on the astral level, the black altar.

Touch your right index finger to your forehead between your eyebrows. Vibrate the syllables of the Hebrew word *ateh* briefly but with power and authority.

"ah-teh"

Feel the resonance in your chest energize your aura, and the vibrations of your aura propel your articulated breath outward to fill the universe.

Touch your right index finger to the end of your sternum in the region of your solar plexus. Vibrate the syllables of the Hebrew word *Malkuth* briefly but with authority.

"Mal-kuth"

Feel the vibrations in your chest energize your aura, and sense that your aura propels your breath outward to fill the universe.

Visualize a white ray extending from the glowing sphere of your heart-center vertically up and down, so that it passes through the top of your skull and between your feet. Conceive this ray to be a laser beam of infinite length.

Touch your right index finger to your right shoulder and vibrate the syllables of the Hebrew words *ve-Geburah* briefly with force.

"veh-Geb-u-rah"

Feel the vibrations in your chest energize your aura, and sense that your aura propels your breath outward to fill the universe.

Touch your right index finger to your left shoulder and vibrate the syllables of the Hebrew words *ve-Gedulah* briefly with force.

"veh-Ged-u-lah"

Feel the vibrations in your chest energize your aura, and sense that your aura propels your breath outward to fill the universe.

Visualize a white ray extending from the glowing sphere of your heart-center horizontally to the left and right so that it passes out the sides of your body below the level of your armpits. Conceive this ray to be a laser beam of infinite length. This horizontal ray intersects the vertical ray at right angles at the center of your heart-center.

Press your hands together in front of your solar plexus in the traditional prayer gesture so that your extended fingers point directly upward, and cup your palms slightly to make a narrow space between them. Vibrate the Hebrew words *le-olam* strongly to create a resonance in your chest.

"leh-oh-lam"

Feel the vibrations in your chest energize your aura, and sense that your aura propels your breath outward to fill the universe.

Visualize a white ray extending from the glowing sphere of your heart-center horizontally in front and behind, so that it passes out of your body through the center of your chest between your joined hands and out the center of your back. This horizontal ray intersects the first two rays at right angles in your heart-center.

Raise your united hands above the level of your head with your fingertips pointing upward. Vibrate the Hebrew word *amen* strongly to create a resonance in your chest. Extend the final syllable so that the remaining air in your lungs is expelled.

"ah-mennnnn"

Feel the vibrations in your chest energize your aura, and sense that your aura propels your breath outward to fill the universe. Lower your joined hands to the level of your solar plexus, then allow them to part and fall to your sides as you assume the standing posture.

Remain motionless in this posture for a minute or so, breathing normally, and contemplate with your inner sight the large golden sphere of your expanded aura, the smaller gold-white sphere of your heart-center, and the three brilliant-white rays that extend from the three axes of your astral body. Mentally withdraw the three rays back into the sphere of your heart-center, but continue to be aware of its radiance. Allow your aura to contract slowly to its usual elongated shape nearer the surface of your skin.

Walk around the altar and stand in the east facing east. Adopt the posture of projection with your left palm pressed into the hollow area of your chest just above the end of your sternum, and your right arm extended in front of you toward the east at the level of your heart. Concentrate awareness in the sphere of your heart-center. Draw energy from this sphere through your chest and into your left palm, then send it circulating in an expanding spiral along your left arm, across your shoulders, and down your right arm. Project this occult energy in a thin stream of white astral fire upon the air in front of you to the edge of the room, area, or structure you intend to purify. The astral fire is not obstructed by physical objects and can be mentally projected through walls to the outer boundaries of buildings.

As you begin to project the stream of fire, turn on your own body axis toward your right but continue to point with your right index finger to the east, so that your right forearm crossed in front of your chest. Walk in a complete circle around the altar clockwise, projecting a line of astral fire as you go. Take care to join the end of this circle of fire with its beginning when you return to the east.

Stand in the east facing east with your arms at your sides and visualize this circle of fire completely filling the room or structure to be cleansed. If you are cleansing an entire house, visualize the circle surrounding the outer walls of the house.

Turn to face the south. Continue to visualize with your astral perception that you stand within the astral temple. Be aware of the white candle burning on top of the black marble altar, and of the flaming astral circle that floats upon the air at heart level at the limits of the place you intend to cleanse.

Walk in a complete circle clockwise around the altar, speaking the following in a clear voice so that your words resonate inwardly in the astral temple.

"See that holy and formless fire, which darts and flashes through the hidden depths of the universe."

As you walk, visualize a swirling vortex of light form in the air above the altar. It is shaped like the inverted funnel of a tornado, but bright instead of gray, and it turns clockwise instead of counterclockwise. The funnel of the vortex of light has its focus in the blue-white star high overhead and opens wider as it extends downward to surround the flame of the candle on the altar. Within the center of the spinning funnel, a column of white light gradually forms between the flame of the candle and the white star high above in the heavens. With your astral perceptions, hear the rushing sound of the light as it swirls down from the star into the circle.

When you reach the eastern quarter once again, stop and stand facing south. Inhale a deep breath, and as you do so, raise your arms gradually upward on each side with your elbows locked, so that as your lungs reach their full capacity, your arms are extended almost straight above your head in a narrow V with your palms turned inward toward each other. Retain the breath four slow beats as you visualize the Hebrew mother letter *Mem* written within the sphere of your heart-center.

מ

Step forward about a foot with your right leg. As you shift your center of gravity toward the south, cast your arms and hands downward and forward with your elbows still locked so that your stiffened fingers extend to the south, and you gaze with a lowered head along the tops of your forearms and over the backs of your touching hands.

As you make this modified Sign of the Enterer that you learned in exercise 26, expel your breath and vibrate the Hebrew letter *Mem* strongly so that the air of the astral temple resounds. The beginning and end of the sound are extended and vibrate within the nose and throat:

"Mmmmmmm-mem-mmmmmmm"

Visualize a pulse of blue light form upon the ring of astral fire to the east. The sound of your voice sends this pulse racing around the circle in a clockwise direction and turns the circle blue. The revolution of the pulse of blue light makes the vortex above the altar rotate more strongly. When the pulse returns to the east, it dissolves into the band of the magic circle. Continue to visualize the circle as blue while sounding the Hebrew letter. When you reach the end of your breath and fall silent, the circle reverts to its usual golden-white color. Lower your arms to your sides, pull back your extended right foot, and resume the standing posture.

After a few seconds of contemplation, walk clockwise in a second circle around the altar. Speak the following words clearly so that they resound in the astral temple.

**"Such a fire existeth, extending through the rushings of air,
a fire formless whence cometh the image of a voice."**

Visualize the light of the vortex above the candle intensify, and the column of light linking the candle with the star become thicker and brighter. The spiritual radiance drawn down the inside of its inverted funnel cascades over the candle and spreads outward to fill the circle with light. Visualize light flooding into the circle from above. The sound of the swirling vortex becomes louder.

When you reach the eastern quarter once again, stop and stand facing south. Inhale a deep breath and raise your arms gradually upward on each side with your elbows locked so that your arms are extended almost straight above your head in a narrow V with your palms turned toward each other. Retain the breath four beats and visualize within your heart-center the Hebrew mother letter *Shin*.

שׁ

Step forward with your right leg without moving your left foot. As you shift your center of gravity toward the south, cast your arms and hands downward and forward to the south, and gaze southward from beneath your eyebrows along the tops of your arms.

As you make this Sign of the Enterer, expel your breath and vibrate the Hebrew mother letter *Shin* strongly so that the air of the astral temple resounds. The beginning and end of the sound should be extended and vibrate within the nose and throat:

"Sheeeeeeeeeee-innnnnnnnnnnn"

Visualize a pulse of ruby light form upon the ring of astral fire to the east. The sound of your voice sends this pulse racing around the circle in a clockwise direction and turns the entire circle red. The revolution of the pulse of ruby light makes the vortex above the altar rotate more strongly. When the pulse returns to the east, it dissolves into the band of the magic circle. Continue to visualize the circle as red while sounding the Hebrew letter. When you reach the end of your breath and fall silent, the circle reverts to its usual golden-white color. Lower your arms to your sides, pull back your extended right foot, and resume the standing posture.

After a few seconds of silent contemplation, walk clockwise in a third circle around the altar. Speak the following words so that they resound in the astral temple.

"A flashing light, abounding, revolving, whirling forth, crying aloud. Hear the voice of Fire!"

Visualize the whirling vortex above the altar intensify and brighten, drawing down a flood of light that fills the entire circle. This light shining from the beam above the candle is so concentrated, it makes the astral temple glow, and may even be seen on the air of the physical temple. Hear the rushing of the light as it descends. It sounds similar to roaring fire caught in a powerful downdraft.

When you reach the eastern quarter once again, stop and stand facing south. Inhale a deep breath and raise your arms gradually upward so that they form a narrow V over your head with your palms turned inward toward each other. Retain the breath four slow beats as you visualize the Hebrew mother letter *Aleph* written within the sphere of your heart-center.

א

Step forward a short distance with your right leg without moving your left foot, and cast your arms and hands downward and forward to the south while gazing southward from beneath your eyebrows along the tops of your arms and hands.

As you make this Sign of the Enterer, expel your breath and vibrate the Hebrew mother letter *Aleph* strongly so that the air of the astral temple resounds. The beginning and end of the sound should be extended and vibrate within the nose and throat:

"Aaaaaaaaaaay-leeeeeeeeeph"

Visualize a pulse of deep yellow light form upon the ring of astral fire to the east. The sound of your voice sends this pulse racing around the circle in a clockwise direction and turns the entire circle yellow. The revolution of the pulse of saffron light makes the vortex above the altar rotate more strongly. When the pulse returns to the east, it dissolves into the band of the magic circle. Continue to visualize the circle as deep yellow while sounding the Hebrew letter. When you reach the end of your breath and fall silent, the circle reverts to its usual pale golden-white color. Lower your arms to your sides, pull back your extended right foot, and resume the standing posture.

After standing in the east facing south for a few seconds of silent contemplation, turn to the west and approach the altar. Observe the flaming candle on the central altar with your physical sight. At the same time you are regarding the physical candle, see with your astral vision the astral candle in the astral temple, and the inverted, funnel-shaped astral vortex or tourbillion that surrounds it. Listen with your astral hearing to the rustling and roaring of this vortex.

Begin to perform the fourfold breath with pore breathing while keeping your gaze focused upon the candle flame. Draw in a deep breath for four silent beats, and as you inhale, visualize the light that swirls in the ritual circle flowing in the form of countless tiny particles into your body through the pores of your skin.

Hold your breath with your lungs comfortably filled with air for the same four silent beats, and visualize the light that now fills your entire body circulating along every vein and nerve channel.

Exhale for four silent beats, and visualize the air flowing from your nostrils to be a dull silvery-gray in color. All of its astral light has been absorbed and retained within your body.

Hold your breath with your lungs comfortably empty of air for four beats, and visualize the light that is circulating throughout your body concentrate itself in the golden-white sphere of your heart-center.

Repeat this cycle of the fourfold breath four times. As you perform the breath, visualize the inverted vortex above the candle gradually lose its whirling energy and fade from your astral perceptions, leaving the vertical beam of light that links the candle with the star. Visualize the light that fills the circle become fainter as more and more of it is drawn into your body through the pores of your skin.

Breathe normally. For a minute or two, contemplate the flame of the candle on the altar, the beam of light extending upward from its tip, and the air within the circle. At the same time remain aware of the brightness of your heart-center.

Spread your arms wide in the posture of Osiris Slain so that your body forms a great cross. While gazing at the flame of the candle, draw a deep breath and hold it four beats as you energize your heart-center by making it vibrate and spin more intensely. Expand your aura into a sphere that surrounds the altar. Vibrate the word *LVX* on your breath.

"Lux!"

Raise your right arm straight overhead while continuing to hold your left arm out to the side, and bow your head slightly to the left so that your body forms the Sign of the Mourning of Isis. Draw another deep breath and hold it four beats to charge your heart-center, then vibrate the following words.

"I come in the Power of the Light."

Lower your right arm slightly and raise your left arm so that your arms form a V-shape. Straighten your neck. Stand in the Sign of Typhon and Apophis while continuing to gaze at the flame of the candle. Draw a deep breath and hold it four beats to energize your heart-center. Vibrate the following words.

"I come in the Light of Wisdom."

Cross your forearms upon your chest in the Sign of Osiris Risen, with your hands flat and your fingertips at the fronts of your shoulders. Continue to regard the candle. Draw a deep breath and hold it four beats while energizing your heart-center. Vibrate the following words.

"I come in the Mercy of the Light."

Spread wide your arms so that your body forms a great cross, and stand in the Sign of Osiris Slain once again. Visualize that your arms have become white, feathered wings. Regard the flame on the candle. Draw a deep breath, hold it four beats while energizing your heart-center, then vibrate the following words.

"The Light hath healing in its Wings."

Slowly raise your extended arms, and your visualized astral wings, at an angle and at the same time elevate your gaze upward to the white star that is high overhead. Speak in a clear voice the following Adoration of the Light so that the words resonate within your body, and within the astral temple.

**"Holy Art Thou, Lord of the Universe,
Holy Art Thou, Whom Nature hath not Formed,
Holy Art Thou, the Vast and the Mighty One,
Lord of the Light and of the Darkness."**

Lower your arms to your sides. Make the Sign of Harpocrates by pressing the tip of your left index finger against the little hollow just above your upper lip, so that the first segment of your finger crosses both lips. Take a few moments to listen to the silence as you hold this pose. Even if there is noise coming from the street or another room, concentrate on the stillness within the astral temple as you gaze inwardly at the candle burning on the top of the black marble altar.

Press your hands together in front of your heart-center in the traditional gesture of prayer, and clap them three times, leaving an interval of three seconds of silence between each clap, to signify the beginning of the ritual proper. Assume the standing posture. Speak the following declaration of intention.

**"By the powers of the four elements the space
within this circle of art will be cleansed and purified."**

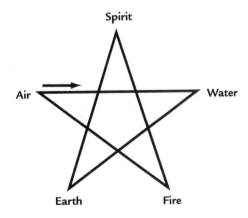

Figure 38-1.
Golden Dawn banishing
pentagram of Air

Allow your expanded aura to contract to its usual elongated shape close to your body. Take the incense stick from its holder and light it in the flame of the white candle. Observe the smoke rising from the glowing top of the incense stick for several breaths, and be aware of its fragrance.

Rotate on your body axis clockwise to face the east. Go to the eastern limit of the room or area in which you are working and stand facing east in the posture of projection, with your feet together, the incense stick in your extended right hand, and your left palm pressed to your chest just above the end of your sternum.

Project through the incense stick a yellow Golden Dawn banishing pentagram of Air upon the east, so that it floats at the level of your heart-center. Begin to trace the pentagram from its upper-left point and proceed clockwise. When the pentagram is complete, visualize it flaming with yellow fire, and mentally expand it and project it to the east so that it fills the entire eastern side of the place you are cleansing. Visualize the white astral band of the magic circle crossing through the center of the pentagram.

Draw a deep breath. Hold it four beats while energizing the sphere of your heart-center. Do not expand your aura. Speak these words strongly so that they resonate within you, and within the astral temple.

"By the power of Air, I banish the region of the east."

Bend your right elbow to raise and lower the incense stick in your right hand three times with a slow shaking motion. Each time you shake downward and point the incense at the pentagram, use your will to project the fragrance of the incense through the center of the pentagram to the eastern quarter.

With the incense stick, inscribe a white cross of equal arms within the center of the yellow pentagram to seal the east against malicious forces of an airy nature. First draw the column of the cross from top to bottom, then the beam from left to right. The intersection of the cross is located on the band of the ritual circle. Allow both the yellow pentagram and white cross to fade from your astral perceptions, leaving only the band of the circle flaming upon the air in the east.

Turn to face the south and, with the incense stick held vertically between the palms of your hands over your heart-center, walk around the inner circumference of the circle to stand in the south facing south. Adopt the posture of projection. Using the incense stick, project a yellow Golden Dawn banishing pentagram of Air to the south and enlarge it to fill the southern quarter. It is made in the same way you made the banishing pentagram of Air in the east. Draw a deep breath and hold it four beats while energizing your heart-center. Vibrate the following words strongly to the south.

"By the power of Air, I banish the region of the south."

Shake the incense stick downward three times with a gentle motion, and use your will to project the fragrance of the incense through the center of the pentagram to the southern quarter.

With the glowing point of the incense stick, inscribe a white cross in the center of this yellow pentagram to seal the south against intrusions of an airy kind. Allow both the pentagram and cross to fade from your astral perceptions, leaving only the band of the circle flaming upon the air in the south.

Turn to face the west. Walk around the inner circumference of the circle, the incense stick between your palms before your chest, to stand in the west facing west. Project a yellow Golden Dawn banishing pentagram of Air to the west and enlarge it to fill the western quarter. Draw a deep breath and hold it four beats to energize your heart-center. Vibrate the following words strongly to the west.

"By the power of Air, I banish the region of the west."

Shake the incense stick forward three times with a gentle motion by bending and straightening your right elbow. Each time you shake downward and point at the pentagram, use your will to project the fragrance of the incense through the center of the pentagram to the western quarter.

Inscribe a white cross in the center of this yellow pentagram to seal the west against intrusions of an airy kind. Allow both the pentagram and cross to fade from your astral perceptions, leaving only the band of the circle flaming upon the air in the west.

Turn to face the north and walk around the inner circumference of the circle to stand in the north facing north. Project a yellow Golden Dawn banishing pentagram of Air to the north and enlarge it to fill the northern quarter. Draw a deep breath and hold it four beats to energize your heart-center. Vibrate the following words strongly to the north.

"By the power of Air, I banish the region of the north."

Shake the incense stick downward and forward three times with a gentle motion. Each time you shake downward and point with the incense to the pentagram, use your will to project the fragrance of the incense through the center of the pentagram to the northern quarter.

Project a white cross in the center of this yellow pentagram to seal the north against intrusions of an airy kind. Allow both the pentagram and cross to fade from your astral perceptions, leaving only the band of the circle flaming upon the air in the north.

Turn to face the east and walk around the inner circumference of the circle to stand in the east facing east, with the incense stick held between the palms of your hands in front of your heart-center. Spend a minute or so contemplating with your astral awareness the ritual circle, and the beam of light above the flame of the candle in the astral temple.

Rotate clockwise on your body axis and approach the altar. Replace the incense stick in its holder on the eastern quarter of the altar. Move clockwise around the altar to the southern quarter and stand facing north with the altar in front of you. Take up the red candle in its holder and light it from the flame of the central white

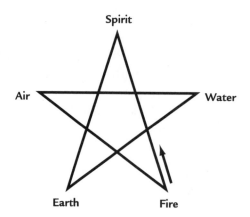

Figure 38-2.
Golden Dawn banishing
pentagram of Fire

candle, while visualizing with your astral sight the pure beam of white light that descends upon the flame of the white candle from the star above. Observe the flame of the red candle. Be aware of its light and warmth.

Rotate on your body axis clockwise to face the south. Go to the southern limit of the room or area in which you are working and stand facing south in the posture of projection, with the red candle in its holder vertical in your extended right hand and your left palm pressed to your chest just above the end of your sternum.

Project through the flame of the red candle a red Golden Dawn banishing pentagram of Fire upon the south, so that it floats at the level of your heart-center. Begin to trace the pentagram from its lower-right point and proceed counterclockwise. When the pentagram is complete, visualize it flaming with bright red fire, and mentally expand it and project it to the south so that it fills the entire southern side of the place you are cleansing. Visualize the golden-white astral band of the magic circle crossing through the center of the pentagram.

Draw a deep breath. Hold it four beats while energizing the sphere of your heart-center. Speak these words strongly so that they resonate within you, and within the astral temple.

"By the power of Fire, I banish the region of the south."

Shake the red candle downward three times with a gentle motion by bending and straightening your right elbow. Avoid a violent motion that would throw the wax across the floor. Each time you shake downward, use your will to project the heat and light of the candle flame through the center of the pentagram to the southern quarter.

With the flame of the red candle, project a white cross of equal arms into the center of this pentagram to seal the south against malicious intrusions of a fiery nature. First draw the column of the cross from top to bottom, then the beam from left to right. The intersection of the cross is located on the band of the ritual circle. Allow both the red pentagram and white cross to fade from your astral perceptions, leaving only the band of the circle flaming upon the air in the south.

Turn to face the west and with the red candle held vertically between your hands in front of your heart-center, walk around the inner circumference of the circle to stand in the west facing west. Adopt the posture of projection. Using the flame of the red candle, project a red banishing pentagram of Fire to the west and enlarge it to fill the western quarter. Draw a deep breath and hold it four beats while energizing your heart-center. Vibrate the following words strongly to the west.

"By the power of Fire, I banish the region of the west."

Shake the red candle downward three times with a gentle motion by bending and straightening your right elbow. Each time you shake downward, use your will to project the heat and light of the candle flame through the center of the pentagram to the western quarter.

Project a white cross in the center of this red pentagram to seal the west against intrusions of a fiery kind. Allow both the pentagram and cross to fade from your astral perceptions, leaving only the band of the circle flaming upon the air in the west.

Turn to face the north and walk around the inner circumference of the circle to stand in the north facing north. Project a red banishing pentagram of Fire to the north and enlarge it to fill the northern quarter. Draw a deep breath and hold it four beats to energize your heart-center. Vibrate the following words strongly to the north.

"By the power of Fire, I banish the region of the north."

Shake the red candle downward three times with a gentle motion by bending and straightening your right elbow. Each time you shake downward, use your will to project the heat and light of the candle flame through the center of the pentagram to the northern quarter.

Project a white cross in the center of this red pentagram to seal the north against intrusions of a fiery kind. Allow both the pentagram and cross to fade from your astral perceptions, leaving only the band of the circle flaming upon the air in the north.

Turn to face the east and walk around the inner circumference of the circle to stand in the east facing east. Project a red banishing pentagram of Fire to the east and enlarge it to fill the eastern quarter. Draw a deep breath and hold it four beats while energizing your heart-center. Vibrate the following words strongly to the east.

"By the power of Fire, I banish the region of the east."

Shake the red candle downward three times with a gentle motion by bending and straightening your right elbow. Each time you shake downward, use your will to project the heat and light of the candle flame through the center of the penta-gram to the eastern quarter.

Project a white cross in the center of this red pentagram to seal the east against intrusions of a fiery kind. Allow both the pentagram and cross to fade from your astral perceptions, leaving only the band of the circle flaming upon the air in the east.

Turn to face the south and walk around the inner circumference of the circle to stand in the south facing south, with the red candle in its holder between your hands in front of your heart-center. Spend a minute or so contemplating with your inner sight the ritual circle and the beam of light above the flame of the white candle on the black marble altar in the astral temple.

Rotate clockwise on your body axis and approach the altar. Replace the red candle on the southern quarter of the altar. Move clockwise around the altar to the western quarter and stand facing east with the altar in front of you. Open the decanter of water and carefully pour water into the goblet until it is about half full. Try not to spill water on the altar. As you do this, visualize with your astral sight the pure beam of white light that descends upon the flame of the central white candle from the star above. Observe the water in the goblet. Be aware of its coolness and wetness.

Rotate on your body axis clockwise to face the west. Go to the western limit of the room or area in which you are working and stand facing west in the posture of projection with your feet together, the goblet held vertical in your extended right

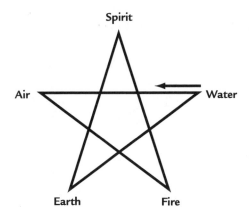

Figure 38-3.
Golden Dawn banishing
pentagram of Water

hand, and your left palm pressed to your chest just above the end of your sternum.

Project through the water in the goblet a blue Golden Dawn banishing penta-gram of Water upon the west, so that it floats at the level of your heart-center. Begin to trace the pentagram from its upper-right point and proceed counter-clockwise. When the pentagram is complete, visualize it flaming with deep-blue fire, and mentally expand it and project it to the west so that it fills the entire west-ern side of the place you are cleansing. Visualize the white astral band of the magic circle crossing through the center of the pentagram.

Draw a deep breath. Hold it four beats while energizing the sphere of your heart-center. Speak these words strongly so that they resonate within you, and within the astral temple.

"By the power of Water, I banish the region of the west."

Transferring the goblet to your left hand, dip the fingers of your right hand into the water. Shake your right hand three times by bending and straightening your right elbow. Flick your fingers to scatter droplets of water beyond the ritual circle to the west. Each time you shake outward, use your will to project the wet-ness and coolness of the water through the center of the pentagram to the western quarter.

With the goblet in your right hand and your left palm pressed to your chest, pro-ject through the water in the goblet the lines of a white cross of equal arms into the center of this pentagram to seal the west against malicious intrusions of a watery nature. First draw the column of the cross from top to bottom, then the beam from left to right. The intersection of the cross is located on the band of the ritual circle. Allow both the blue pentagram and white cross to fade from your astral per-ception, leaving only the band of the circle flaming upon the air in the west.

Turn to face the north and with the goblet held between your hands in front of your heart-center, walk around the inner circumference of the circle to stand in the north facing north. Adopt the posture of projection. Using the goblet in your right hand, project a blue banishing pentagram of Water to the north and enlarge it to fill the northern quarter. Draw a deep breath and hold it four beats while energiz-ing your heart-center. Vibrate the following words strongly to the north.

"By the power of Water, I banish the region of the north."

With the goblet in your left hand, dip the fingers of your right hand into the water. Shake your right hand three times by bending and straightening your right elbow, and at the same time flick your fingers to scatter droplets of water beyond the ritual circle to the north. Each time you shake outward, use your will to project the wetness and coolness of the water through the center of the pentagram to the northern quarter.

Return the goblet to your right hand and use it to inscribe a white cross in the center of this blue pentagram to seal the north against intrusions of a watery kind. Allow both the pentagram and cross to fade from your astral perceptions, leaving only the band of the circle flaming upon the air in the north.

Turn to face the east and walk around the inner circumference of the circle to stand in the east facing east. Holding the goblet in your right hand with your left hand pressed to your chest, project a blue banishing pentagram of Water to the east through the water of the goblet and enlarge it to fill the eastern quarter. Draw a deep breath and hold it four beats while energizing your heart-center. Vibrate the following words strongly to the east.

"By the power of Water, I banish the region of the east."

Transfer the goblet to your left hand and dip the fingers of your right hand into the water. Shake your right hand three times by bending and straightening your right elbow, and at the same time flick your fingers to scatter droplets of water beyond the ritual circle to the east. Each time you shake outward, use your will to project the wetness and coolness of the water through the center of the pentagram to the eastern quarter.

Inscribe with the goblet in your right hand a white cross in the center of this blue pentagram to seal the east against intrusions of a watery kind. Allow both the pentagram and cross to fade from your astral perceptions, leaving only the band of the circle flaming upon the air in the north.

Turn to face the south and walk around the inner circumference of the circle to stand in the south facing south. Project a blue banishing pentagram of Water to the south and enlarge it to fill the southern quarter. Draw a deep breath and hold it four beats while charging your heart-center. Vibrate the following words strongly to the south.

"By the power of Water, I banish the region of the south."

Dip the fingers of your right hand into the water. Shake your right hand three times by bending and straightening your right elbow, and at the same time flick your fingers to scatter droplets of water beyond the ritual circle to the south. Each time you shake outward, use your will to project the wetness and coolness of the water through the center of the pentagram to the southern quarter.

With the goblet in your right hand, project a white cross in the center of this blue pentagram to seal the south against intrusions of a watery kind. Allow both the pentagram and cross to fade from your astral perceptions, leaving only the band of the circle flaming upon the air in the south.

Turn to face the west and walk around the inner circumference of the circle to stand in the west facing west, with the goblet of water between your hands in front of your heart-center. Spend a minute or so contemplating with your inner sight the ritual circle and the beam of light above the flame of the white candle on the black marble altar in the astral temple.

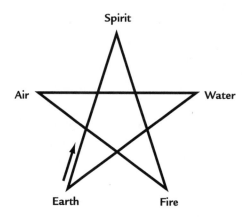

Figure 38-4.
Golden Dawn banishing
pentagram of Earth

Rotate clockwise on your body axis and approach the table that serves as a physical alter. Replace the goblet on the western side of the table. Dry your fingers on a small towel placed on the table for this purpose. Move clockwise around the altar to the northern quarter and stand facing south with the altar in front of you. Open the container holding the salt and carefully pour salt onto the flat dish until it forms a small pile. Try not to spill salt grains on the altar. As you do this, visualize with your astral sight the pure beam of white light that descends upon the flame of the white candle from the star above. Observe the salt crystals on the dish. Be aware of their hardness and their cubic shape.

Rotate on your body axis clockwise to face the north. Go to the northern limit of the room or area in which you are working and stand facing north in the posture of projection, with the dish held flat in your extended right hand and your left palm pressed to your chest just above the end of your sternum.

Project through the salt on the dish a green Golden Dawn banishing pentagram of Earth upon the north, so that it floats at the level of your heart-center. Begin to trace the pentagram from its lower-left point and proceed clockwise. When the pentagram is complete, visualize it flaming with dark-green fire, and mentally expand it and project it to the north so that it fills the entire northern side of the place you are cleansing. Visualize the white astral band of the magic circle crossing through the center of the pentagram.

Draw a deep breath. Hold it four beats while energizing the sphere of your heart-center. Speak these words strongly so that they resonate within you, and within the astral temple.

"By the power of Earth, I banish the region of the north."

Transferring the dish to your left hand, take a pinch of salt between the index finger and thumb of your right hand. Shake your right hand three times by bending and straightening your right elbow. Each time, release a small amount of the salt by rolling it between your thumb and forefinger, so that the salt scatters beyond the ritual circle to the north. The third time you shake your hand, flick your thumb and index finger apart to release the remainder of the pinch of salt. Use your will to project the hardness and dryness of the salt through the center of the pentagram to the northern quarter.

With the dish in your right hand and your left palm pressed to your chest, project through the salt on the dish a large white cross of equal arms into the center of this pentagram to seal the north against malicious intrusions of an earthy nature. First draw the column of the cross from top to bottom, then the beam from left to right. The intersection of the cross is located on the band of the ritual circle. Allow both the green pentagram and white cross to fade from your astral perceptions, leaving only the band of the circle flaming upon the air in the north.

Turn to face the east and with the dish held between your hands in front of your heart-center, walk around the inner circumference of the circle to stand in the east facing east. Adopt the posture of projection. Using the dish in your right hand, project a green banishing pentagram of Earth to the east and enlarge it to fill the eastern quarter. Draw a deep breath and hold it four beats while energizing your heart-center. Vibrate the following words strongly to the east.

"By the power of Earth, I banish the region of the east."

Take a pinch of salt between the fingers of your right hand. Shake your right hand three times by bending and straightening your right elbow, and at the same time roll your fingers to scatter grains of salt beyond the ritual circle to the east. Each time you shake outward, use your will to project the hardness and dryness of the salt through the center of the pentagram to the eastern quarter.

Inscribe a white cross in the center of this green pentagram with the dish held in your right hand, sealing the east against intrusions of an earthy kind. Allow both the pentagram and cross to fade from your astral perceptions, leaving only the band of the circle flaming upon the air in the east.

Turn to face the south and walk around the inner circumference of the circle to stand in the south facing south. Project a green banishing pentagram of Earth to the south with the dish and enlarge it to fill the southern quarter. Draw a deep breath and hold it four beats while energizing your heart-center. Vibrate the following words strongly to the south.

"By the power of Earth, I banish the region of the south."

Take a pinch of salt between the fingers of your right hand. Shake your right hand three times by bending and straightening your right elbow, and at the same time roll your fingers to scatter grains of salt beyond the ritual circle to the south.

Each time you shake outward, use your will to project the hardness and dryness of the salt through the center of the pentagram to the southern quarter.

With the dish in your right hand, project a white cross in the center of this green pentagram to seal the south against intrusions of an earthy kind. Allow both the pentagram and cross to fade from your astral perceptions, leaving only the band of the circle flaming upon the air in the south.

Turn to face the west and walk around the inner circumference of the circle to stand in the west facing west. Project a green banishing pentagram of Earth to the west and enlarge it to fill the western quarter. Draw a deep breath and hold it four beats while energizing your heart-center. Vibrate the following words strongly to the west.

"By the power of Earth, I banish the region of the west."

Take a pinch of salt between the fingers of your right hand. Shake your right hand three times by bending and straightening your right elbow, and at the same time roll your fingers to scatter grains of salt beyond the ritual circle to the west. Each time you shake outward, use your will to project the hardness and dryness of the salt through the center of the pentagram to the western quarter.

With the dish in your right hand, project a white cross in the center of this green pentagram to seal the west against intrusions of an earthy kind. Allow both the pentagram and cross to fade from your astral perceptions, leaving only the band of the circle flaming upon the air in the west.

Turn to face the north and walk around the inner circumference of the circle to stand in the north facing north, with the dish of salt between your hands in front of your heart-center. Spend a minute or so contemplating with your inner sight the ritual circle and the beam of light above the flame of the white candle on the black marble altar in the astral temple.

Rotate clockwise on your body axis and approach the altar. Replace the dish of salt on the northern side of the altar. Walk clockwise to stand in the eastern quarter facing west. Gaze at the flame of the white candle in the center of the altar, and with your astral sight contemplate the beam of white light descending onto the flame vertically from the white star high overhead. Be aware of the purity of circle, cleansed by the powers of the four elements.

Press your palms together in front of your heart-center with your fingers pointing upward in the traditional prayer gesture. While looking at the flame of the white candle, speak the following declaration.

"By the powers of the four elements, the space within this circle of art has been cleansed and purified."

To signify the fulfillment of your ritual purpose, clap your hands together four times, allowing an interval of four seconds of silence between each clap. Allow your hands to fall to your sides.

Turn to the north. Walk around the altar in a counterclockwise direction while speaking the following in a strong voice that vibrates within your body and resounds in the astral temple.

"Hear the voice of fire! A flashing light abounding, revolving, whirling forth, crying aloud."

As you walk, visualize a counterclockwise vortex of silver-gray begin at the top of the candle flame and extend upward into a funnel, expanding as it rises. This vortex completely surrounds the beam of white light that connects the candle flame with the white star in the heavens. It is wider at its top, narrower at its base.

When you reach the eastern quarter once again, stop and stand facing north. Inhale a deep breath and raise your arms gradually upward on each side with your elbows locked so that your arms are extended almost straight above your head in a narrow V with your palms turned inward toward each other. Hold the breath four beats and visualize the Hebrew letter *Aleph* in your heart-center. Step forward a short distance with your right leg, without moving your left foot. As you shift your center of gravity toward the north, cast your arms and hands downward and forward with your elbows still locked so that your stiffened fingers extend to the north and your thumbs touch. Gaze northward from beneath your eyebrows along the tops of your arms and hands.

As you make this Sign of the Enterer, expel your breath and vibrate the Hebrew mother letter *Aleph* strongly so that the air of the astral temple resounds. The beginning and end of the sound should be extended and vibrate within the nose and throat:

"Aaaaaaaaaaay-leeeeeeeeeph"

Visualize a pulse of deep yellow light form upon the ring of astral fire in the east. The sound of your voice sends this pulse racing around the circle in a counter-clockwise direction and turns the entire circle yellow. The revolution of the pulse of saffron light makes the vortex above the altar rotate more strongly. When the pulse returns to the east, the pulse dissolves into the band of the magic circle. Continue to visualize the circle as deep yellow while sounding the Hebrew letter. When you reach the end of your breath and fall silent, the circle reverts to its usual pale golden-white color. Lower your arms to your sides, pull back your extended right foot, and resume the standing posture.

Walk in a second circle counterclockwise around the altar. When you return to the east, speak these words so that they vibrate in your chest and resound in the astral temple.

"Such a fire existeth, extending through the rushings of air, a fire formless whence cometh the image of a voice."

Visualize the counterclockwise vortex strengthening and extending upward above the candle. Hear with your astral senses the rushing of its rotation. See it begin to absorb the radiance of the white ray connecting the candle flame with the star, so that the vortex slowly turns from silvery gray to a golden white.

When you reach the eastern quarter once again, stop and stand facing north. Inhale a deep breath and, as you hold it four beats, be aware of the Hebrew letter *Shin* in your heart-center. Make the Sign of the Enterer to the north.

As you expel your breath, vibrate the Hebrew mother letter *Shin* strongly so that the air of the astral temple resounds. The beginning and end of the sound should be extended and vibrate within the nose and throat:

"Sheeeeeeeeeee-innnnnnnnnnn"

Visualize a pulse of ruby light form upon the ring of astral fire in the east. The sound of your voice sends this pulse racing around the circle in a counterclockwise direction and turns the entire circle red. The revolution of the pulse of ruby light makes the vortex above the altar rotate more strongly. When the pulse returns to the east, it dissolves into the band of the magic circle. Continue to visualize the circle as bright red while sounding the Hebrew letter. When you reach the end of your breath and fall silent, the circle reverts to its usual pale golden-white color. Lower your arms to your sides, pull back your extended right foot, and resume the standing posture.

Walk counterclockwise for a third circuit. Speak these words so that they vibrate in your chest and resound in the astral temple.

"See that holy and formless fire, which darts and flashes through the hidden depths of the universe."

When you reach the eastern quarter once again, stop and stand facing north. Inhale a deep breath, hold it four beats as you visualize the Hebrew letter *Mem* in your heart-center, and make the Sign of the Enterer to the north.

As you expel your breath, vibrate the Hebrew mother letter *Mem* strongly so that the air of the astral temple resounds. The beginning and end of the sound should be extended and vibrate within the nose and throat:

"Mmmmmmm-mem-mmmmmmm"

Visualize a pulse of deep blue light form upon the ring of astral fire in the east. The sound of your voice sends this pulse racing around the circle in a counterclockwise direction and turns the entire circle blue. The revolution of the pulse of blue light makes the vortex above the altar rotate more strongly. When the pulse returns to the east, it dissolves into the band of the magic circle. Continue to visualize the circle as deep blue while sounding the Hebrew letter. When you reach the end of your breath and fall silent, the circle reverts to its usual pale golden-white color. Lower your arms to your sides, pull back your extended right foot, and resume the standing posture.

Turn to face the west. For a few moments, contemplate the counterclockwise vortex above the astral altar. The funnel has turned completely white and whirls furiously around the beam linking the candle with the star. The beam has become pale and flickers along its length.

- Declaration of intention
- Cleansing by Air
- Cleansing by Fire
- Cleansing by Water
- Cleansing by Earth
- Declaration of fulfillment
- Reverse circumambulation
- Absorption of the circle
- Kabbalistic Cross

As a general rule, while working rituals in the circle, all rotation on your body axis and all movement around the ritual altar should be done in a clockwise direction. When you turn your body no more than a quarter-turn, you may, if you wish, overlook this rule for the sake of convenience, but when you rotate more than a quarter-turn, always rotate clockwise. For example, when you stand in front of the altar in the eastern quarter facing west, and turn to face south, it is permissible to turn counterclockwise rather than rotating three-quarters of a turn clockwise. But if you stand in the eastern quarter facing east, and turn to the west to face the altar, you must rotate clockwise. It is a good habit at the beginning of practice to always rotate clockwise, even for quarter turns of your body. This general rule does not apply when you are absorbing the circle, or circumambulating widdershins to release the light.

EXERCISE 39

Supreme Invoking Ritual of the Pentagram

FIND AN OPEN floor where you have room to walk around the inner circumference of a circle seven feet or larger in diameter. If necessary due to lack of space, the ritual can be done by standing in one spot and rotating on your own axis to form a lesser circle, but it is better to use a greater circle.

Stand in the middle of the floor facing east. Adopt the standing pose, with your feet together, arms at your sides, back straight, and head erect. Direct your gaze straight ahead and look through the wall at the unseen, distant horizon. Take several long, deep breaths to focus your resolve and prepare for what you are about to do.

Visualize high over your head a blue-white star that blazes with pure spiritual energy. Ascend in your inner awareness to this star and enter it. Allow the star's brilliant radiance to completely surround you and saturate your awareness with cooling light.

Extend a ray of white light from the star straight downward through the top of your skull to your heart-center. Visualize this

250

center expand into a three-inch transparent sphere of glowing golden radiance, the color of sunlight. Focus the white ray from the star on the center of the transparent golden sphere.

Allow your awareness to slide down this white ray to your heart-center. Continue to draw spiritual energy down the ray until your heart-center turns from yellow to soft radiant white with a slight golden tint. Sever your link with the star as you hold your awareness in your heart-center.

Take a deep breath. As you inhale, your body expands to godlike proportions. Your head and shoulders rise through the ceiling of your practice chamber, continuing upward above the level of the clouds, until your body projects into starry space.

Hold the air in your lungs for four slow beats as you visualize the warm light from your heart-center radiate outward to expand your aura into a sphere.

Touch your right index finger to your forehead between your eyebrows. Vibrate the syllables of the Hebrew word *ateh* briefly but with power and authority.

"ah-teh"

Feel the resonance in your chest energize your aura, and the vibrations of your aura propel your articulated breath outward to fill the universe.

Touch your right index finger to the end of your sternum, just above your solar plexus. Vibrate the syllables of the Hebrew word *Malkuth* briefly but with authority.

"Mal-kuth"

Feel the vibrations in your chest energize your aura, and sense that your aura propels your breath outward to fill the universe.

Visualize a white ray extending from the glowing sphere of your heart-center vertically up and down, so that it passes through the top of your skull and between your feet. Conceive this ray to be a laser beam of infinite length.

Touch your right index finger to your right shoulder and vibrate the syllables of the Hebrew words *ve-Geburah* briefly with force.

"veh-Geb-u-rah"

Feel the vibrations in your chest energize your aura, and sense that your aura propels your breath outward to fill the universe.

Touch your right index finger to your left shoulder and vibrate the syllables of the Hebrew words *ve-Gedulah* briefly with force.

"veh-Ged-u-lah"

Feel the vibrations in your chest energize your aura, and sense that your aura propels your breath outward to fill the universe.

Visualize a white ray extending from the glowing sphere of your heart-center horizontally to the left and right so that it passes out the sides of your body below the level of your armpits. Conceive this ray to be a laser beam of infinite length. This horizontal ray intersects the vertical ray at right angles at the center of your heart-center.

Press the palms of your hands together in front of your solar plexus so that your extended fingers point upward. Vibrate the Hebrew words *le-olam* strongly to create a resonance in your chest.

"leh-oh-lam"

Feel the vibrations in your chest energize your aura, and sense that your aura propels your breath outward to fill the universe.

Visualize a white ray extending from the glowing sphere of your heart-center horizontally in front and behind, so that it passes out of your body through the center of your chest between your joined hands and the out-center of your back. This horizontal ray intersects the first two rays at right angles in your heart-center.

Raise your united hands in a prayer gesture above the level of your head, while still gazing forward into infinity and visualizing the three rays from your heart-center. Vibrate the Hebrew word *amen* strongly to create a resonance in your chest. Extend the final syllable so that the remaining air in your lungs is expelled.

"ah-mennnnn"

Feel the vibrations in your chest energize your aura, and sense that your aura propels your breath outward to fill the universe.

Allow your arms to fall to your sides and adopt the standing pose. Remain in this posture for a minute or so, breathing normally, and contemplate with your inner sight the large golden sphere of your expanded aura, the smaller gold-white sphere of your heart-center, and the three brilliant-white rays that extend from the three axes of your gigantic astral body. Mentally in-draw the three rays into your heart-center, but continue to be aware of the radiance of its sphere. Allow your aura to contract slowly to its usual elongated shape nearer the surface of your skin, and cause your expanded astral form to shrink down to the dimensions of your physical body.

Step forward and stand in the eastern quarter of your practice area still facing east. Assume a posture of projection with your left hand over your heart-center and your right arm extended. Inhale a deep breath and hold it four beats. Do not enlarge your aura. With your breath stopped, visualize the five English letters of the Enochian word *Exarp* shining blue-white within the sphere of your heart-center.

Project with brilliant white fire the equilibrated active invoking pentagram of Spirit upon the air toward the east, beginning at the lower-right point of the star and proceeding clockwise. As you are in the process of emitting a stream of white astral fire from the tip of your right index finger to form this pentagram, vibrate upon your breath the Enochian word of power *Exarp* so that each letter of the word is sounded separately. Use all of your breath for this vibration.

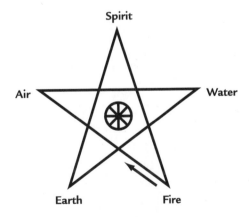

Figure 39-1.
Golden Dawn equilibrated active
invoking pentagram of Spirit

"Ee-ex-ay-ar-pay"

Take another deep breath and hold it four beats as you intensify the radiance of your heart-center. While your breath is stopped, visualize the Hebrew letters of the divine name *Eheieh* (A = א, H = ה, I = י, H = ה) written in brilliant blue-white flame from right to left within the sphere of your heart-center.

ה י ה א

Inscribe within the center of the pentagram a wheel with eight spokes, using the stream of astral fire that flows from your index finger. The manner of forming the wheel is as follows: first make the rim of the wheel beginning at the top and proceeding clockwise; mark a vertical line through the center of the wheel from top to bottom; intersect this with a horizontal line of white fire that is drawn across the wheel from left to right; draw a diagonal line through the center of the wheel beginning at the upper-left and ending at the lower-right of the rim; cross this with another diagonal beginning at the upper-right and ending at the lower-left.

As you are in the process of inscribing this wheel of Spirit upon the air, vibrate the divine name of power *Eheieh* upon your breath, articulating each Hebrew letter separately so that the sounds resonate within your body and expand to fill the universe.

"Ah-heh-aye-yah"

Lower your arms to your sides and stand contemplating this white pentagram of Spirit and the white wheel of Spirit at its center for a few seconds. Intensify the brightness of the pentagram in your imagination. Make the gesture of Rending the Veil by bringing your hands up in front of your heart-center and turning them so that they are back to back. Spread your hands apart as though opening the two sides of a closed curtain. The final posture is with your arms extended on either side of your body at the level of your solar plexus, your palms turned outward as though pushing apart a curtain.

As you make the gesture of Rending the Veil, visualize your hands opening an aperture in the very fabric of space itself that is shaped like an eye turned on its side. This pointed oval shape is called a mandorla. It begins to open at the center of the white pentagram of Spirit and extends above and below it so that the pentagram is contained within its limits. Visualize this aperture as if it were formed by the parting of two sides of a curtain attached together at their top and bottom.

Stand with your arms at your sides contemplating the white pentagram within the mandorla. Allow the flaming image of the pentagram of Spirit and its central wheel to gradually fade from your astral awareness, but maintain the opening of the mandorla.

Assume the posture of projection, left palm over your heart-center and right hand extended. Take a breath, hold it four beats, and visualize the Enochian words of power *Oro Ibah Aozpi* written across the golden sphere of your heart-center in scintillating blue-white flame. With your right index finger, trace a flaming yellow invoking pentagram of Air in the east exactly over the top of the fading image of the pentagram of Spirit. Begin from the upper-right point of the star and draw its line counterclockwise. Visualize it glowing brightly with rich yellow flame.

While you are in the process of inscribing this pentagram of Air, vibrate the Enochian words of power so that they resonate throughout your body and extend outward to fill the universe, causing space itself to ring like a vast bell.

Figure 39-2.
Golden Dawn invoking
pentagram of Air

"Oh-roh, Ee-bah-hay, Ah-oh-zode-pee"

Inhale another deep breath, and hold it four beats while visualizing the Hebrew letters of the name IHVH (I = י, H = ה, V = ו, H = ה) written from right to left within the sphere of your heart-center. The letters flame brilliantly with a dazzling blue-white radiance.

י ה ו ה

Inscribe with your index finger in the center of the yellow pentagram of Air the sign of the zodiac sign Aquarius—two zigzag lines one above the other, each with three peaks. First draw the upper zigzag line, then the lower line. As you project this symbol with yellow astral fire into the pentagram, vibrate on your breath the letters of the divine name so that the sound resonates in your chest, throat, and nose, and expands outward to the limits of the universe.

"Yud-Heh-Vav-Heh"

Continue pointing to the center of the pentagram with your right index finger. The vibrations of the holy name cause a pillar of white light to extend downward from the single blue-white star at the zenith of the heavens. This pillar of light touches the earth behind the yellow pentagram in the east. Allow your arms to fall to your sides and contemplate this pillar of light through the aperture of the mandorla.

Make the sign of elemental Air by raising your hands to a level just above your head, with your elbows turned outward, palms turned up, and fingertips directed inward toward each other and about eight inches apart, so that it appears that you are holding up the sky itself. As you lift your hands, tilt up your head slightly and raise your gaze heavenward.

Resume the standing posture with arms at your sides and contemplate the yellow pentagram of Air in the east for five seconds or so. Lay your left palm across your heart-center and point with your right index finger at the center of the pentagram. Turn your body to the right so that your right forearm crosses in front of your chest, but continue to point your right index finger at the center of the pentagram of Air.

Walk along one quarter of the circumference of an imaginary circle to the south, projecting from your right index finger a line of golden-white fire upon the air at heart level as you go. This line of white astral fire begins in the center of the eastern pentagram. Feel the vital energy in your heart-center flow through your chest into your left palm, up your left arm, across your shoulders, and down your right arm to exit in a flaming stream from your right index finger. The expanding spiral it follows as it circulates through your body increases its force. Continue to sustain in your awareness the pentagram in the east while projecting this line of fire.

Stand in the southern quarter of your practice area facing south, with your left hand over your heart-center and your right arm extended. Inhale a deep breath and hold it four beats. With your breath stopped, visualize the five English letters of the Enochian word *Bitom* shining blue-white within the sphere of your heart-center.

Project with brilliant white fire the equilibrated active invoking pentagram of Spirit upon the air toward the south, beginning at the lower-right point of the star and proceeding clockwise. As you are in the process of emitting a stream of white astral fire from the tip of your right index finger to form this pentagram, vibrate upon your breath the Enochian word of power *Bitom* so that each letter of the word is sounded separately. Use all of your breath for this vibration.

"Be-eye-tay-oh-em"

Figure 39-3.
Golden Dawn equilibrated active
invoking pentagram of Spirit

Take another deep breath and hold it four beats as you intensify the radiance of your heart-center. While your breath is stopped, visualize the Hebrew letters of the divine name *Eheieh* (A = א, H = ה, I = י, H = ה) written in brilliant blue-white flame from right to left within the sphere of your heart-center.

$$\text{ה י ה א}$$

Inscribe within the center of the pentagram a white wheel with eight spokes in the manner already described, using the stream of astral fire that flows from your index finger.

As you are in the process of inscribing this wheel of Spirit upon the air, vibrate the divine name of power *Eheieh* upon your breath, articulating each Hebrew letter separately so that the sounds resonate within your body and expand to fill the universe.

"Ah-heh-aye-yah"

Lower your arms to your sides and stand contemplating this white pentagram of Spirit and the wheel of Spirit at its center for a few seconds. Intensify the brightness of the pentagram in your imagination. Make the gesture of Rending the Veil as you previously did in the east, by bringing your hands up in front of your heart-center so that they are six inches or so apart, and turning them back to back. Spread your hands apart as though opening the two sides of a closed curtain, so that you stand with your arms extended on either side of your body at the level of your solar plexus, your palms turned outward as though pushing apart a curtain.

As you make the gesture of Rending the Veil, visualize your hands opening a mandorla aperture in the very fabric of space itself. It begins to open at the center of the white pentagram of Spirit in the south and extends above and below it so that the pentagram is contained within its limits.

Stand with your arms at your side contemplating the white pentagram within the mandorla. Allow the flaming image of the pentagram of Spirit and its central wheel to gradually fade from your astral awareness, but maintain the opening of the mandorla.

Assume the posture of projection with feet together, left palm over your heart-center and right hand extended. Take a breath, hold it four beats, and visualize the Enochian words of power *Oip Teaa Pedoce* written across the golden sphere of your heart-center in scintillating blue-white flame. With your right index finger, trace a flaming red invoking pentagram of Fire in the south exactly over the top of the fading image of the pentagram of Spirit. Begin from the uppermost point of the star and draw its line clockwise. Visualize it glowing brightly with rich ruby flame.

While you are in the process of inscribing this pentagram of Fire, vibrate the Enochian words of power so that they resonate throughout your body and extend outward to fill the universe, causing space itself to ring like a vast bell.

"Oh-ee-pay, Tay-ay-ay, Pay-doh-cay"

Inhale another deep breath, and hold it four beats while visualizing the Hebrew letters of the name *Elohim* (A = א, L = ל, H = ה, M = מ) written from right to left within the sphere of your heart-center. The letters flame brilliantly with a dazzling blue-white radiance.

$$\text{א ל ה מ}$$

Inscribe with your index finger in the center of the ruby pentagram of Fire the red glyph of the zodiac sign Leo—an arched line with a curl on each end that vaguely resembles the mane of a lion. Draw this glyph of Leo from left to right. As

Figure 39-4.
Golden Dawn invoking
pentagram of Fire

you project this symbol into the pentagram, vibrate on your breath the letters of the divine name so that the sound resonates in your chest, throat, and nose, and expands outward to the limits of the universe.

"Ay-loh-hay-em"

Continue pointing to the center of the pentagram with your right index finger. The vibrations of the holy name cause a pillar of white light to extend downward from the single blue-white star at the zenith of the heavens. This pillar of light touches the earth behind the red pentagram in the south. Allow your arms to fall to your sides and contemplate this pillar of light through the aperture of the mandorla.

Make the sign of elemental Fire by raising your hands to your forehead with the palms turned to the front, the tips of your thumbs and the tips of your index fingers touching so that the space between your joined thumbs and index fingers defines an upward-pointing triangle of Fire. Hold this pose for several seconds, gazing forward.

Resume the standing posture with arms at your sides and contemplate the red pentagram of Fire in the south for five seconds or so. Lay your left palm across your heart-center and point with your right index finger at the center of the penta-gram. Turn your body to the right so that your right forearm crosses in front of

Figure 39-5.
Golden Dawn equilibrated passive
invoking pentagram of Spirit

your chest, but continue to point your right index finger at the center of the penta-gram of Fire.

Walk along one quarter of the circumference of an imaginary circle from the south to the west, projecting from your right index finger a line of golden-white flame upon the air at heart level as you go. This line of white astral fire begins in the center of the southern pentagram. Feel the vital energy in your heart-center flow through your chest into your left palm, up your left arm, across your shoulders, and down your right arm to exit in a flaming stream from your right index finger. The expanding spiral it follows as it circulates through your body increases its force. Continue to sustain in your awareness the pentagrams burning upon the air in the east and the south while projecting this line of fire.

Stand in the western quarter of your practice area facing west, with your left hand over your heart-center and your right arm extended. Inhale a deep breath and hold it four beats. With your breath stopped, visualize the five English letters of the Enochian word *Hcoma* shining blue-white within the sphere of your heart-center.

Project with brilliant white fire the equilibrated passive invoking pentagram of Spirit upon the air toward the west, beginning at the lower-left point of the star and proceeding counterclockwise. As you are in the process of emitting a stream of white astral fire from the tip of your right index finger to form this pentagram, vibrate upon your breath the Enochian word of power *Hcoma* so that each letter of the word is sounded separately. Use all of your breath for this vibration.

"Ha-cay-oh-em-ah"

Take another deep breath and hold it four beats as you intensify the radiance of your heart-center. While your breath is stopped, visualize the Hebrew letters of the divine name *AGLA* (A = א, G = ג, L = ל, A = א) written in brilliant blue-white flame from right to left within the sphere of your heart-center.

$$\text{א ל ג א}$$

Inscribe within the center of the pentagram a wheel with eight spokes in the way already described, using the stream of astral fire that flows from your index finger.

As you are in the process of inscribing this white wheel of Spirit upon the air, vibrate the divine name of power *AGLA* upon your breath, articulating each

Hebrew letter of this compound name separately so that the sounds resonate within your body and expand to fill the universe.

"Ah-Geh-Lah-Ah"

Lower your arms to your sides and stand contemplating this white pentagram with the wheel of Spirit at its center for a few seconds. Intensify the brightness of the pentagram in your imagination. Make the gesture of Rending the Veil as already described, by bringing your hands up in front of your heart-center and turning them back to back, then spreading your hands apart as though opening the two sides of a closed curtain.

As you make the gesture of Rending the Veil, visualize your hands opening a mandorla-shaped aperture in the very fabric of space. It begins to open at the center of the white pentagram of Spirit in the west and extends above and below it so that the pentagram is contained within its limits.

Stand with your arms at your sides contemplating the white pentagram within the mandorla. Allow the flaming image of the pentagram of Spirit and its central wheel to gradually fade from your astral awareness, but maintain the opening of the mandorla.

Assume the posture of projection, left palm over your heart-center and right hand extended. Take a breath, hold it four beats, and visualize the Enochian words

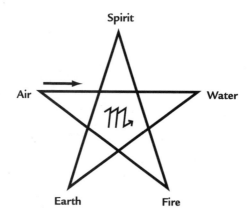

Figure 39-6.
Golden Dawn invoking
pentagram of Water

of power *Mph Arsl Gaiol* written across the golden sphere of your heart-center in scintillating blue-white flame. With your right index finger, trace a flaming blue invoking pentagram of Water in the west exactly over the top of the fading image of the pentagram of Spirit. Begin from the upper-left point of the star and draw its line clockwise. Visualize it glowing brightly with deep blue flame.

While you are in the process of inscribing this pentagram of Water, vibrate the Enochian words of power so that they resonate throughout your body and extend outward to fill the universe, causing space itself to ring like a vast bell.

"Em-pay-hay, Ar-sel, Gah-ee-ol"

Inhale another deep breath, hold it for four beats while visualizing the Hebrew letters of the divine name *Al* (A = א, L = ל) written from right to left within the sphere of your heart-center. The letters flame brilliantly with a dazzling blue-white radiance.

$$ל \quad א$$

Inscribe with your index finger in the center of the blue pentagram of Water the glyph of the zodiac sign Scorpio—a pointed letter *M* with a barbed tail on its end. Form this blue glyph from left to right. As you project this symbol into the pentagram, vibrate on your breath the letters of the divine name so that the sound resonates in your chest, throat, and nose, and expands outward to the limits of the universe.

"Ay-el"

Continue pointing to the center of the pentagram with your right index finger. The vibrations of the holy name cause a pillar of white light to extend downward from the single blue-white star at the zenith of the heavens. This pillar of light touches the earth behind the blue pentagram in the west. Allow your arms to fall to your sides and contemplate this pillar of light through the aperture of the mandorla.

Make the sign of elemental Water by raising your hands to the level of your lower belly, with palms turned inward to your body, the thumbs and index fingers touching so that the space between them forms a downward-pointing triangle of Water. As you form this sign, continue to gaze forward to the west.

Resume the standing posture with arms at your sides and contemplate the blue pentagram of Water in the west for five seconds or so. Lay your left palm across your heart-center and point with your right index finger at the center of the pentagram. Turn your body to the right so that your right forearm crosses in front of your chest, but continue to point your right index finger at the center of the pentagram of Water.

Walk along one quarter of the circumference of an imaginary circle to the north, projecting from your right index finger a line of golden-white fire upon the air at heart level as you go. This line of white astral fire begins in the center of the western pentagram. Feel the vital energy in your heart-center flow through your chest into your left palm, up your left arm, across your shoulders, and down your right arm to exit in a flaming stream from your right index finger. The expanding spiral it follows as it circulates through your body increases its force. Continue to sustain in your awareness the pentagrams in the east, south, and west while projecting this line of fire.

Stand in the northern quarter of your practice area facing north, your left hand over your heart-center and your right arm extended northward. Inhale a deep breath and hold it four beats. With your breath stopped, visualize the five English letters of the Enochian word *Nanta* shining blue-white within the sphere of your heart-center.

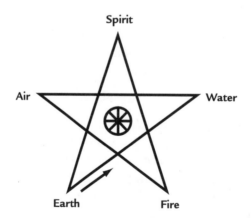

Figure 39-7.
Golden Dawn equilibrated passive
invoking pentagram of Spirit

Project with brilliant white fire the equilibrated passive invoking pentagram of Spirit upon the air toward the north, beginning at the lower-left point of the star and proceeding counterclockwise. As you are in the process of emitting a stream of white astral fire from the tip of your right index finger to form this pentagram, vibrate upon your breath the Enochian word of power *Nanta* so that each letter of the word is sounded separately. Use all of your breath for this vibration.

"En-ay-en-tay-ah"

Take another deep breath and hold it four beats as you intensify the radiance of your heart-center. While your breath is stopped, visualize the Hebrew letters of the divine name *AGLA* (A = א, G = ג, L = ל, A = א) written in brilliant blue-white flame from right to left within the sphere of your heart-center.

$$\text{א ל ג א}$$

Inscribe within the center of the pentagram a white wheel with eight spokes in the manner already described, using the stream of astral fire that flows from your index finger.

As you are in the process of inscribing this wheel of Spirit upon the air, vibrate the divine name of power *AGLA* upon your breath, articulating each Hebrew letter separately so that the sounds resonate within your body and expand to fill the universe.

"Ah-Geh-Lah-Ah"

Lower your arms to your sides and stand contemplating this white pentagram of Spirit and the wheel of Spirit at its center for a few seconds. Intensify the brightness of the pentagram in your imagination. Make the gesture of Rending the Veil as previously indicated, by bringing your hands up in front of your heart-center and spreading them apart as though opening the two sides of a closed curtain.

As you make the gesture of Rending the Veil, visualize your hands opening a mandorla-shaped aperture in the very fabric of space itself. It begins to open at the center of the white pentagram of Spirit in the north and extends above and below it so that the pentagram is contained within its limits.

Stand with your arms at your sides contemplating the white pentagram within the mandorla. Allow the flaming image of the pentagram of Spirit and its central wheel to gradually fade from your astral awareness, but maintain the opening of the mandorla.

Assume the posture of projection, left palm over your heart-center and right hand extended. Take a breath, hold it four beats, and visualize the Enochian words of power *Mor Dial Hctga* written across the golden sphere of your heart-center in scintillating blue-white flame. With your right index finger, trace a flaming dark green invoking pentagram of Earth in the north exactly over the top of the fading image of the pentagram of Spirit. Begin from the uppermost point of the star and draw its line counterclockwise. Visualize it glowing brightly with rich evergreen flame.

While you are in the process of inscribing this pentagram of Earth, vibrate the Enochian words of power so that they resonate throughout your body and extend outward to fill the universe, causing space itself to ring like a vast bell.

"Em-or, Dee-al, Hec-tay-gah"

Inhale another deep breath, hold it for four beats while visualizing the Hebrew letters of the name *Adonai* (A = א, D = ד, N = נ, I = י) written from right to left within

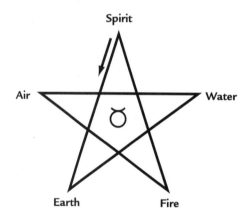

Figure 39-8.
Golden Dawn invoking
pentagram of Earth

the sphere of your heart-center. The letters flame brilliantly with a dazzling blue-white radiance.

א נ ד י

Inscribe with your index finger in the center of the green pentagram of Earth the glyph of the zodiac sign Taurus—a circle with a crescent on its top. First draw the crescent from left to right, then the circle below it beginning at the top of the circle and proceeding clockwise. As you project this green symbol into the pentagram, vibrate on your breath the letters of the divine name so that the sound resonates in your chest, throat, and nose, and expands outward to the limits of the universe.

"Ah-doh-en-aye"

Continue pointing to the center of the pentagram with your right index finger. The vibrations of the holy name cause a pillar of white light to extend downward from the single blue-white star at the zenith of the heavens. This pillar of light touches the earth behind the evergreen pentagram in the north. Allow your arms to fall to your sides and contemplate this pillar of light through the aperture of the mandorla.

Make the sign of elemental Earth by raising your right arm high above your head to point upward at the heavens, while pointing at the ground with your left index finger beside your left thigh. As you make this double gesture, continue to gaze forward to the north.

Resume the standing posture with arms at your sides and contemplate the dark green pentagram of Earth in the north for five seconds or so. Lay your left palm across your heart-center and point with your right index finger at the center of the pentagram. Turn your body to the right so that your right forearm crosses in front of your chest, but continue to point your right index finger at the center of the pentagram of Earth.

Walk along one quarter of the circumference of an imaginary circle to your starting place in the east, projecting from your right index finger a line of golden-white fire upon the air at heart level as you go. This line of white astral fire begins in the center of the northern pentagram. Feel the vital energy in your heart-center flow through your chest into your left palm, up your left arm, across your shoulders, and down your right arm to exit in a flaming stream from your right index finger. The expanding spiral it follows as it circulates through your body increases its force. Continue to sustain in your awareness the pentagrams in the east, south, west, and north while projecting this line of fire.

Join the end of the line of golden fire to its beginning in the center of the eastern pentagram. Drop your arms to your sides and step backward to the center of the flaming astral circle. Assume the standing pose. Gaze straight ahead, and focus your eyes on the distant eastern horizon that lies in front of you beyond the wall and other intervening obstructions. Extend your astral awareness to the circle around you, and to the invoking pentagrams of Air, Fire, Water, and Earth that are set in its golden-white band. Contemplate the circle and the different colors of the pentagrams for several minutes. Strive to hold the complete, unbroken circle in your mind. Be aware of the four white pillars beyond the circle.

Spread your arms wide so that your body forms the shape of a cross. Draw a long, deep inhalation. As you do so, visualize the air filling your body and expanding it to gigantic stature. Hold the breath for four slow beats and visualize the light from your heart-center shining outward to enlarge the outer surface of your aura into a perfect transparent sphere of palest gold.

Vibrate upon your breath the following words so that your chest, throat, and nose resonate inwardly:

"Be-fore me, Raph-a-el."

Exhale the remainder of your breath while maintaining your enlarged stature and your expanded aura. Visualize the yellow of the eastern pentagram transfer itself into the pillar. As the pillar turns yellow, the pentagram fades to a clear golden-white.

The yellow pillar thickens and solidifies into the towering, yellow-robed angel Raphael. The angel stands barefoot beyond the circle, gazing down at you with vigilant awareness in its pale gray eyes. Its golden hair is the same color as its robe. The human face of the angel glows with the residual energy of your vibrated words. Watch with your astral awareness as the angel opens wide its white wings to fill the eastern quarter.

Draw a deep breath and hold it for four slow beats as you focus your awareness in your heart-center.

Vibrate upon your breath the following words.

"Be-hind me, Gab-ri-el."

Exhale the remainder of your breath while maintaining your enlarged stature and your expanded aura. Visualize the blue of the western pentagram transfer itself into the pillar behind you. As the pillar turns deep blue, the western pentagram fades to a clear golden-white.

The blue pillar thickens and solidifies into the towering, blue-robed angel Gabriel. The angel stands barefoot beyond the circle, gazing down at you with vigilant awareness in its bronze-colored eyes. The golden-brown eagle's head of the angel glows with the residual energy of your vibrated words. Watch with your astral awareness as the angel opens wide its white wings to fill the western quarter.

Vibrate upon your breath the following words.

"At my right hand, Mich-a-el."

Exhale the remainder of your breath while maintaining your enlarged stature and your expanded aura. Visualize the bright red of the southern pentagram transfer itself into the pillar. As the pillar turns red, the pentagram fades to a clear golden-white.

The red pillar thickens and solidifies into the towering, scarlet-robed angel Michael. The angel stands barefoot beyond the circle, gazing down at you with vigilant awareness in its golden eyes. The maned lion's head of the angel glows with the residual energy of your vibrated words. Watch with your astral awareness as the angel opens wide its white wings to fill the southern quarter.

Vibrate upon your breath the following words.

"At my left hand, Aur-i-el."

Exhale the remainder of your breath while maintaining your enlarged stature and your expanded aura. Visualize the dark green of the northern pentagram transfer itself into the pillar. As the pillar turns green, the pentagram fades to a clear golden-white.

The green pillar thickens and solidifies into the towering, green-robed angel Auriel. The angel stands barefoot beyond the circle, gazing down at you with vigilant awareness in its dark eyes. The brown bull's head of the angel glows with the residual energy of your vibrated words. Watch with your astral awareness as the angel opens wide its white wings to fill the northern quarter.

Contemplate the four angels standing outside the circle. Hold simultaneously in your awareness the circle, the pentagrams that have been drained of their color, and the angels as you continue to stand with your arms spread into a cross.

Visualize your heart-center. Use its energy to expand forward through the center of your chest a white pentagram that hangs upon the air inside the circle about two feet in front of your chest. At the same time expand backward from your heart-center a white hexagram that hangs upon the air inside the circle about two feet behind your back. Make both the pentagram and hexagram three feet across. The hexagram is formed of two interlocking triangles, one upright and the other inverted.

Draw a deep breath. Hold it four slow beats while focusing your awareness upon the pentagram before you and the hexagram behind your back. Vibrate the following words.

"Before me flames the pentagram— behind me shines the six-rayed star."

Lower your arms and adopt the standing pose. For several minutes hold in your mind the white pentagram in front, the white hexagram behind, the golden-white circle with its four inset pentagrams around you, and the four angels at the quarters.

Allow your expanded aura to contract to its normal shape, and reduce your enlarged astral form so that it fits within your physical body.

Turn your attention to the pentagram and hexagram and draw them into your heart-center through your chest and back.

Focus awareness on the four guardian angels beyond the circle and elongate them into pillars of colored light that stretch upward to the star high overhead. When the pillars touch the star, they immediately turn blue-white and scintillate with brilliant radiance. Let them withdraw themselves upward into the star.

Become aware of the four white pentagrams on the magic circle. Mentally reduce them in size until they merge with the circle and disappear.

Step forward to the eastern part of the circle and stand facing east. Place your right hand upon your chest over your heart-center, and extend your left arm in front of you. Concentrate on your heart-center, and begin to draw the energy of the circle into your body through the tip of your left index finger as though sucking air in through the nozzle of a vacuum cleaner. This breaks the band of the circle in the east.

Turn your body a quarter-turn to the left while still pointing east with your left index finger, so that your left forearm extends across your chest. Slowly walk counterclockwise around the inside of the circle, drawing in its flaming white band as you go, until you have returned to the eastern quarter, and the circle has been completely reabsorbed into your heart-center.

Turn to face east and let your arms fall to your sides. Step backward to the center of your practice area and adopt the standing posture. Draw several normal breaths. Focus your attention inward and contemplate the warm light of your heart-center for a minute or two. Expand your awareness so that you are conscious of your physical body, but keep the main focus of your attention on the golden-white sphere in the center of your chest.

Take a deep breath. As you inhale, your body stretches to godlike proportions, until your head is above the level of the clouds. Hold the air four slow beats as you visualize the light from your heart-center expand your aura into a sphere.

Touch your right index finger to your forehead between your eyebrows. Vibrate the syllables of the Hebrew word *ateh* briefly but with power and authority.

"ah-teh"

Feel the resonance in your chest energize your aura, and the vibrations of your aura propel your articulated breath outward to fill the universe.

Touch your right index finger to the end of your sternum in the region of your solar plexus. Vibrate the syllables of the Hebrew word *Malkuth* briefly but with authority.

"Mal-kuth"

Feel the vibrations in your chest energize your aura, and sense that your aura propels your breath outward to fill the universe.

Visualize a white ray extending from the glowing sphere of your heart-center vertically up and down, so that it passes through the top of your skull and between your feet. Conceive this ray to be a laser beam of infinite length.

Touch your right index finger to your right shoulder and vibrate the syllables of the Hebrew words *ve-Geburah* briefly with force.

"veh-Geb-u-rah"

Feel the vibrations in your chest energize your aura, and sense that your aura propels your breath outward to fill the universe.

Touch your right index finger to your left shoulder and vibrate the syllables of the Hebrew words *ve-Gedulah* briefly with force.

"veh-Ged-u-lah"

Feel the vibrations in your chest energize your aura, and sense that your aura propels your breath outward to fill the universe.

Visualize a white ray extending from the glowing sphere of your heart-center horizontally to the left and right so that it passes out the sides of your body below the level of your armpits. Conceive this ray to be a laser beam of infinite length. This horizontal ray intersects the vertical ray at right angles at the center of your heart-center.

Press the palms of your hands together in front of your solar plexus with your extended fingers pointing directly upward. Vibrate the Hebrew words *le-olam* strongly to create a resonance in your chest.

"leh-oh-lam"

Feel the vibrations in your chest energize your aura, and sense that your aura propels your breath outward to fill the universe.

Visualize a white ray extend from the glowing sphere of your heart-center horizontally in front and behind, so that it passes out of your body through the center of your chest between your joined hands and out the center of your back. This horizontal ray intersects the first two rays at right angles in your heart-center.

Raise your united hands above your head so that your fingertips point upward to the heavens. Vibrate the Hebrew word *amen* strongly to create a resonance in your chest. Extend the final syllable so that the remaining air in your lungs is expelled.

"ah-mennnnn"

Feel the vibrations in your chest energize your aura, and sense that your aura propels your breath outward to fill the universe.

Allow your arms to fall to your sides and stand motionless in this posture for a minute or so, breathing normally, while you contemplate with your inner sight the large golden sphere of your expanded aura, the smaller gold-white sphere of your heart-center, and the three brilliant-white rays that extend from the three axes of your gigantic astral body. Mentally withdraw the three rays back into your heart-center, but continue to be aware of its radiance. Allow your aura to contract slowly to its usual elongated shape nearer the surface of your skin, and cause your expanded astral form to shrink down to the dimensions of your physical body.

Close your eyes for a few seconds to rest them. Press the palms of your hands upon your face and slide them down as though drawing off a skin-tight mask. Relax and stretch gently, then go on with your day.

Commentary

As you can see by comparing this exercise with exercise 33, the Lesser Invoking Ritual of the Pentagram is a simplification of the Supreme Invoking Ritual. Instead of four similar Earth pentagrams to represent the four elements, as in the Lesser Ritual, four separate elemental pentagrams are projected to the quarters. Each is accompanied by a pentagram of Spirit.

The elements assigned to the east and south by the Golden Dawn are the active elements Air and Fire. They are termed active because of their rapid, violent motions, and because in their natural state they tend to rise upward. The Spirit pentagram drawn in these quarters balances the active lower elements of Air and Fire. Note that the first segment of the Spirit pentagram extends upward from the point of Fire to the point of Air. For this reason the pentagram is known as the Equilibrated Active Invoking Pentagram of Spirit. "Equilibrated" because it serves to equilibrate or balance the elements, "active" because it is used in conjunction with Air and Fire, the active elements, and "invoking" because it is used with the invoking pentagrams of the elements, and because it invokes Spirit or Light.

The elements linked to the west and north by the Golden Dawn are the passive lower elements of Water and Earth. They are termed passive because they tend to contract in upon themselves and remain inactive unless stirred into motion by an outside force, and because in their natural states they tend to fall downward. The Spirit pentagram that accompanies them is the Equilibrated Passive Invoking Pentagram of Spirit. Note that its first line segment extends upward from the point of passive Earth to the point of passive Water.

As a result of the placement of the spirit pentagrams, there is a passive and an active equilibrated pentagram of spirit on each axis of the magic circle. Spirit is invoked on all four quarters, but on the east and south it is projective Spirit, and on the west and north it is receptive Spirit.

Specific physical gestures were employed in the grade rituals of the Golden Dawn. The signs of the four so-called elemental grades appear in this pentagram ritual. The grade of Theoricus relates to Air, that of Philosophus to Fire, that of Practicus to Water, and that of Zelator to Earth. In the pentagram ritual, a fifth sign is used in connection with spirit. This is the sign known as the Rending of the Veil, and occurs in the Portal Grade Ritual of the Golden Dawn, a transition ritual connecting the lower elemental grades with the higher grades of adepthood. I mention this only to indicate that these physical gestures have precise and important meanings.

The Enochian words *Exarp, Hcoma, Nanta,* and *Bitom* occupy the central cross of the Enochian Great Table of the Four Watchtowers. A Watchtower is a grid of twelve columns and thirteen rows, each cell of which contains its own letter. In the Golden Dawn system of magic the four connecting words were placed upon their own table of four rows and five columns known as the Tablet of Union, because these words unite the four Watchtowers and allow them to constitute the Great Table. They were assigned to the uppermost point of the pentagram and to the element of Spirit or Light. This is why these words are used in connection with the equilibrated pentagrams of Spirit in the Supreme Ritual of the Pentagram.

The other four Enochian word sets are derived from the beams of the central crosses of the four Watchtowers. In the Golden Dawn system of magic, the Watchtower of the East has on its central row the letters *Oro Ibah Aozpi.* The Watchtower of the South contains on its central row the letters *Oip Teaa Pdoce.* The Watchtower of the West contains *Mph Arsl Gaiol.* The Watchtower of the North contains *Mor Dial*

Hctga. Since the cross of each Watchtower may be regarded as its spiritual heart, and the arm of the cross balances its energies, these word sets are appropriate for the balancing pentagrams of elemental Spirit.

It will readily be seen that these words cannot be pronounced in the usual way. Vowel sounds must be added, or each letter must be pronounced separately. The Golden Dawn combined both of these workarounds when voicing these Enochian words. In the exercise, I have provided the pronunciations that were used by the Golden Dawn in its ritual. Unfortunately, they obscure the very important number symbolism of three letters, four letters, and five letters in each word set. For this reason, I have also indicated the original spelling of the words in the body of the exercise.

It would not be possible to fully explain the meanings of the Enochian words in this little book. Those interested in Enochian magic should consult my *Enochian Magic for Beginners*. However, it is not necessary to understand the meanings of the words to work the ritual effectively, provided it is understood that each Enochian word from the Tablet of Union and corresponding set of words from the central row of the Watchtower relates to the spiritual energy of its associated lower element. For example, *Exarp* and *Oro Ibah Aozpi* activate the spiritual energies of elemental Air and the northern quarter of space.

This ritual is described in outline form in the original Golden Dawn documents presented by Israel Regardie in his book *The Golden Dawn*. I have expanded it to make it clearer and more useful for beginners, while taking care not to alter its basic structure. The greatest defect of its presentation in the Order papers is a lack of any instructions on visualization. Members of the Order were expected to understand what they should visualize while performing the ritual. Modern practitioners attempting to perform the ritual based only on the original outline, without the addition of visualization, are inevitably disappointed. They can walk through the mechanical aspects of the ritual but can never infuse it with life.

By substituting for the invoking pentagrams of the elements their corresponding banishing pentagrams, and for the invoking pentagrams of Spirit the corresponding banishing pentagrams, this ritual can be transformed into the Supreme Banishing Ritual of the Pentagram. When making this inversion, you should visualize the guardian angels of the quarters as facing outward, away from the circle, rather than inward to its center.

EXERCISE 40

Evoking Into
the Triangle

THIS GENERAL METHOD may be used to evoke any lower spirit within the triangle. As an example, the evocation of Paralda, the king of the airy elementals known as Sylphs, will be described.

Lay out on the floor of the practice area a circle seven feet in diameter and an equilateral triangle three-feet long on each side, so that the base of the triangle is one foot away from the edge of the circle, and the apex of the triangle points toward the quarter associated with the spirit that is to be evoked. The triangle of Paralda points toward the east. For the circle use twelve pennies positioned at the hours of the clock. For the triangle, use ten dimes to form the tetractys, a triangular figure defined by ten dots. Three dimes mark its points, two dimes occupy each side, and a single dime resides at its center.

Upon the central dime in the triangle place an elemental focus for the spirit you seek to evoke. In the present example, a dish containing four cones of smoking incense may be used as a focus for Paralda. Arrange the incense cones in the shape of a square to signify materialization.

Place a knife with a straight steel blade on the floor just inside the circle in the east so that its blade points toward the south.

Assume the standing pose in the center of the physical circle, facing east. Direct your gaze straight ahead and focus your eyes on the unseen distant horizon. Take several deep breaths to calm your thoughts and prepare for what will follow.

Visualize yourself standing in the center of your astral temple, in the place usually occupied by the black marble altar, facing the upright solid yellow triangle on the east wall. On the floor in the eastern side of the astral temple the outline of a yellow triangle has been painted. Its base is about a foot away from the outer edge of the circle and its apex points east. The line of the triangle is three inches wide— the same width as the painted white astral circle surrounding you. Where there is a coin in your physical temple, a candle burns on the floor of your astral temple. The exception to this rule is the center of the triangle, which contains a dish with four smoking incense cones similar to the dish of smoking incense that occupies the physical triangle in your practice area. Lying just inside the circle of the astral

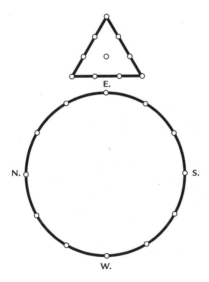

Figure 40-1. Circle and triangle laid out using coins

temple in the east is a dagger with a straight steel blade that points toward the south.

Clap your hands together sharply three times with three-second intervals between the claps, and speak the following declaration of intention.

"This ritual evocation of Paralda, King of Air, is well and truly commenced."

Raise your arms slowly out to your sides with your elbows locked until they are angled slightly above your head. Turn your palms up and spread your fingers. At the same time tilt your head back and elevate your gaze so that it is directed upward at the white star high in the heavens. See this star shining in the darkness of space through the domed skylight of your astral temple with your astral sight. Take care not to hunch your shoulders or lock your neck—keep your shoulders relaxed and stretch upward with your face.

Speak the cleansing prayer in a clear voice that vibrates within you and makes the astral temple resonate. As you speak the words of the prayer, visualize cooling streams of silvery water shower down from this star and pass through the roof of your astral temple to fall upon your upturned face and hands and cascade along your arms and down the length of your body.

"Have mercy upon me, O Lord, Blot out my transgressions. Wash me thoroughly from my iniquities And cleanse me from my sins. Asperge me with hyssop, and I shall be clean; Wash me, and I shall be whiter than snow. Create in me a clean heart, O Lord, And renew a right spirit within me."

Feel the astral rain from the star penetrate through your skin and wash away all obstructions to your purpose. Feel the cooling rain wash through your brain and sweep away the chaos of your thoughts, leaving only a quiet clarity. Feel it cleanse your heart of hurtful emotions. Feel it wash through your bowels and groin and sweep away all base urges. Feel it wash out through the soles of your feet and carry with it any sickness or weakness that was afflicting your body.

Add the following coda to the cleansing prayer, which is used only during evocations.

"By these holy waters am I cleansed, purified, and renewed, so that no lower spirit may harm me or abide within me."

As the words of the prayer end, the silvery rain from the star ceases. Resume the standing posture with your arms at your sides and gaze east at the unseen distant horizon.

Take a deep breath. As you inhale, your body expands to godlike proportions. Your head and shoulders rise through the ceiling of your astral temple, continuing upward above the level of the clouds, until your body projects into starry space.

Hold the air in your lungs for four slow beats as you visualize the warm light from your heart-center radiate outward to expand your aura into a sphere.

Touch your right index finger to your forehead between your eyebrows. Vibrate the syllables of the Hebrew word *ateh* briefly but with power and authority.

"ah-teh"

Feel the resonance in your chest energize your aura, and the vibrations of your aura propel your articulated breath outward to fill the universe.

Touch your right index finger to the end of your breastbone in the area of your solar plexus. Vibrate the syllables of the Hebrew word *Malkuth* briefly but with authority.

"Mal-kuth"

Feel the vibrations in your chest energize your aura, and sense that your aura propels your breath outward to fill the universe.

Visualize a white ray extending from the glowing sphere of your heart-center vertically up and down, so that it passes through the top of your skull and between your feet. Conceive this ray to be a laser beam of infinite length.

Touch your right index finger to your right shoulder and vibrate the syllables of the Hebrew words *ve-Geburah* briefly with force.

"veh-Geb-u-rah"

Feel the vibrations in your chest energize your aura, and sense that your aura propels your breath outward to fill the universe.

Touch your right index finger to your left shoulder and vibrate the syllables of the Hebrew words *ve-Gedulah* briefly with force.

"veh-Ged-u-lah"

Feel the vibrations in your chest energize your aura, and sense that your aura propels your breath outward to fill the universe.

Visualize a white ray extending from the glowing sphere of your heart-center horizontally to the left and right so that it passes out the sides of your body below the level of your armpits. Conceive this ray to be a laser beam of infinite length. This horizontal ray intersects the vertical ray at right angles at your heart-center.

Press the palms of your hands together in front of your solar plexus with your extended fingers pointing upward in the traditional gesture of prayer, and cup your palms slightly to form a hollow between them. Vibrate the Hebrew words *le-olam* strongly to create a resonance in your chest.

"leh-oh-lam"

Feel the vibrations in your chest energize your aura, and sense that your aura propels your breath outward to fill the universe.

Visualize a white ray extending from the glowing sphere of your heart-center horizontally in front and behind, so that it passes out of your body through the center of your chest between the palms of your joined hands and out the center of your back. This horizontal ray intersects the first two rays at right angles in your heart-center.

Raise your united hands above the level of your head while continuing to gaze forward. Vibrate the Hebrew word *amen* strongly to create a resonance in your chest. Extend the final syllable so that the remaining air in your lungs is expelled.

"ah-mennnn"

Feel the vibrations in your chest energize your aura, and sense that your aura propels your breath outward to fill the universe.

Lower your joined hands to the level of your solar plexus, then allow your palms to part and your arms to fall to your sides. Stand motionless in this posture for a minute or so, breathing normally, and contemplate with your inner sight the large golden sphere of your expanded aura, the smaller gold-white sphere of your heart-center, and the three brilliant-white rays that extend from the three axes of your gigantic astral body.

Mentally draw the three rays into your heart-center, but continue to be aware of its radiance. Allow your aura to contract slowly to its usual elongated shape nearer the surface of your skin, and cause your expanded astral form to shrink down to the dimensions of your physical body.

With your inner perception continue to be aware of the aura surrounding your physical body, but direct your main focus to your heart-center. Press your left palm over your chest just above the end of your sternum, and extend your right arm directly in front of you in the gesture of projection. Point with your right index finger to the east at the level of your heart.

Use the force of your will to make the golden-white energy filling the sphere of your heart-center fountain through your chest into the palm of your left hand. Guide it in an expanding spiral up your left arm, across your shoulders, and down your right arm. Project this spiritual energy in the form of white fire in a stream from the tip of your right index finger to the boundary of the circle of pennies surrounding your physical form. At the same time, in the astral temple project the stream of gold-white fire to the boundary of the circle of candle flames.

As you begin projecting the fire, rotate clockwise on your own body axis and trace a circle of brilliant white flame around you at the level of your heart. The projected ring of astral flame hangs directly above the circle of pennies in the physical workspace, and directly above the circle of candles in the astral temple. Take care to join the end of the ring of astral fire to its beginning.

Let your arms fall to your sides as you resume the standing pose. Contemplate the circle around you, and the golden-white sphere in the center of your chest. Hold both of these dynamic astral forms in your consciousness at the same time for a dozen seconds, then shift your attention to your heart-center.

Visualize the Hebrew letters of the name *IHVH* (I= י, H= ה, V= ו, H= ה) written within the shining sphere of your heart-center from right to left. They blaze with brilliant white light that is edged with electric blue against the softer, slightly yellow background of the sphere. The letters are blindingly intense, similar in color to the light of the star.

ה ו ה י

Take a slow, deep breath. Imagine as you inhale that your body is being expanded by the indrawn air to gigantic proportions. Your head and shoulders rise through the ceiling of your astral temple as though passing through a shadow. They continue upward through the roof of the building, further upward into the sky above the level of the clouds, until you find yourself with almost all of your body projected above the atmosphere into the starry midnight of space. As you grow larger, the astral circle of fire around your form enlarges at the same rate and remains at the level of your heart.

Retain your breath within your lungs for four slow beats. During the retention, visualize the warm white light from your heart-center radiating outward to expand the envelope of your aura into a sphere that surrounds your entire gigantic form.

Pronounce the four Hebrew letters of the name *IHVH* individually so that the resonant sound of your voice sets every part of your body vibrating in sympathetic response. The letters are vibrated with a regular rhythm, their sounds of equal duration and drawn out upon the breath. The vibration of the name empties most of the air from your lungs but does not leave you gasping.

"Yod-Heh-Vav-Heh"

This resonant sound-force fills your transparent golden aura and sets it vibrating in sympathy. The vibrations of your aura send the air issuing from between your lips outward in all directions, expanding at an exponential rate until the vibration of your voice saturates the entire universe to its uttermost limits. Feel with your astral awareness the entire universe humming with this vibration as though it were a giant crystal bell.

Visualize the energy of the sounds rebound from the outer limits of the universe and return to focus in the east, just beyond the shining ring of the magic circle. The sounds become ever more concentrated, until they assume a vaguely humanoid shape that is bright yellow. As you watch with your astral vision, this shape defines itself into an angel of vast size, taller even than your enlarged astral body. The angel has a human head, golden hair, a beautiful male face, and white wings that hang downward on its back almost to its bare feet. It wears a long robe of a light yellow color.

Extend your consciousness to the angel. As the angel becomes aware of your existence, gaze directly into its pale gray eyes. Mentally will the angel to turn outward. Visualize the angel nod in acknowledgement, then turn and spread its white wings so that they fill the entire region of the east. The wings conceal the head and body of the angel like a shimmering, semitransparent curtain of pale white light, so that the head and body of the angel vanish, but you are able to see through the curtain of light to the stars beyond.

Draw several normal breaths and allow the expanded balloon of your aura to contract to its normal shape nearer to the limits of your form. Allow your giant form to shrink back into your physical body within your practice chamber. The astral circle shrinks with you. Maintain an awareness of the opened wings of the angel in the east towering above you like a vast translucent curtain of pale light. Through this curtain see with your astral vision the eastern wall of the astral temple, and with your physical vision the eastern side of your practice area. The curtain of light formed by the wings of the angel divides the magic circle from the triangle.

Turn one quarter of a revolution clockwise on your body axis and assume the standing pose facing the south. Continue to maintain an awareness of the glowing ball of your heart-center and the flaming circle around you. Look straight ahead and focus your physical eyes on the distant southern horizon beyond your chamber.

Visualize written within your heart-center from right to left the four Hebrew letters of the name *Adonai* (A= א, D= ד, N= נ, I= י). These letters blaze with blinding blue-white intensity against the softer yellow-white of the sphere.

$$\text{א ד נ י}$$

Draw in a deep breath. As you inhale imagine your body enlarging to gigantic proportions so that your upper body leaves the atmosphere of the Earth and projects into space. You are surrounded by stars. The flaming astral circle grows with you and remains at the level of your heart. Retain the breath four slow beats, and visualize the warm light from your heart-center radiating out through your skin to expand your aura into a complete sphere around your enlarged form.

Extend the pronunciation of the name *Adonai* so that there is one sound for each Hebrew letter. The sound of your voice sets your entire body resonating in sympathetic response.

"Ah-doh-en-aye"

This resonance travels outward to fill your transparent golden aura and sets it vibrating in sympathetic response to your body. The air issuing from your lips is driven forth in all directions by the vibrations of your aura with rapidly increasing force until the vibrations of the name fill every part of the universe, and cause a sympathetic vibration in the universe itself.

Visualize the energy of the sounds rebound from the outer limits of the universe and return to focus in the south, just beyond the shining ring of the magic circle. The sounds become ever more concentrated, until they assume a vaguely humanoid shape that is bright red, the color of fresh blood. As you watch with your astral vision, this shape defines itself into an angel of vast size, taller even than your enlarged astral body. The angel has the maned, golden-red head of a male lion, and white wings that hang down on its back almost to its bare feet. It wears a long robe of a bright red color.

Extend your consciousness to the angel. As the angel becomes aware of your existence, gaze directly into its golden eyes. Silently will the angel to turn away from the circle and spread its wings. Visualize the angel nod its leonine head in acknowledgement and turn its back to the circle, then spread its white wings so that they fill the entire region of the south. The wings conceal the head and body of the angel, and hang like a translucent curtain of light, wrapping around the southern quarter of the astral circle and extending endlessly up and down.

Draw several normal breaths and allow the expanded balloon of your aura to contract to its normal shape nearer to the limits of your projected form. Allow your giant form to shrink back into your physical body within your practice chamber. The magic circle shrinks to remain at the level of your heart. Hold an awareness of the opened wings of the angel in the south towering above you like a shining radiant curtain.

Turn a quarter-revolution clockwise to face the west. Adopt the standing pose. Gaze on the unseen western horizon and maintain the inner perception of your glowing heart-center and the flaming circle that surrounds you.

Visualize written within this golden-white, transparent orb from right to left the four Hebrew letters of the name *Eheieh* (A= א, H= ה, I= י, H= ה). These letters shimmer and almost blind your inner sight with their blue-white intensity.

א י ה ה

Draw in a deep breath and imagine as you do so that your body enlarges through the ceiling of your ritual chamber, past the level of the clouds, until it projects gigantically into the darkness of space. Hold the breath for four slow beats as you visualize the light from your heart-center shining outward in all directions to expand the envelope of your aura into a perfect sphere that is colored a transparent pale gold.

Extend the pronunciation of the name *Eheieh* so that there is a separate sound for each of the four Hebrew letters. Your entire physical body vibrates with the force of the sound.

"Ah-heh-aye-yah"

The sound energy expands outward from its source in your heart-center and sets the sphere of your aura resonating in sympathy. The breath that issues from between your lips is driven away in all directions by your energized aura so that it fills the entire universe. The universe itself begins to vibrate with the combined sounds of the letters.

Visualize the energy as the sounds rebound from the outer limits of the universe and return to focus in the west, just beyond the shining ring of the magic circle. The sounds become ever more concentrated, until they assume a vaguely humanoid shape that is a beautiful dark blue. As you watch with your astral vision, this shape defines itself into an angel of vast size, taller even than your enlarged astral body. The angel has the light-brown, feathered head and hooked beak of a golden eagle. Long white wings hang down its back almost to its bare feet. It wears a long robe of a rich, dark blue color.

Extend your conscious to the angel. As the angel becomes aware of your existence, gaze directly into its bronze-colored eyes. Mentally will the angel to turn and spread its wings. Visualize the angel nod its feathered head in acknowledgement, then turn away from the circle and spread its white wings so that they fill the entire region of the west like a vast curtain of translucent light. The head and body of the angel vanish behind its wings, but through them you can see the distant stars.

Draw several normal breaths and allow the expanded balloon of your aura to contract to its normal shape nearer to the limits of your form. Allow your giant form to shrink back into your physical body within your practice chamber. Maintain an awareness of the opened wings of the angel in the west towering above you like a vast curtain of pale light.

Turn a quarter-revolution clockwise to face the north and assume the standing posture. Let your physical eyes focus on the distant, unseen horizon, while you maintain your inner concentration on your glowing heart-center and the astral circle that surrounds you.

Visualize written from right to left within the warmly glowing orb in the middle of your chest the four Hebrew letters of the name *AGLA* (A= א, G= ג, L= ל, A= א). These letters scintillate with blazing blue-white intensity against the softer radiance of your heart-center.

אלגא

Draw a long, deep inhalation. As you do so, visualize the air fill your body and expand it to gigantic stature. You project into the midnight of space, surrounded by stars. The astral circle expands at the same rate and continues to float at the level of your heart. Hold the breath for four slow beats and visualize the light from your heart-center shining outward to enlarge the envelope of your aura into a perfect transparent sphere of palest gold.

Pronounce the name *AGLA* with a separate sound for each of its four Hebrew letters so that your entire body tingles with the vibrations resonating within your expanded chest.

"Ah-Geh-Lah-Ah"

The force of the sounds expanding outward from your heart-center causes your aura to tremble and vibrate in sympathetic resonance. Simultaneously, the air issuing from your lungs is energized and driven outward in all directions by your aura the way sound expands from the vibrating diaphragm of a stereo speaker. It fills all of space and sets the universe vibrating in harmony.

Visualize the energy of the sounds rebound from the outer limits of the universe and return to focus in the north, just beyond the shining ring of the magic circle. The sounds become ever more concentrated, until they assume a vaguely humanoid shape that is a beautiful dark green, the color of evergreen trees. As you watch with your astral vision, this shape defines itself into an angel of vast size, taller even than your enlarged astral body. The angel has the dark-brown, horned head of a bull, and white-feathered wings that hang down its back almost to its bare feet. It wears a long robe of a deep evergreen color.

Extend your consciousness to the angel. As the angel becomes aware of your existence, gaze directly into its dark-brown eyes. Silently will the angel with the force of your mind to turn away from the circle and spread its wings. Visualize the angel nod its horned head in acknowledgement, turn its back upon the circle, and spread its white wings so that they fill the entire region of the north like a shimmering, translucent curtain of pale light. The head and body of the angel are concealed behind its wings, but through them the stars are visible.

Draw several normal breaths and allow the expanded balloon of your aura to contract to its normal shape nearer to the limits of your body. Allow your giant form to shrink back into your physical body within your practice chamber. Maintain an awareness of the open wings of the angel in the north, towering above you like a vast curtain of light.

Turn a quarter-revolution clockwise to face the east and assume the standing pose. Be aware of the wings of all four angels completely enclosing the magic circle as they touch tip to tip.

Spread your arms wide so that your body imitates the shape of a cross. Draw a long, deep inhalation. As you do so, visualize the air fill your body and expand it to gigantic stature. The magic circle grows in proportion to your body. Hold the breath four slow beats and visualize the light from your heart-center shining outward to enlarge the envelope of your aura into a perfect transparent sphere of palest gold.

Vibrate upon your breath the following words so that your chest, throat, and nose resonate inwardly.

"Be-fore me, Raph-a-el."

Visualize the shimmering wings of the angel Raphael in the east glow bright yellow with the energy of your vibrated words. After a few moments, the wings fade once again from yellow to white. Exhale the remainder of your breath and draw in another deep inhalation while maintaining your enlarged stature and your expanded aura. Hold it four slow beats as you focus your awareness in your heart-center.

Vibrate upon your breath the following words.

"Be-hind me, Gab-ri-el."

Without turning your head, visualize the open wings of the angel Gabriel behind you in the west glowing dark blue with the energy of your vibrated words. After a moment or two, they revert to a pallid white. Exhale the remainder of your breath and draw in another deep inhalation while maintaining your enlarged stature and your expanded aura. Hold the breath four slow beats as you focus your awareness in your heart-center.

Vibrate upon your breath the following words.

"At my right hand, Mich-a-el."

Visualize the expanded wings of the angel Michael on your right side in the south, glowing red with the energy of your vibrated words. After a moment or two the wings pale to white. Exhale the remainder of your breath and draw in another deep inhalation while continuing to maintain your enlarged stature and expanded aura. Hold the breath four slow beats as you focus your awareness in your heart-center.

Vibrate upon your breath the following words.

"At my left hand, Aur-i-el."

Visualize the widespread wings of the angel Auriel on your left side in the north, glowing dark green with the energy of your vibrated words. The green persists for a few moments, then the wings revert to their former translucent white. Let the rest of your breath leave your lungs silently.

Drop your arms to your sides and adopt the standing posture. Draw several normal breaths and contract the pale-golden sphere of your aura to its usual shape nearer to the limits of your form. Allow your giant astral body to shrink back into your physical body within your practice chamber. As your astral form reduces in size, the circle of gold-white fire shrinks in proportion to remain at the level of your heart.

Hold the awareness of the four angels of the quarters towering above you unseen behind unbroken curtain of their expanded conjoined wings. Feel their strength both shield you and protect your circle.

Spread your arms wide so that your body forms a great cross. Raise your arms slightly and turn your palms up while opening your fingers and tilting your face upward. Be aware that as you stand within the astral temple and gaze upward through the domed skylight that forms the central part of its ceiling, you can see the single brilliant blue-white star shining in the blackness of space directly overhead. Spin slowly clockwise on your body axis while speaking the following in a clear voice so that your words resonate inwardly in the astral temple.

"See that holy and formless fire, which darts and flashes through the hidden depths of the universe."

As you rotate, visualize a swirling vortex of light form in the air all around you. It is shaped like a bright cone and turns clockwise. The inverted funnel of the vortex of light has its focus in the blue-white star high overhead and opens wider as it extends downward to surround your body. Within the center of the spinning cone, a column of white light descends from the white star high above in the heavens to touch your upturned face between your eyebrows and pierce downward to the sphere of your heart-center. Feel it enter and energize your body. With your astral perceptions, hear the rushing sound of the larger vortex of light as it swirls down from the star into the circle.

When you have turned a complete rotation and face the eastern quarter once again, continue spinning in a second circle on your body axis. Speak the following words clearly so that they resound in the astral temple.

"Such a fire existeth, extending through the rushings of air, a fire formless whence cometh the image of a voice."

Visualize the brightness of the vortex all around you intensify, and the column of light linking your heart-center with the star become thicker and more intense.

The spiritual radiance drawn down the inside of the inverted funnel of the vortex cascades over your body and spreads outward to fill the entire circle with light. Visualize light flooding into the circle from above. The sound of the swirling vortex becomes louder.

When you complete your second rotation and once again face the eastern quarter, continue spinning slowly in a third clockwise rotation on your body axis. Speak the following words so that they resound in the astral temple.

"A flashing light, abounding, revolving, whirling forth, crying aloud. Hear the voice of Fire!"

Visualize the whirling vortex around your body intensify and brighten, drawing down a flood of light that fills the entire circle. This light shining from the beam that links the star with your heart-center is now so concentrated, it makes the astral temple glow, and can even be seen on the air of the physical temple. Hear the rushing of the light as it descends. It sounds similar to roaring fire caught in a powerful downdraft.

When you complete the third rotation, stop the turning of your body so that you face the direction of the spirit you intend to evoke into the triangle. In the present example, you stop turning with your body facing east, because east is the quarter of Paralda. If you were evoking a spirit associated with elemental Water and the west, you would complete the third rotation and continue to turn until you faced west, then stop. Continue to gaze upward at the star with your arms spread wide and your palms turned up.

Visualize written within your heart-center from right to left the Hebrew letters of the divine name *Shaddai El Chai* (Sh = שׁ, D = ד, I = י, A = א, L = ל, Ch = ח, A = א, I = י) so that the letters burn with brilliant white light that is edged by electric blue flame.

$$ \text{י   א   ח   ל   א   י   ד   שׁ} $$

Take a deep breath, and as the air enters your lungs, visualize your body enlarging to gigantic proportions, so that your head rises upward through the roof of your astral temple and you are surrounded by stars. The astral circle expands with you and remains at the level of your heart. Hold the breath four beats, and visualize the radiant light from the sphere of your heart-center expand your aura into a glowing golden sphere.

Sound the name *Shaddai El Chai* upon your breath so that each syllable is articulated separately, and your chest vibrates. The sounds of the name expand outward from your heart-center to the limits of your aura, and the sympathetic resonance of your aura sends them expanding endlessly to fill the universe.

"Shad-dai, El Chai"

Take several normal breaths and allow your aura to contract to its usual shape close to your skin. Reduce the size of your astral body so that it once again is contained within the astral temple.

While continuing to gaze up at the star with your arms spread, speak the following invocation to the ruler of the east and the element of Air.

"I, _____, invoke thee, Shaddai El Chai, lord of the east and of the region of Air, and of all the spiritual creatures that dwell therein. Descend from your throne in the sphere of Yesod and fill this circle of art with your presence. Enter my body and fill me with your light. Enter my heart-center and empower my will with authority to rule over all the creatures of the Air element in your name, by the supreme power and authority of Yod-Heh-Vav-Heh upon which the universe is formed."

Take a deep breath, and as you inhale, visualize the air flowing into your lungs enlarge your body to gigantic dimensions, so that your head rises through the roof of the astral temple and is surrounded by stars. Hold the breath four beats, and expand your aura to a sphere. Vibrate the individual Hebrew letters of the divine name *IHVH,* so that your heart-center transmits the sound to your expanded aura, and your aura conveys it outward to fill the universe.

"Yod-Hey-Vav-Hey"

As you complete the vibration of the holy name *IHVH,* the whirling vortex of light surrounding your body turns a deep, rich yellow, the color of elemental Air.

Breathe normally, contract your aura to its usual shape close to your skin, and reduce the size of your astral body until you are contained within the astral temple.

Lower your arms to your sides and assume the standing pose facing the direction in which the triangle points—in the present example, the east. Continue to be aware of the beam of white light that passes through the top of your skull to link your heart-center with the blue-white star in the heavens, and of the swirling clockwise vortex of yellow light that fills the circle and surrounds your body.

Begin to perform the fourfold breath with pore breathing while keeping your physical gaze focused upon the unseen distant eastern horizon. Draw in a deep breath for four silent beats, and as you inhale, visualize the yellow light that swirls in a clockwise vortex around the ritual circle flowing in the form of countless tiny glowing particles into your body through the pores of your skin.

Hold your breath with your lungs comfortably filled with air for the same four silent beats, and visualize the light that now fills your entire body circulating along every vein and nerve channel.

Exhale for four silent beats, and visualize the air flowing from your nostrils to be silvery-gray in color. All of its yellow airy energy has been absorbed and retained within your body.

Hold your breath with your lungs comfortably empty of air for four beats, and visualize the light that circulates throughout your body concentrate itself in the golden-white sphere of your heart-center. Feel your will become strong with the indwelling presence and authority of *Shaddai El Chai.*

Repeat this cycle of the fourfold breath four times. As you perform the breath, visualize the inverted yellow vortex around your body gradually lose its whirling energy and fade from your astral perceptions, leaving only the vertical white beam of light that links your heart-center with the star. Visualize the light that fills the circle become fainter as more and more of it is drawn into your body through the pores of your skin.

Breathe normally. For a minute, contemplate the beam of light extending upward from your heart-center to the star, and the stillness of the air within the circle. Deliberately sever the beam, so that it snaps upward to the star like a rubber band released at one end. Remain aware of the accumulated brightness in your heart-center that is the power and authority of *Shaddai El Chai.*

Pick up the dagger from the floor in the east and stand facing the triangle on the floor in the posture of projection with the knife extended in your right hand at heart level and your left palm pressed to the center of your chest. Make sure that when the dagger is fully extended its blade passes through the ring of the astral circle that you have established in the air above the ring of pennies on the floor. Take care that your hand does not pass beyond the limit of this circle. At the same time, inwardly visualize yourself standing within your astral temple, the blade of the dagger projecting eastward through the ring of astral fire that floats upon the air above the circle of burning candles.

Raise the point of the dagger about a foot and a half above the level of the astral circle, and use it to trace a triangle vertically on the air counterclockwise from its apex. The standing astral triangle should be the same size as the physical triangle defined in dimes on the floor of the practice area, which is the same size as the astral triangle that is painted in a band of yellow on the floor of the astral temple. Project a beam of yellow fire from the point of the dagger through the protective curtain of the wings of the angels. This beam has its focus on a vertical plane that rises from the base line of the triangle on the floor.

Take a deep breath, and as you project the left side of this vertical triangle downward from its apex, vibrate the Hebrew mother letter of elemental Air, *Aleph* (א), in two sounds, the first sound extended as you draw the line of the side, the second short and cut off abruptly as you point to the end of the line.

"Aaaaaaaay-leph!"

Take a second breath, and as you project the base of the vertical triangle in a line of yellow fire from left to right, vibrate the Hebrew mother letter of elemental Water, *Mem* (מ), in two sounds, the first extended as you draw the line of the base, the second short and cut off abruptly as you point to the end of the line.

"Emmmmmmm-mah!"

Take a third breath, and as you project the right side of the vertical triangle in a line of yellow fire from the lower-right point back to its apex, vibrate the Hebrew mother letter of elemental Fire, *Shin* (ש), in two sounds, the first extended as you trace the line of the side, the second short and abrupt as you point to the end of the line.

"Sheeeeeee-enh!"

Project a spiral of yellow fire that begins at the apex of the vertical triangle and is drawn in three and one-half inward revolutions clockwise within the triangle, so that it terminates and has its focus in the center of the triangle. Visualize the spiral turning inward, so that it creates an endless tunnel through the center of the vertical triangle.

On top of this project an equal-armed cross of yellow fire, first the vertical segment, then the horizontal segment, so that the intersection of the cross is at the center of the spiral and the triangle. As you draw the vertical column of the cross from top to bottom, vibrate the name *Shaddai*.

"Shad-dai"

As you draw the horizontal beam of the cross from left to right, vibrate the name *El Chai*.

"El-Chai"

Allow the glowing lines of the cross to contract into a point at the center of the opened spiral and fade from your inner vision. Point with the dagger at the center of the triangle as it floats upon the air in the east above the base line of

Figure 40-2.
Clockwise-inward spiral
of three and one-half turns

the physical triangle defined in dimes on the floor. The center of the vertical astral triangle is on the level of your heart-center. Speak in a clear voice the following evocation to Paralda, the king of the Air:

"**Paralda, King of the Sylphs, whose dwelling place is in the east, who governs the spirits of Air, who commands the winds of the world and the products of the intellect, I , _____ , evoke and summon you into this triangle of art, with the authority of Shaddai El Chai, the divine ruler of the east and the Air, who dwells within me and is the voice of my mouth. I evoke and summon you by the archangel Raphael, wise guardian of the east. I evoke and summon you by the angel Chassan, the executor of the acts of Air. I evoke and summon you by the ruler Ariel, swift and graceful herald who conveys the commands of the angels of Air from their lips to your ears.**

Enter this triangle through the gateway of its spiral vortex. Put on the fragrant smoke rising in its center, so that the smoke becomes your body. Manifest tangibly to my awareness in a form that is graceful and pleasing. Heed my words and answer

Figure 40-3.
Counterclockwise-outward spiral
of three and one-half turns

me truly without evasion or deception. Be obedient in all things, for I evoke and summon you with the authority and presence of Shaddai El Chai, lord of the east."

With the point of your dagger project in yellow fire an expanding counterclockwise vortex that begins at the center of the vertical astral triangle and makes three and one-half revolutions to pass through the base of the vertical triangle and terminate at the dish of incense in the physical triangle constructed of dimes.

Withdraw the knife and hold it between your hands in front of your chest with its point up. Continue to gaze attentively, but without anxiety for any specific result, through the vertical astral triangle at the rising smoke of the incense cones. Be aware of any small signs that a spiritual presence has entered the physical triangle. It may manifest itself by a sudden drop in temperature, currents in the air of the practice chamber, motions in the rising smoke, moving brightness or shadow within the triangle, or sudden sounds. Be aware of any unusual sounds that may occur beyond the limits of the practice chamber.

If you receive some indication of a spiritual presence, clearly state the task that you wish Paralda to accomplish. He does not act directly, but instructs his elementals to fulfill your instructions. For purposes of practice, this can be some general

Figure 40-4.
Counterclockwise-inward spiral
of three and one-half turns

task, such as help in acquiring the texts and teachings needed to become expert in the art of magic. The airy element controls intellectual pursuits and the articulation and transmission of knowledge. Remember that Paralda is a king, and accord him the respect and dignity of his office. At the same time, never forget that you evoke him with the authority of the divine name *Shaddai El Chai,* a name that Paralda by his nature is bound to obey.

After instructing Paralda, press your left palm over your heart-center and point with the dagger in your right hand at the dish of incense that sits in the center of the physical triangle. Project a beam of yellow fire from your heart-center through the dagger and use it to draw an inward-turning counterclockwise spiral of three and one-half revolutions that begins at the dish of incense in the physical triangle on the floor and rises upward through the base of the vertical astral triangle to focus upon the open tunnel at the center of the vertical triangle.

Visualize the spiral spinning in a counterclockwise direction, and drawing upward from the physical triangle on the floor the spiritual presence of Paralda into the vertical astral triangle. Be aware of the spirit within the open tunnel at the center of the vertical triangle.

Speak the following license to depart that will release the spirit Paralda from the triangle.

Figure 40-5.
Clockwise-outward spiral
of three and one-half turns

"By the power and authority of Shaddai El Chai, the divine ruler of the east and of the Air, who dwells within me and is the voice of my mouth, I, _____, license Paralda, King of Sylphs, to depart from this triangle of art. Go in peace, and fare you well."

On top of the counterclockwise-inward spiral project an equal-armed cross of yellow fire, first the vertical segment, then the horizontal segment, so that the intersection of the cross is at the center of the spiral and the astral triangle. As you draw the vertical column of the cross from top to bottom, vibrate the name *Shaddai*.

"Shad-dai"

As you draw the horizontal beam of the cross from left to right, vibrate the name *El Chai*.

"El-Chai"

Allow the glowing lines of the cross to contract into a point at the center of the spiral and fade from your inner vision. The spiral itself gradually fades from your awareness.

Point with the dagger at the open tunnel in the center of the astral triangle, through which Paralda has passed and departed. Project in a stream of yellow fire an expanding clockwise spiral that begins at its center over this tunnel and loops outward in three and one-half revolutions to terminate at the apex of the astral triangle. Visualize the tunnel gradually diminish and narrow until it is completely sealed. Allow the spiral to fade from your awareness.

Transfer the dagger to your left hand and press your right palm over your heart-center. Point at the apex of the astral triangle, and will the line of the triangle to separate at its apex. Began to absorb the triangle by tracing it clockwise. Draw its flaming line into the dagger, up your left arm, across your shoulders, down your right arm, and project it through your right palm into your heart-center.

Take a deep breath, and as you absorb the right side of the vertical triangle in a line of yellow fire from the apex down to the lower-right point, vibrate the Hebrew mother letter of elemental Fire, *Shin* (שׁ), in two sounds, the first extended as you draw into the dagger the line of the side, the second short and abrupt as you point to the end of the line.

"Sheeeeeee-enh!"

Take a second breath, and as you absorb the base of the vertical triangle in a line of yellow fire from right to left, vibrate the Hebrew mother letter of elemental Water, *Mem* (מ), in two sounds, the first extended as you draw the line of the base, the second short and cut off abruptly as you point to the end of the line.

"Emmmmmmm-mah!"

Take a third breath, and as you absorb the left side of this vertical triangle upward from its lower-left point to its apex, vibrate the Hebrew mother letter of elemental Air, *Aleph* (א), in two sounds, the first sound extended as you draw the line of the side, the second short and cut off abruptly as you point to the end of the line.

"Aaaaaaaay-leph!"

Contemplate the emptiness of the eastern quarter for a minute. The astral triangle has been drawn completely into your heart-center. With your inner sight, be aware of the stillness in the eastern side of the astral temple. Set the dagger down upon the floor to the east just inside the circle of pennies, so that the point of the knife points toward the north. Step back to the center of the circle facing east.

Spread your arms wide so that your body forms a great cross. Raise your arms slightly and turn your palms up while opening your fingers and tilting your face upward. Be aware that you stand within the astral temple and gaze upward through the skylight at the single brilliant blue-white star shining in the blackness of space directly overhead. Extend your awareness upward to link your heart-center with the star.

Visualize written within your heart-center from right to left the Hebrew letters of the divine name *Shaddai El Chai* so that the letters burn with brilliant white light that is edged by electric blue flame. Take a deep breath, and as the air enters your lungs, visualize your body enlarging to gigantic proportions, so that your head rises upward through the roof of your astral temple and you are surrounded by stars. The astral circle expands with you and remains at the level of your heart. Hold the breath four beats, and visualize the radiant light from the sphere of your heart-center expand your aura into a glowing golden sphere.

Sound the name *Shaddai El Chai* upon your breath so that each syllable is articulated separately, and your chest vibrates. The sounds of the name expand outward from your heart-center to the limits of your aura, and the sympathetic resonance of your aura sends them expanding endlessly to fill the universe.

"Shad-dai, El Chai"

Take several normal breaths and allow your aura to contract to its usual shape close to your skin. Reduce the size of your astral body so that it once again is contained within the astral temple.

While continuing to gaze up at the star with your arms spread, speak the following formula of release to the ruler of the east and the element of Air.

"I, _____, release thee, Shaddai El Chai, lord of the east and of the region of Air, and of all the spiritual creatures that dwell therein. Go up from my heart-center. Ascend from my body. Arise and resume your throne in the sphere of Yesod. Depart this circle, by the supreme power and authority of IHVH upon which the universe is formed."

Take a deep breath, and as you inhale, visualize the air flowing into your lungs enlarge your body to gigantic dimensions, so that your head rises through the roof of the astral temple and is surrounded by stars. Hold the breath four beats, and expand your aura to a sphere. Vibrate the individual Hebrew letters of the divine name *IHVH*, so that your heart-center transmits the sound to your expanded aura, and your aura conveys it outward to fill the universe.

"Yod-Hey-Vav-Hey"

Take several normal breaths and allow your aura to contract to its usual shape close to your skin. Reduce the size of your astral body so that it once again is contained within the astral temple. Keep your arms spread wide and your face elevated.

Begin to spin slowly counterclockwise on your body axis while speaking the following in a clear voice so that your words resonate inwardly in the astral temple.

"A flashing light, abounding, revolving, whirling forth, crying aloud. Hear the voice of Fire!"

As you rotate, visualize a swirling vortex of light form in the air all around you. It is shaped like the funnel of a tornado, but bright instead of gray, and it turns counterclockwise. The funnel of the vortex of light opens wider as it extends upward. Within the center of the spinning funnel, a column of white light ascends from the sphere of your heart-center through your upturned forehead between your eyebrows and touches the white star high above in the heavens. Feel the energizing power of the light withdraw from your body. With your astral perceptions, hear the rushing sound of the vortex as it swirls upward from the circle.

When you have turned a complete rotation and face the eastern quarter once again, continue spinning in a second counterclockwise rotation on your body axis. Speak the following words clearly so that they resound in the astral temple.

"Such a fire existeth, extending through the rushings of air, a fire formless whence cometh the image of a voice."

Visualize the light of the vortex all around you weakening, and the column of light linking your heart-center with the star become thin and pale. The spiritual radiance that fills your body fountains up through the inside of the connecting beam of light that links your heart-center with the star, driven heavenward by the spinning funnel of the vortex. The sound of the swirling vortex becomes louder.

When you complete your second rotation and once again face the eastern quarter, continue spinning slowly in a third counterclockwise rotation on your body axis. Speak the following words so that they resound in the astral temple.

"See that holy and formless fire, which darts and flashes through the hidden depths of the universe."

Visualize the whirling vortex around your body darken and weaken. The light shining upward through the beam that links the star with your heart-center is now very pale and weak. It is barely visible to your inner perception.

When you complete the third rotation, stop turning with your body facing eastward. Continue to gaze upward at the star with your arms spread wide and your palms turned up. Allow the weakened beam of light to separate itself from your heart-center and rise quickly upward to the star. Let the last traces of the vortex fall silent. Lower your arms to your side and assume the standing posture with your gaze directed at the unseen eastern horizon beyond the wall of your practice chamber.

Visualize the pale, glowing curtain of light that surrounds the circle. Mentally will the guardian angels of the four quarters to close their wings. As the angels obey, the unbroken curtain around the circle becomes four separate panels. These narrow and become brighter. As you watch them with your inner awareness, they lengthen and narrow into four identical pillars of white light. The pillars come together high above your head to focus upon the distant white star. Mentally release the angels and watch astrally as the pillars are drawn upward into the star.

Turn your attention inward and contemplate the warm light of your heart-center for a minute or two. Expand your awareness so that you are conscious of your physical body, but keep the main focus of your attention on the golden-white sphere in the center of your chest.

Press your right palm over your chest just above the end of your sternum, and extend your left arm directly in front of you. Point with your left index finger to the circle in the eastern quarter. Begin to draw the golden-white fire of the circle into the tip of your left index finger, up your left arm, across your chest, down your right arm, and out your right palm into your heart-center. As you do so, rotate counterclockwise on your own body axis a full turn so that the circle is completely absorbed.

Facing east, clap your hands together sharply four times with four-second intervals between the claps, and speak this declaration of fulfillment:

"This ritual evocation of Paralda, King of Air, into the triangle of art is well and truly fulfilled."

Let your arms fall to your sides as you resume the standing pose facing east. Continue breathing easily for half a minute or so. Close your eyes for a few seconds to rest them. Press the palms of your hands upon your face and slide them down as though drawing off a skin-tight mask. Relax and stretch gently, then go on with your day.

Commentary

Higher spirits such as angels are invoked into the circle, which is an extension of the self; hence, these spirits are invoked into our own bodies and personalities, where for a time they become a part of us. Lower spirits such as demons or elementals are evoked outside the circle, beyond the boundary of the self, usually into a triangle. We invoke spirits to acquire their wisdom and authority for the purposes of improving our nature and commanding lower spirits; we evoke spirits to use them for manifest or material ends. Invocation of higher spirits elevates the soul, but invocation of lower spirits would degrade and endanger the soul, which is why lower spirits are evoked outside the circle. The role of the circle is primarily defensive during evocation.

Lower spirits may be defined as spirits that dwell below the sphere of the moon. These include all earthly spirits of particular objects or places, such as spirits of woodlands, stones, trees, meadows, springs, rivers, buildings, and geographical regions. Also classed as lower spirits are the spirits of the four lower elements, which may or may not have specific local habitations—the Sylphs of Air, the Salamanders of Fire, the Undines of Water, and the Gnomes of Earth. The infernal spirits, such as the demons of hell, who traditionally are supposed to dwell beneath the surface of the earth, are also lower spirits, as are the Qlippoth or Shells of Kabbalistic doctrine. Higher spirits are those that dwell in or above the sphere of the moon. They are associated with the spheres, successively, of the moon, Mercury, Venus, the sun, Mars, Jupiter, Saturn, and the sphere of the fixed stars, or zodiac.

This traditional division of the world into successive shells or spheres about the Earth should be understood in a symbolic sense. Lower spirits are those involved with the senses, emotions, desires, health of the body, and physical substances. Higher spirits are concerned with aspirations, intuition, inspiration, ideals, morals, destiny, and the soul. In general, lower spirits are of a materialistic nature, higher spirits are of a spiritual nature. The moon is the portal between the earthly realm and the higher spheres, and as a result, lunar spirits are concerned with fantasies, dreams, illusions, delusions, manias, obsessions, and mental health, and partake of a mixture of the lower and higher natures.

If you have a floor that will accept tape, you can outline the circle and triangle in this way, but do not draw or paint a permanent circle and triangle, since the direction in which the triangle points will vary from evocation to evocation. When using tape, define the circle with white tape, and the triangle with either yellow for east, red for south, blue for west, or green for north.

Those with a deck of Tarot cards may use the twenty-two trumps to define the circle and triangle of evocation. Consider the circle as the face of a great clock, with 12:00 at the east. The cards should be positioned with their bases directed inward to the center of the circle. At 12:00 place the Star, at 1:00 the Lovers, at 2:00 the Emperor, at 3:00 Strength, at 4:00 Temperance, at 5:00 the Chariot, at 6:00 Death, at 7:00 the Moon, at 8:00 the Devil, at 9:00 the Hierophant, at 10:00 the Hermit, and at 11:00 Justice.

The cards of the triangle should all be upright with their bases perpendicular to the base of the triangle. At the apex place the Fool; on the left side of the second row put the Universe; on the right of the second row, the Wheel; on the left of the third row, the Empress; in the center of the third row, the Magician; on the right of the third row, the Tower; on the left of the bottom row, the Hanged Man; second from left, the High Priestess; third from left, the Sun; at the right of the bottom row put the Last Judgment.

The ten number cards of the suit corresponding to the direction in which the triangle points should be placed under these ten trumps that define the triangle. For Air and the east, use Swords; for Fire and the south, use Wands; for Water and the west, use Cups; for Earth and the north, use Pentacles. Beneath the Fool put the Ace; beneath the Universe, the Two; beneath the Wheel, the Three; beneath the Empress, the Four; beneath the Magician, the Five; beneath the Tower, the Six; beneath the Hanged Man, the Seven, beneath the High Priestess, the Eight; beneath the Sun, the Nine; beneath the Last Judgement, the Ten.

The use of Tarot trumps to form the circle and triangle is superior to the methods of tape or coins, since the arrangement of the trumps creates a powerful symbolic machine that aids in evocation. In this present exercise trumps are placed according to Golden Dawn occult associations. The twelve trumps linked to the signs of the zodiac in the Golden Dawn system constitute the circle. Trumps of the fixed zodiac signs are placed in the four directions, because these are the signs of the Kerubic beasts and the archangels of the elements, and each direction has its own element. In each quarter, the trump corresponding to the cardinal sign of that quarter's element is put on the left of the trump for the fixed sign, and the trump for the mutable sign on the right of the trump for the fixed sign, from the perspective of the center of the circle.

The remaining ten trumps on the triangle are associated with the elements and planets. The three trumps for the pure elements (as opposed to the compound element Earth) define the points of the triangle. The seven trumps of the seven planets of traditional astrology define the body of the triangle and its center. At its base, the trump associated with the moon is put on the left next to the trump of Water, and the trump of the sun on the right next to the trump of Fire. The trumps of the lunar planets, Jupiter and Saturn, occupy the left side, and the trumps of the solar planets, Venus and Mars, the right side. In the center is placed the trump linked with the planet Mercury, the planet of balance and union that contains both solar and lunar principles.

In the coin method, pennies are used to define the circle because they are composed of bronze, a mixture of copper (metal of Venus) and tin (metal of Jupiter). The influence of both these planets is benign—Jupiter is known as the Greater Fortune, and Venus as the Lesser Fortune. Twelve is the number of the zodiac, the circular band of stars that surrounds the Earth. Dimes are used to define the triangle because they signify a value of ten, the number of the tetractys, and dimes are composed of nickel and iron, metals used in the making of the swords and knives that are traditionally employed to control or punish lower spirits. Copper is the metal of Venus, whose symbolic shape is round; iron is the metal of Mars, whose symbolic shape is pointed.

In a more general sense, coins are used because the coin is one of the alternative emblems for the Tarot suit of Pentacles, the suit related to elemental Earth, the element of manifestation. Money is perhaps the ultimate symbol of materialism, and in evocation the purpose is to bring into material presence a spirit within the triangle. When the value of the coins is added, the sum is 112, which by Pythagorean addition results in the number 4 (1+1+2 = 4). Four is the number of materialization. The sum 112 may be considered as 4 x 28—28 is the number of the lunar cycle, the number of days it takes the moon, boundary of the lower sphere of the elements (*aulam yesodoth*), to describe a complete circle in the heavens. The sum 112 may also be considered as 100 + 12, or by Pythagorean addition, 10 + 12.

Elements	Air (East)	Fire (South)	Water (West)	Earth (North)
Divine Names	Shaddai El Chai שדי אל חי	IHVH Tzabaoth יהוה צבאות	Elohim Tzabaoth אלהים צבאות	Adonai ha-Aretz אדני הארץ
Archangels	Raphael רפאל	Michael מיכאל	Gabriel גבריאל	Auriel אוריאל
Angels	Chassan חשן	Aral אראל	Taliahad טליהד	Phorlakh פירלאך
Rulers	Ariel אריאל	Seraph שרף	Tharsis תרשיס	Kerub כרוב
Kings	Paralda	Djin	Nichsa	Ghob
Elementals	Sylphs	Salamanders	Undines	Gnomes

It is not necessary to understand fully this analysis of the structure of the circle and triangle to practice the exercise. It is inserted to show that the arrangement of the Tarot trumps and the selection and placement of the coins have a basis in occult symbolism, and should not be arbitrarily changed.

The procedure in this exercise can be used to evoke any lower spirit into the triangle, but it is necessary to know the names of power that rule over that spirit before evoking it. For purposes of practice, the four kings of the elements should be used. Evocation of these kings alone can accomplish most of the material goals that might arise during the practice of ritual magic. When an understanding is gained of other lower spirits and their place in the earthly or infernal hierarchies, this method can be employed to call them forth into the triangle.

The four kings of the elements and the divine, archangelic, angelic, and ruling beings placed over them, according to Golden Dawn teachings, are shown in the accompanying table. Remember that Hebrew is written and read from right to left.

The apex of the triangle points in the direction most appropriate for the spirit or spirits that will be evoked into it. In the Golden Dawn system, elemental spirits of Air are evoked into a triangle pointing east; spirits of Fire into a triangle pointing south; spirits of Water into a triangle pointing west; spirits of Earth into a triangle pointing north. It is usually possible to determine an elemental affinity for any evoked spirit, and to point the triangle in the direction appropriate for that spirit.

Intellectual, emotionless spirits are airy; willful, violent spirits are fiery; loving, emotional spirits are watery; practical, tangible spirits are earthy.

All materials used in the evocation exercise should be cleansed prior to laying them out on the circle and triangle. The easiest way to do this is with the cleansing prayer described in exercise 37. After cleansing, they can be wrapped in clean white cloth to keep them ritually pure between uses. As a focus for Air spirits, the smoke of burning incense can be employed; as a focus for Fire spirits, the flame of a candle or small oil lamp; as a focus for Water spirits, an open dish of water; as a focus for Earth spirits, a large natural stone. The material should be placed in the triangle shortly before beginning the ritual, and removed immediately after the ritual. When discarding any ritual substance, inscribe a cross of equal arms over it with your right index finger and vibrate the words "Return to Earth, remain undefiled."

When practicing the evocation of Djin, the king of elemental Fire and the Salamanders, the following invocation to the divine ruler of the south, *IHVH Tzabaoth*, would be used.

"I, _____, invoke thee, IHVH Tzabaoth, lord of the south and of the region of Fire, and of all the spiritual creatures that dwell therein. Descend from your throne in the sphere of Netzach and fill this circle of art with your presence. Enter my body and fill me with your light. Enter my heart-center and empower my will with authority to rule over all the creatures of the Fire element in your name, by the supreme power and authority of Yod-Heh-Vav-Heh upon which the universe is formed."

When practicing the evocation of Nichsa, king of elemental Water and the Undines, the following invocation to the divine ruler of the west, *Elohim Tzabaoth*, would be used.

"I, _____, invoke thee, Elohim Tzabaoth, lord of the west and of the region of Water, and of all the spiritual creatures that dwell therein. Descend from your throne in the sphere of Hod and fill this circle of art with your presence. Enter my body and fill me with your light. Enter my heart-center and empower my will with authority to rule over all the creatures of the Water element in

your name, by the supreme power and authority of Yod-Heh-Vav-Heh upon which the universe is formed."

When practicing the evocation of Ghob, king of elemental Earth and the Gnomes, the following invocation to the divine ruler of the north, *Adonai ha-Aretz,* would be used.

"I, _____, invoke thee, Adonai ha-Aretz, lord of the north and of the region of Earth, and of all the spiritual creatures that dwell therein. Descend from your throne in the sphere of Malkuth and fill this circle of art with your presence. Enter my body and fill me with your light. Enter my heart-center and empower my will with authority to rule over all the creatures of the Earth element in thy name, by the supreme power and authority of Yod-Heh-Vav-Heh upon which the universe is formed."

It should not be too difficult for anyone using this exercise in evocation to make the changes in the wording of the ritual necessary for different spirits. Always bear in mind that the name of a spirit should be accompanied by its specific titles, offices, and associations, and that a spirit is ruled by the authority of the divine and angelic names that are set over it—spirits of Water are ruled by the divine names presiding over Water, and by the angels of Water, for example. A name of power can only be used effectively by a ritualist if the angelic or divine quality signified by that name has been invoked. The magician must become *Shaddai El Chai* before he or she can rule lower spirits by the authority of *Shaddai El Chai.* This is why the exercise of evocation contains within it an invocation.

Those familiar with my writings will know that I have objections to some of the forms of the divine names used by the Golden Dawn. However, to avoid confusion for beginners new to occult correspondences, I adhere in the present work to the traditional Golden Dawn divine names that rule over the four elements and four directions of the compass.

There should not be an expectation that an evoked spirit will appear as a being of flesh and blood physically within the triangle. This sometimes occurs when the practitioner has a natural psychic ability or performs the evocation in a highly excited emotional state. More commonly, the spirit is perceived in subtle ways, by movements in the air, sounds, sensations, odors, and indistinct forms or shadows. The purpose of evocation is not to bring forth a spirit in physical form, but to command a lower spirit into the triangle beyond the boundary of the magic circle where it can be used safely. It is the nature of lower spirits to be more material than higher spirits. The lower they are in the spiritual hierarchy, the denser and more tangible their evoked forms.

It is necessary to learn evocation when seeking a complete understanding of the art of magic because evocation outside the circle is the only safe way to deal with infernal demons, and with the more dangerous elementals. Undines can usually be summoned without the protection of a circle, provided the magician is mentally stable. Often this is also true of Sylphs. It is best to evoke Gnomes, and Salamanders should always be evoked. Demons are best left alone entirely, but if they must be used for some grossly material purpose, they should always be evoked into the triangle beyond the limit of the circle.

PRACTICE SCHEDULE

Forty-Week
Study Guide

THIS FORTY-WEEK outline for practice is designed to teach the mechanics of the exercises contained in this book, and to show how they interact with each other. The exercises are grouped in weekly cycles. The only constant is the presence of a breathing exercise each day. Learning is reinforced by repetition.

The most important aspect of training is the clear visualization of astral forms during the exercises. These visualizations create structures on the astral level, and attract the notice of spiritual intelligences, who will begin to make their presence known to you during training by affecting one of more of your senses. Interaction with spirits is vital to successful training in ritual magic. Spirits make subtle changes in your physiology necessary to the successful performance of magic. The presence of spirits during the exercises should be observed with a tranquil and receptive mind and balanced emotions. Fear must not be permitted to arise when the spirits manifest, as it will inhibit or destroy the benefits they would otherwise confer.

If the exercises are done properly, by the end of the 280 days of training, you will notice a profound difference both inwardly and in the greater world. There will be heightened intuition, enhanced perception of the thoughts, emotions, and intentions of other human beings, increased physical vitality and clarity of thinking, and the more frequent occurrence of significant coincidences that have a bearing on your training. These synchronicities become very common when you are making good progress.

It is best to obtain a loose-leaf binder at the beginning of the training period, and record any dreams that occur during the forty weeks, along with a day-to-day record of changes in the condition of the mind and body, and any strange or remarkable happenings that take place in the greater world, and appear to be connected in some way with the training. Such a record of progress can be illuminating at a later period, and can provide guidance when seeking to progress further in magic.

First Quarter

Week 1

Monday: 1, 4, 11, 14
Tuesday: 1, 4, 11, 14
Wednesday: 1, 4, 11, 14
Thursday: 1, 4, 11, 14
Friday: 1, 4, 11, 14
Saturday: 1, 4, 11, 14
Sunday: 1, 4, 11, 14

Week 2

Monday: 2, 4, 11, 15
Tuesday: 2, 4, 11, 15
Wednesday: 2, 4, 11, 15
Thursday: 2, 4, 11, 15
Friday: 2, 4, 11, 15
Saturday: 2, 4, 11, 15
Sunday: 2, 4, 11, 15

Week 3

Monday: 3, 5, 11, 16
Tuesday: 3, 5, 11, 16
Wednesday: 3, 5, 11, 16
Thursday: 3, 5, 11, 16
Friday: 3, 5, 11, 16
Saturday: 3, 5, 11, 16
Sunday: 3, 5, 11, 16

Week 4

Monday: 1, 6, 12, 17
Tuesday: 1, 6, 12, 17
Wednesday: 1, 6, 12, 17
Thursday: 1, 6, 12, 17
Friday: 1, 6, 12, 17
Saturday: 1, 6, 12, 17
Sunday: 1, 6, 12, 17

Week 5

Monday: 2, 6, 12, 18
Tuesday: 2, 6, 12, 18
Wednesday: 2, 6, 12, 18
Thursday: 2, 6, 12, 18
Friday: 2, 6, 12, 18
Saturday: 2, 6, 12, 18
Sunday: 2, 6, 12, 18

Week 6

Monday: 3, 7, 12, 19
Tuesday: 3, 7, 12, 19
Wednesday: 3, 7, 12, 19
Thursday: 3, 7, 12, 19
Friday: 3, 7, 12, 19
Saturday: 3, 4, 12, 19
Sunday: 3, 4, 12, 19

Week 7

Monday: 7, 11, 14
Tuesday: 7, 11, 15
Wednesday: 7, 11, 16
Thursday: 7, 11, 17
Friday: 7, 11, 14
Saturday: 5, 11, 15
Sunday: 5, 11, 16

Week 8

Monday: 8, 12, 20
Tuesday: 8, 12, 20
Wednesday: 8, 12, 20
Thursday: 8, 12, 20
Friday: 8, 12, 20
Saturday: 8, 12, 20
Sunday: 8, 12, 20

Week 9

Monday: 9, 13, 21
Tuesday: 9, 13, 21
Wednesday: 9, 13, 21

Thursday: 9, 13, 21
Friday: 9, 13, 21
Saturday: 9, 13, 21
Sunday: 9, 13, 21

Week 10

Monday: 10, 13, 22
Tuesday: 10, 13, 22
Wednesday: 10, 13, 22
Thursday: 10, 13, 22
Friday: 10, 13, 22
Saturday: 10, 13, 22
Sunday: 10, 13, 22

Second Quarter

Week 11

Monday: 7, 13, 17
Tuesday: 7, 13, 18
Wednesday: 7, 13, 19
Thursday: 7, 13, 17
Friday: 7, 13, 18
Saturday: 5, 13, 19
Sunday: 6, 13, 20

Week 12

Monday: 4, 11, 23
Tuesday: 4, 11, 23
Wednesday: 4, 11, 23
Thursday: 4, 11, 23
Friday: 4, 11, 23
Saturday: 4, 11, 23
Sunday: 4, 11, 23

Week 13

Monday: 5, 12, 24
Tuesday: 5, 12, 24
Wednesday: 5, 12, 24
Thursday: 5, 12, 24
Friday: 5, 12, 24
Saturday: 5, 12, 24
Sunday: 5, 12, 24

Week 14

Monday: 6, 13, 25
Tuesday: 6, 13, 25
Wednesday: 6, 13, 25
Thursday: 6, 13, 25
Friday: 6, 13, 25
Saturday: 6, 13, 25
Sunday: 6, 13, 25

Week 15

Monday: 8, 12, 26
Tuesday: 8, 12, 23
Wednesday: 8, 12, 26
Thursday: 8, 12, 24
Friday: 8, 12, 26
Saturday: 8, 12, 25
Sunday: 8, 12, 26

Week 16

Monday: 9, 11, 27
Tuesday: 9, 11, 27
Wednesday: 9, 11, 27
Thursday: 9, 11, 27
Friday: 9, 11, 27
Saturday: 9, 11, 27
Sunday: 9, 11, 27

Week 17

Monday: 10, 13, 28
Tuesday: 10, 13, 28
Wednesday: 10, 13, 28
Thursday: 10, 13, 28
Friday: 10, 13, 28
Saturday: 10, 13, 28
Sunday: 10, 13, 28

Week 18

Monday: 4, 12, 23
Tuesday: 5, 12, 24
Wednesday: 6, 12, 25
Thursday: 4, 12, 26
Friday: 5, 12, 27

Saturday: 6, 12, 28
Sunday: 4, 12, 28

Week 19

Monday: 7, 11, 14
Tuesday: 7, 11, 15
Wednesday: 7, 11, 16
Thursday: 7, 11, 17
Friday: 7, 11, 18
Saturday: 6, 11, 19
Sunday: 6, 11, 20

Week 20

Monday: 8, 12, 22
Tuesday: 8, 12, 21
Wednesday: 8, 12, 22
Thursday: 8, 12, 20
Friday: 8, 12, 22
Saturday: 8, 12, 21
Sunday: 8, 12, 22

Third Quarter

Week 21

Monday: 13, 27, 29
Tuesday: 13, 27, 30
Wednesday: 13, 27, 29
Thursday: 13, 27, 30
Friday: 13, 27, 29
Saturday: 13, 27, 30
Sunday: 13, 27, 29

Week 22

Monday: 13, 28, 31
Tuesday: 13, 28, 31
Wednesday: 13, 28, 31
Thursday: 13, 28, 31
Friday: 13, 28, 31
Saturday: 13, 28, 31
Sunday: 13, 28, 31

Week 23

Monday: 13, 20, 23
Tuesday: 13, 21, 24
Wednesday: 13, 22, 25
Thursday: 13, 20, 23
Friday: 13, 21, 24
Saturday: 13, 22, 25
Sunday: 13, 22, 26

Week 24

Monday: 12, 19, 28
Tuesday: 12, 18, 28
Wednesday: 12, 17, 28
Thursday: 12, 19, 28
Friday: 12, 18, 28
Saturday: 12, 17, 28
Sunday: 12, 19, 28

Week 25

Monday: 8, 11, 32
Tuesday: 8, 11, 32
Wednesday: 8, 11, 32
Thursday: 8, 11, 32
Friday: 8, 11, 32
Saturday: 8, 11, 32
Sunday: 8, 11, 32

Week 26

Monday: 9, 12, 23
Tuesday: 9, 12, 24
Wednesday: 9, 12, 25
Thursday: 9, 12, 26
Friday: 9, 12, 27
Saturday: 9, 12, 28
Sunday: 9, 12, 29

Week 27

Monday: 10, 13, 30
Tuesday: 10, 13, 31
Wednesday: 10, 13, 32
Thursday: 10, 13, 29
Friday: 10, 13, 31

Saturday: 10, 13, 32
Sunday: 10, 13, 30

Week 28

Monday: 12, 20, 27
Tuesday: 12, 21, 28
Wednesday: 12, 22, 27
Thursday: 12, 20, 28
Friday: 12, 21, 27
Saturday: 12, 22, 28
Sunday: 12, 23, 27

Week 29

Monday: 11, 17, 28
Tuesday: 11, 18, 28
Wednesday: 11, 19, 28
Thursday: 11, 17, 28
Friday: 11, 18, 28
Saturday: 11, 19, 28
Sunday: 11, 25, 28

Week 30

Monday: 12, 23, 27
Tuesday: 12, 24, 28
Wednesday: 12, 25, 27
Thursday: 12, 23, 28
Friday: 12, 24, 27
Saturday: 12, 25, 28
Sunday: 12, 26, 27

Fourth Quarter

Week 31

Monday: 13, 23, 33
Tuesday: 13, 23, 33
Wednesday: 13, 23, 33
Thursday: 13, 23, 33
Friday: 13, 23, 33
Saturday: 13, 23, 33
Sunday: 13, 23, 33

Week 32

Monday: 13, 24, 34

Tuesday: 13, 24, 34
Wednesday: 13, 24, 34
Thursday: 13, 24, 34
Friday: 13, 24, 34
Saturday: 13, 24, 34
Sunday: 13, 24, 34

Week 33

Monday: 13, 25, 35
Tuesday: 13, 25, 35
Wednesday: 13, 25, 35
Thursday: 13, 25, 35
Friday: 13, 25, 35
Saturday: 13, 25, 35
Sunday: 13, 25, 35

Week 34

Monday: 12, 27, 36
Tuesday: 12, 27, 36
Wednesday: 12, 27, 36
Thursday: 12, 27, 36
Friday: 12, 27, 36
Saturday: 12, 27, 36
Sunday: 12, 27, 36

Week 35

Monday: 11, 28, 37
Tuesday: 11, 28, 37
Wednesday: 11, 28, 37
Thursday: 11, 28, 37
Friday: 11, 28, 37
Saturday: 11, 28, 37
Sunday: 11, 28, 37

Week 36

Monday: 12, 29, 38
Tuesday: 12, 32, 38
Wednesday: 12, 35, 38
Thursday: 12, 30, 38
Friday: 12, 32, 38
Saturday: 12, 35, 38
Sunday: 12, 37, 38

Week 37

Monday: 13, 28, 39
Tuesday: 13, 28, 39
Wednesday: 13, 28, 39
Thursday: 13, 28, 39
Friday: 13, 28, 39
Saturday: 13, 28, 39
Sunday: 13, 28, 39

Week 38

Monday: 13, 34, 40
Tuesday: 13, 34, 40

Wednesday: 13, 34, 40
Thursday: 13, 34, 40
Friday: 13, 34, 36
Saturday: 13, 34, 38
Sunday: 13, 34, 39

Week 39

Monday: 13, 28, 33
Tuesday: 13, 28, 33
Wednesday: 13, 28, 33
Thursday: 13, 28, 33
Friday: 13, 28, 33

Saturday: 13, 28, 33
Sunday: 13, 28, 33

Week 40

Monday: 13, 28, 39
Tuesday: 13, 28, 39
Wednesday: 13, 28, 39
Thursday: 13, 28, 39
Friday: 13, 28, 39
Saturday: 13, 28, 39
Sunday: 13, 28, 39

After you have become familiar with all of the exercises through the forty-week term of training, it is best to adopt a regular routine of practice that can be carried on indefinitely. It should not be too demanding in either time or energy, so that when you wish you can perform new rituals designed to accomplish specific purposes. It is desirable for you to construct your own rituals on the models provided in this book, and work them in conjunction with your daily exercises. The regular practice schedule should be regarded as a kind of maintenance plan designed to sustain the level of skill that has been acquired.

The regular routine of practice should have a cycle long enough to introduce variety, but short enough so that important exercises are repeated often. The suggested four-week schedule below consists of one reclining exercise, one breathing exercise, and one ritual each day. From time to time it is useful to vary the routine to prevent tedium and impatience during the work. If you discover that after a few weeks or months a particular exercise has gone dead for you, and no longer yields any discernable benefit, substitute another in its place. Do not be too quick to discard an exercise, however—there are dry periods during the regular practice of any ritual, but if the work is continued, often these barren periods are followed by a burst of new insights and the release of pent-up energies.

Week One

Monday: 5, 11, 27
Tuesday: 5, 11, 31
Wednesday: 5, 11, 28
Thursday: 5, 11, 31
Friday: 5, 11, 27

Saturday: 5, 11, 31
Sunday: 5, 11, 28

Week Two

Monday: 6, 13, 27
Tuesday: 6, 13, 33
Wednesday: 6, 13, 28

Thursday: 6, 13, 33
Friday: 6, 13, 27
Saturday: 6, 13, 33
Sunday: 6, 13, 28

Week Three

Monday: 8, 12, 27

Tuesday: 8, 12, 34
Wednesday: 8, 12, 28
Thursday: 8, 12, 34
Friday: 8, 12, 27
Saturday: 8, 12, 34
Sunday: 8, 12, 28

Week Four

Monday: 9, 13, 27
Tuesday: 9, 13, 36
Wednesday: 9, 13, 28
Thursday: 9, 13, 36

Friday: 9, 13, 27
Saturday: 9, 13, 36
Sunday: 9, 13, 28

Suggested Reading

THE OVERRIDING CONSIDERATION in compiling this reading list was practicality. Only works that contain important instructions, techniques, or rituals of ceremonial magic are included. These are books in my own library that I have read and reread numerous times. The list is by no means exhaustive, but every book on it is worth intense study, and will repay the energy expended on it many times over.

Agrippa, Cornelius. *Three Books of Occult Philosophy*. Translated from the Latin into English by J. F. Edited and annotated by Donald Tyson. St. Paul: Llewellyn Publications, 1993. First published in Latin in its complete form in 1533. This English edition first published in 1651.

The most important of the older textbooks of Western magic. No other book is so detailed and complete. Every aspect of occultism, from numerology and astrology to the evocation of angels, is presented in exhaustive detail. This book is an essential resource, almost as vital for the modern student as Regardie's *Golden Dawn*.

Bardon, Franz. *Initiation Into Hermetics*. English translation by A. Radspieler. Wuppertal, Germany: Dieter Ruggeberg, 1971. First published as *Der Weg zum wahren Adepten* in 1956 by Verlag Hermann Bauer.

Without question, this is the best book of basic training exercises in the Western tradition of ceremonial magic. No other work approaches it for clarity, usefulness of material, and completeness. An essential text. It should be studied along with *The Practice of Magical Evocation*. Bardon wrote several other books, but they are of no consequence—these two works are his legacy.

——. *The Practice of Magical Evocation*. English translation by Peter Dimai. Wuppertal, Germany: Dieter Ruggeberg, 1975. First published as *Die Praxis der magischen Evokation* in 1956 by Verlag Hermann Bauer.

This is not so good a work as the author's brilliant *Initiation Into Hermetics,* but it is invaluable as a source of specific technical information on the evocation of spirits, which is an essential aspect of the Western tradition of magic.

Crowley, Aleister. *Magick In Theory and Practice*. New York: Dover, 1976. This material was first published in this format in 1929.

All of Crowley's writings on magic are practical, but none more so than this important book, which sets forth his essential understanding of the nature of magic and how to work it.

Fortune, Dion. *Psychic Self-Defence*. York Beach, Maine: Samuel Weiser, 1979. First published in 1930.

This is Fortune's most readable and entertaining book. It contains many practical techniques for defense against occult attacks from human beings or spirits. As a rule, Fortune's books are wordy and vague, but there is useful material here.

Gray, William G. *Inner Traditions of Magic*. York Beach, Maine: Samuel Weiser, 1970.

All of Gray's books are excellent. I have a special fondness for his work because when I was struggling to learn the basics of ritual magic, it was his books that proved the most helpful. Of special utility is the fifth chapter, "How To Build A Magic Circle."

——. *Magical Ritual Methods*. York Beach, Maine: Samuel Weiser, 1980. First published by Helios Books in 1969.

Ideally, this book should be studied along with Gray's *Inner Traditions of Magic*. Although there are no complex rituals described, many vital practical details of ceremonial magic are presented.

——. *Temple Magic*. St. Paul, Minnesota: Llewellyn Publications, 1988.

A complete consideration of the requirements of a working ritual temple.

Griffin, David. *The Ritual Magic Manual*. Beverly Hills, California: Golden Dawn Publishing, 1999.

This large text presents in great detail the practical elements of Golden Dawn ritual magic. It should be studied along with Regardie's *Golden Dawn*.

Kraig, Donald Michael. *Modern Magick: Eleven Lessons in the High Magickal Arts*. St. Paul, Minnesota: Llewellyn Publications, 1997. First copyrighted in 1988.

As the subtitle indicates, the work contains eleven progressive lessons in the techniques of ceremonial magic in the Golden Dawn tradition. This is one of the better basic tutorials. It contains so much concentrated information, it may be a bit hard for beginners to digest at first reading, but it is well worth the effort to master its contents.

Levi, Eliphas. *Transcendental Magic*. York Beach, Maine: Samuel Weiser, 1970. Translated by A. E. Waite. First published in French in two parts as *Dogme de la Haute Magie* (1855) and *Rituel de la Haute Magie* (1856). First published in English as one volume in 1896 by Rider and Company.

This is Levi's most practical book. Although it does not contain detailed exercises or rituals, it does give many bits and pieces of information useful for working ritual magic.

———————

Mathers, Samuel Liddell MacGregor. *The Book of the Sacred Magic of Abramelin the Mage*. New York: Dover Publications, 1975. First published in 1898.

Mathers' translation of this French occult manuscript brought into being one of the seminal preoccupations of the Golden Dawn, the calling forth into visible presence of the tutelary spirit known as the Holy Guardian Angel. It obsessed Aleister Crowley for much of his early career as a magician. To his Guardian Angel, Aiwass, Crowley attributed the transmission of his most important text, *Liber AL: The Book of the Law*. The pursuit of the Guardian Angel has become one of the cornerstones of the Western esoteric tradition. The extended ritual described in exhaustive detail in the Second Book of this work is somewhat different in character than those of most grimoires, in that it is more concerned with inner development and less with outer gestures and objects.

   The Third Book contains a set of magic squares the majority of which are incomplete. Each square is supposed to possess an inherent power of magic. The squares have quite a bad reputation for causing evil to those who even so much as possess them, without knowing what they are for or how to use them. In my view, this is idle superstition. No one should be afraid to study this book, which is the essential teaching on the Holy Guardian Angel.

———————

———. *The Goetia: The Lesser Key of Solomon the King. Lemegeton, Book I, Clavicula Salomonis Regis*. Illustrated second edition, edited and introduced by Aleister Crowley. Further editing by Hymenaeus Beta. York Beach, Maine: Samuel Weiser, 1995. First edition first published 1904.

Almost all the credit for this work belongs to Mathers. Crowley contributed very little, although he did add a few sketches of demons to the second edition. This is not really the *Lesser Key* or *Lemegeton,* but only the first book of that large manuscript. Since it is the best known and most widely available of the grimoires of demonic spirit evocation, it is worth studying for the practical insights into spirit evocation as a whole that it provides the serious practitioner.

———. *The Key of Solomon the King (Clavicula Salomonis)*. York Beach, Maine: Samuel Weiser, 1989. First published in 1888.

It is a tribute to Mathers' skill as an editor that his version of the *Key of Solomon* has survived for more than a century to become the standard grimoire of Western magic. It is invaluable as a practical guide to traditional spirit evocation.

Regardie, Israel. *Ceremonial Magic*. Northamptonshire, England: The Aquarian Press, 1980.

Several rituals derived from the teachings of Aleister Crowley. This is a good introduction to Crowley's rituals. It will be a bit bewildering to those with no prior knowledge of his magic. It should be studied together with Crowley's *Magick In Theory and Practice* and Regardie's *Golden Dawn*. Included is a fairly clear description of the Greater Banishing Ritual of the Pentagram, although as is usually the case when this ritual is described, the necessary internal actions are not presented at all, merely the external physical gestures.

———. *The Golden Dawn*. Sixth Edition. Edited and indexed by David Godwin. St. Paul, Minnesota: Llewellyn Publications, 1990. First published in four volumes 1938–1940 by Aries Press of Chicago.

This is Regardie's greatest work. It consists of an edited collection of the original Golden Dawn teaching documents and grade rituals that circulated among members of that Hermetic Order. Regardie obtained this material in 1934 when he was admitted to the Hermes Lodge of the Stella Matutina. It was the first time these instructional papers had been presented in an honest form, although much of the Golden Dawn teachings had previously appeared in print as part of Aleister Crowley's periodical, *The Equinox*. Crowley tended to present the Golden Dawn teachings as his own, but Regardie returned the credit for their brilliance to the leader of the Golden Dawn, S. L. MacGregor Mathers.

The Golden Dawn is the single most important book on Western ceremonial magic that exists in the world today. It is absolutely essential to a true understanding of Western magic. Godwin's index alone is worth far more than the price of the book.

——. *The One Year Manual.* York Beach, Maine: Samuel Weiser, 1981. First published as *Twelve Steps To Spiritual Enlightenment* in 1969 by The Sangreal Foundation.

Regardie had the right idea in this book, which describes a number of simple ritual exercises that are to be practiced over the course of an entire year. Where it fails, in my opinion, is in its instruction to perform a small number of exercises over a long period of time, which tends to make them repetitious and tedious. However, it illustrates quite well the need for regular practice of the fundamental techniques of ritual, and as far as it goes, its material is quite useful.

——. *The Tree of Life.* York Beach, Maine: Samuel Weiser, 1973. First published in 1932.

A practical overview of Western ceremonial magic in the Golden Dawn tradition. Regardie studied magic under Crowley, and later became a member of an offshoot branch of the Golden Dawn. This is one of his best books.

Sadhu, Mouni. *Concentration.* London: George, Allen and Unwin, 1977. First published in 1959.

A collection of really excellent exercises in concentration. In my opinion, this is Sadhu's best book.

——. *Samadhi.* London: George, Allen and Unwin, 1976. First published in 1962.

Despite its Eastern title, this work contains a great deal of practical advice on matters of Western ceremonial magic. It should be studied together with this author's book, *Concentration.*

Shah, Idries. *The Secret Lore of Magic: Book of the Sorcerers.* London: Sphere Books, 1972. First published in Great Britain in 1957 by Frederick Muller Ltd.

Similar to Waite's *Book of Ceremonial Magic,* but Shah covers some ground that Waite misses, so the two works are both worth having. The advantage of studying the original grimoires is to see how magic was actually worked, at least on the external physical level, in past centuries. Magic has no evolution. The magic of a thousand years ago is essentially the same as the magic of today, varying only in its details. A knowledge of ancient magic illuminates the techniques of modern magic.

Starhawk. *The Spiral Dance: A Rebirth of the Ancient Religion of the Great Goddess.* San Francisco: Harper and Row, 1979.

Starhawk, or Miriam Simos, has written a really wonderful basic textbook on ritual magic from the perspective of modern witchcraft. It contains numerous brief exercises, many of them excellent.

Tyson, Donald. *New Millennium Magic: A Complete System of Self-Realization.* St. Paul, Minnesota: Llewellyn Publications, 1996.

In this work I present in detail my personal system of ceremonial magic. The system is derived from the Golden Dawn model, but differs from it in several important respects, most notably by being Mercury-centric rather than Sol-centric. Most system of magic, that of the Golden Dawn included, place the Sun at the heart of the system—in the center of the planets, the center of the human body, and the center of the Kabbalistic Tree of the Sephiroth. In my system, Mercury is placed at the center, and the Sun moves to the periphery to balance the Moon. This shift is based on the esoteric teachings of alchemy, and on its own internal sense of rightness. This book should be studied after a thorough practice of the exercises in the present work, which adhere to the more traditional Golden Dawn arrangement.

New Millennium Magic is an expanded and corrected version of my earlier book, *The New Magus,* where my personal system of magic was first presented to the world.

———. *Tetragrammaton: The Secret to Evoking Angelic Powers and the Key to the Apocalypse.* St. Paul, Minnesota: Llewellyn Publications, 1995.

Central to the occult tradition of the West is Tetragrammaton, the Hebrew name of God with four letters. This is the first complete examination of this name in the context of the Kabbalah, Enochian angel magic, and the Apocalypse. My primary purpose in this book was to show why Tetragrammaton has maintained so prominent a rank in the teachings of magic for so many centuries. A completely new hierarchy of angels called the Wings of the Winds is presented that relies on the structure of the fourfold name and a hint from Dr. John Dee in his *Hieroglyphic Monad.*

Waite, Arthur Edward. *The Book of Ceremonial Magic: A Complete Grimoire.* Secaucus, New Jersey: Citadel Press. First published in this form in London in 1911. This is a corrected and expanded edition of the author's earlier work, *The Book of Black Magic and of Pacts,* published in London in 1898.

What can be said about Arthur Edward Waite? It is impossible to ignore him when studying the literature of Western magic, but his attitude was so cynical and condescending, and his writing style is so wretched, his works are nearly unreadable. Although he spent the better part of his life studying and writing about the Western esoteric tradition, he frequently expressed an utter contempt for it, and for those who studied it.

This book is an edited collection of rituals, seals, circles, and sigils from the grimoires, an anonymous collection of manuscripts preserving practical techniques of magic. It is one of the better introductions to the grimoires, and should be read along with Idries Shah's *The Secret Lore of Magic,* which is quite similar in its approach and content. Waite mentioned in his book that he had added deliberate errors into the text as a trap for fools, but this claim is not to be taken too seriously. I imagine he wrote this to cover himself for when his readers pointed out the errors that inevitably creep into a work of this type.

Weinstein, Marion. *Positive Magic: Occult Self-Help.* Surrey, British Columbia: Phoenix Publishing, 1981. First published in 1978.

Weinstein has produced one of the two most useful primers of magic for pagans or Wiccans. The other is *The Spiral Dance* by Starhawk. Both are classics of their kind and well worth study by beginners, particularly those with pagan inclinations.

Index